KATHY THE CANNIBAL

SANDRA LEE

KATHY THE CANNIBAL

JOHN BLAKE

Published by John Blake Publishing Ltd,
3, Bramber Court, 2 Bramber Road,
London W14 9PB, England

www.blake.co.uk

First published in Hardback in 2004

ISBN 1844540375

British Library Cataloguing-in-Publication Data:

A catalogue record for this book is available from the British Library.

Design by www.envydesign.co.uk

Printed in Great Britain by Creative Print and Design

1 3 5 7 9 10 8 6 4 2

Papers used by John Blake Publishing are natural, recyclable products
made from wood grown in sustainable forests. The manufacturing processes
conform to the environmental regulations of the country of origin.

Every attempt has been made to contact the relevant copyright-holders,
but some were unobtainable. We would be grateful if the appropriate
people could contact us.

In memory of my mother, Valda May Lee (1932–1994).

And for my dad, Dixie.

Contents

Prologue

The plea

Katherine Knight didn't look like a killer. Tall and slimmish with a tangle of dulling red hair that fell to just below her shoulders and with blue eyes that stared out from no-nonsense steel-framed glasses, she was a handsome woman who'd never been in danger of being called beautiful. She was the type of woman you'd find in almost every Australian family, a familiar character with pursed lips and ruddy cheeks, conspicuous by her awkward attempts to be fashionable which always just missed the mark. She could pass muster as a waitress at the local RSL or behind the bar at the bowling club, pulling beers and calling you 'love' in a hardened and strangled Australian accent as she sloshed a schooner your way.

As she stood in the dock of the New South Wales Supreme Court in East Maitland on Thursday, 18 October 2001, Katherine Knight, then forty-five, did not look like someone who could have confessed to murdering her de facto husband of six years. But, on this third day of what was to have been her murder trial, she did just that. She pleaded guilty to murdering John Charles Thomas Price, thereby sparing a jury of twelve ordinary Australians the stomach-turning task of hearing the gruesome details of what she had done.

The previous day, Justice Barry O'Keefe had taken up his position on the bench and, looking down on the swell of potential jurors before him, warned them of the horrific nature of the trial ahead. Wearing the red cloak of authority with his dusted wig atop his balding pate, the judge used words that needed no help to inflame the imagination.

'The evidence will be graphic and grisly,' he told the one hundred and twenty men and women, selected at random from the electoral roll, soon after they'd filed into court to do their civic duty.

There was a shuffling of feet as they twisted in their seats wondering nervously how grisly it could be. A few stole a look at Katherine Knight, a normal-looking mother of four and grandmother of three, to see if a monster was hiding in those matronly clothes. The judge continued, unconsciously lapsing into the tortured language of the legal profession.

'The evidence as to the circumstances of and surrounding the death of the deceased will involve the members of the jury being exposed to quite explicit material; it is material which is quite gruesome and such as to be likely to shock and upset even those who may be fairly phlegmatic by nature,' he said. His open, round face, with its practised look of gravitas, had concern etched all over it. He looked at the faces peering up at him and continued: 'It may be capable of causing significant distress to anyone who is squeamish or made ill by the sight of blood or human remains, even in pictorial form, or who may be affected by graphic verbal descriptions of such matters. For anyone who is extremely sensitive, it could cause very considerable upset.'

Justice O'Keefe then offered the jurors an exit, telling them that if they felt the task ahead might be too disturbing, too frightening, too macabre, they could excuse themselves from the panel, after explaining their reasons. Extreme images of blood and human remains might affect them, and if it did, either physically or mentally, then they should take their leave as soon as he had finished what he had to say. They could perform their duty as responsible and active members of the community another time.

After years of sitting on the bench, Barry O'Keefe understood that the range of emotional and physical reactions to violence could be extreme and unpredictable. Mrs Knight, he had instructed them, was innocent until a jury of her peers decided otherwise, and she was entitled to a fair and impartial trial. He didn't want that fundamental right affected by a weak stomach or a fainting spell. The wheels of justice were not to be stopped by a spontaneous squeal of fright when a shocking crime scene picture was held before them.

Justice O'Keefe – known as 'the mild one', a play on the stage name of his brother, 1950s rocker Johnny O'Keefe, who was known as the Wild One – knew what was ahead. A couple of the policemen who worked on the case, collecting evidence soon after John Price was murdered, were still undergoing counselling eighteen months later, haunted and traumatised by what they had seen. One had been unable to return to work. The judge had to make sure the twelve men and women who were to be accepted as a group of reasonable, fair-minded peers would be able to weather what was ahead, in all its bloodiness. This was no ordinary murder. In fact it was a very rare one, according to Robert Keppel, one of America's most respected criminal profilers and investigators and the author of several books on murders and serial killers. 'I don't think I have ever heard of a case like this before, that does the things that this woman did.'

Keppel, who started as a homicide detective investigating sexually related murders, has worked on more than 2000 murder cases in the United States, and was on the original team whose work led to the capture of serial killer Ted Bundy, believed to have killed thirty-six women before dying in the electric chair in Florida in 1989.

'This is so far up the continuum of psychopathological behaviour. This person is full blown; you have gone through the elements of voyeurism, you have gone through the elements of enjoying torture before death, you have gone through the elements of enjoying torture after death, you have got the consumption, the cannibalism . . . you know, total necrophiliac behaviours,' Keppel said.

While Justice O'Keefe was explaining the mechanics of justice to the potential jurors, Katherine Mary Knight, the woman accused of the horrific crime he was talking about, sat silently in the wooden dock, staring blankly over the phalanx of highly polished lawyers, who stood in sharp relief to her in their spiffy suits and black robes and their neatly combed hair. Piles of legal references and briefs tied in pink cotton ribbon cast shadows on the floor from the bar table.

She seemed remote, out of place. The lawyers were talking about her, but they weren't talking to her. They couldn't even see her. She was sitting behind them and they rarely turned around or paid her any mind. To the strangers in the jury panel, it must have seemed incongruous. Katherine Knight didn't look like a monster at all. Her youngest brother Shane Knight, the baby of the family, was in court, a symbol of familial love and support. How could *this* woman be accused of such an extraordinary crime, one that the judge had warned was graphic, gruesome and grisly? An outsider could be forgiven for thinking it was all a big mistake.

Until 29 February 2000, Katherine Knight had led a life so routine that she could have slipped quietly into semi-rural suburban anonymity. She came from a large and respected family that traced its lineage in Aberdeen – situated roughly halfway between Newcastle and Tamworth in northeastern New South Wales – back about a hundred years. Her father, Kenneth Charles Knight, grew up with his five brothers and sisters in a little wooden shack on top of a hill known as the Needles, at the foot of the Barrington Tops Mountains.

When she was sixteen, Kathy followed in her father's footsteps and got a job as a slicer and packer at the Aberdeen meatworks, the biggest show in town at the time. For the next fourteen years she worked in one abattoir or another in New South Wales and, for a short time, in Queensland. For eight hours a day she would stand shoulder to shoulder with fellow slicers, usually women, over a waist-high bench wielding a knife and trimming excess fat and imperfections off lumps of meat, or scraping out congealed blood from a cattle carcass killed the day before. It was tough, physical work and she loved it. But in 1985 she was laid off after hurting her back and had been unemployed ever since, collecting a fortnightly invalid pension.

Known variously as Katherine, Kathy or Kath, she was easy enough to like and was well known in Aberdeen. All the Knights were. With a selfconscious vanity the result of middle age, she liked to keep fit and most mornings walked from her house up to her twin sister Joy Hinder's home a few blocks away. With Joy and her husband John Hinder, she would cut an arm-pumping swathe around the streets of Aberdeen, and sometimes they repeated the exercise in the afternoon; occasionally they were joined by other relatives or friends eager for social exercise.

She played bingo in Muswellbrook twice a week, Tuesdays and Thursdays, took a sewing class each Wednesday night, and made her own clothes. She enjoyed and excelled at knitting and crafts, her lace quilts being especially coveted. Kathy was also a good mother, and few people doubted her ability. She was the first in line to help people out if they needed a ride, happily transporting friends and family to the doctors or into town on a shopping excursion in her red Toyota people mover. She'd offer to baby-sit kids, or take them to the park for a day out. A heart of gold, some people said.

But just as she was easy to like, Katherine Knight was easy enough to dislike. Some of the boys at the pub, and even her de facto John Price, called her 'the speckled hen' or 'the red hen', a nod to her hair colour. They said it with a laugh, but if the truth be told, it was a less than affectionate sobriquet. She could be scratchy. You had to watch Kathy Knight, the locals warned. She armed herself with a fiery temper that threatened violence and a vocabulary choked with profanities. You didn't want to get on the wrong side of her. Like a feared black cat on Friday the 13th, some people crossed the road to avoid making contact with her. They didn't want to be struck by the invective-filled language that shot out of her mouth like poisoned darts, fired at random at whoever was unlucky enough to make eye contact with her when she was out of sorts. Still, her mercurial personality and foul language didn't seem to deter male company, and Kathy Knight was never left wanting, moving from one relationship to the next without much time in between.

Kathy had been married once, to David Stanford Kellett. It was no grand affair. She didn't walk down the aisle on her dad's arm – instead, she hopped on her powerful motorbike and rode to her wedding at the registry office in Muswellbrook with Kellett spooned behind her as pillion passenger, his arms wrapped firmly around her waist, holding on for dear life as they roared up over the hill and into town. It was 1974 and she was eighteen. Kathy didn't invite her family, which upset her mother, and Kellett's mum only met her a few months later.

Theirs was never an easy marriage, littered as it was with violence and furies that erupted when she imagined David had been unfaithful to her. They had two daughters: Melissa, born on Mother's Day in 1976, and Natasha, who arrived four years later. Finally, in October 1986, they were divorced.

The following year she took up with David Saunders and in 1988 had a baby with him, a girl she named Sarah*. In 1989 Kathy, David and the three children moved into a two-bedroom weatherboard house he bought in MacQueen Street, next door to the Aberdeen General Store. She paid off the house later using her $15 000 compensation payout, and stayed there after she left David Saunders in 1990. Next came John Chillingworth, who she met in a pub and was several years older than her. Within three years, Kathy had notched up another failed romance, also marked by violence. She had her fourth child, a boy she named Eric*.

By the time Kathy Knight started her affair with John Price at the end of 1993, she was closing in on forty. She was a single mother of four children aged from seventeen to two. Her track record with men was abysmal. She hated breakups yet seemed unable to stop them. She had another shot at romance and she wanted this one to last.

John Charles Thomas Price was like many Australian men of a certain age and born outside the big city limits. He was a worker who, at the end of twelve hours of hard yakka, liked nothing more than to shoot the breeze with his mates in the local pub, with a schooner of Tooheys New, his favourite brew, puffing away on a packet of Winfield Red. As the air around him turned a dirty grey with smoke, and with one foot planted firmly on the carpet, the other resting on the barstool, Pricey would chat with his mates about their respective days. Nothing too personal, mind you, just life in general. Male conversation tended towards the weather and its effect on stock, the latest league results if it was winter, or cricket if it was summer, or plans for the next week-long fishing expedition, nutting out the details of who would bring the bait, the beer and the beds.

Pricey, as he was known, was your average bloke. There was nothing overwhelming or underwhelming about him. He didn't live dangerously. Risky, life-threatening behaviour was not part of his normal routine. Perhaps the greatest risk he'd taken, and was ever likely to take, was crossing, late at night after knocking back one too many schooners at the top pub, the dimly lit two-lane New England Highway that splits in half the quiet country town of Aberdeen where he lived about a ten-minute walk away from Kathy Knight.

John Price had been married and divorced, once each, and had three children, Johnathon, Rosemary and Jackie*. Pricey and his wife Colleen had separated in 1988 after fifteen years of marriage for the simple reason that they were incompatible, a description so vast and intangible that one never knows where to start to join the dots of marital failure. But he was a nice bloke, a regular guy, and his carefree nature meant that his relationship with Colleen always remained friendly. They were best mates, she said.

His two eldest children, Johnathon and Rosemary, had grown into healthy, well-adjusted young adults with their own families. Johnathon lived in Aberdeen, two blocks away from his father, with his partner and their young daughter. John Price's youngest child, Jackie, a teenager in high school, lived with her mum a couple of hundred kilometres due north up the highway in Tamworth. He owned his own modest house, a neat three-bedroom, red brick veneer on the high side of the street, had a decent job and a recent promotion, drove a company car and loved to fish for trout and drink in his spare time, not necessarily in that order. The more beer he drank the louder and more boisterous he became, as if the boy had never left the man.

John Price was a nuggety bloke, of average height and above average weight. At forty-four he had seen better days after years of working hard and playing just as hard. He was no oil painting but wasn't bad looking either, with tousled dark brown curly hair and an impish smile that slid into a grin that squeezed his eyes nearly shut and formed deep laugh crevasses tracking horizontally to his ears. Pricey was the archetypal larrikin, friendly, good natured, loved a joke and didn't mind if it bordered on lewd. Probably better if it did, just to get a rise. And could he swear!

Since starting work at fifteen Pricey had always been one of the boys, whether he was driving trucks or working in a coal mine. He enjoyed being a labourer, mucking in, doing his job, going home to a cold beer and leaving the responsibilities of management to someone else. Any ambition he had was hidden under a bushel until midway through 1999, when he was promoted to foreman at an earth moving equipment company where he had worked for just a year. He supervised a team of no-nonsense blokes just like him who drove massive Caterpillar scrapers and dozers worth more than a million dollars each. And he was good at it. Pricey was a doer, not a gunna. If the weather had been a bit dodgy overnight, he'd be at the mine site well before 6 am to ensure it was safe to work. He'd roll his shirtsleeves up and look out for his crew, and his men loved him for it, maybe just a little less when he was ripping into them or giving them a mouthful if something wasn't up to scratch.

He followed a strict routine: up around 5 am, out of the house by five-thirty, work by six, despite the hangover if there was one. Pricey knocked off roughly twelve hours after he started and each night, without fail, drove the 15-kilometre route along the New England Highway from the Bayswater colliery on the southern side of Muswellbrook to the front bar of the top pub in Aberdeen where he was a regular. Depending on the traffic, he could be knocking back his first beer by six-twenty. Life for Pricey was that simple: wake, work, family, friends, beer, bed.

The Aberdeen Hotel is known by pragmatic locals as the top pub simply because it stands at the top of the hill, about a kilometre up the road from the bottom pub, the Commercial, which is at the bottom of the hill and the second last building you see on the left as you leave Aberdeen heading north towards Scone. In most of the small towns that pepper the Australian countryside there are, usually, only two degrees of separation. Almost everyone who walked into the Aberdeen pub and spotted John Price gave him a friendly slap on the back followed by a 'G'day, Pricey' as they sauntered to the bar to order. Pricey never had to worry about drinking alone at the top pub.

It was no surprise that Pricey met Kath in the top pub. She remembered the date exactly as 8 October. Pricey was everything she wanted: employed, liked a bit of a good time, and single. Kath fell madly in love and was determined to make this relationship last.

By February 2000, Kathy and Pricey had been together for more than six years but their romance danced a clunky minuet from passion one moment to loathing the next. They were on and off, it was just the way they were, the locals said with a shrug. In 1998 Price severed all contact after they had a blue, and for nearly two months they kept their distance. It was a bitter separation, the scars of which never fully healed, but for reasons only they could explain, they got back together again.

During the Christmas and New Year of 1999, the relationship with Kath was wearing on Pricey. He coped, somehow, with her fiery personality, but he was coming to the end of his tether. On Sunday 27 February they had another dust-up and the police were called. On Monday, acting on Kathy's behalf, police served an Apprehended Violence Order on Pricey.

It instructed him to keep away from Kathy, but it was a joke. She was at his house when it was issued, making a mockery of the paper it was written on. Kathy rebuked the police, saying she had never asked for the AVO, and she stayed the night at Pricey's, her two youngest children sleeping in the spare bedrooms. Before they went to bed, they agreed they couldn't go on the way they were. Pricey wanted her out of the house, but Kath didn't want to leave.

On Tuesday, Pricey went to court to get his own AVO against Kath. It was official. He wanted her out of his life. Pricey had a copy of the AVO but it was never served. That night, as he lay in bed after they made love, Kath picked up a 31.5 centimetre knife, its 17 centimetre blade curved like a pirate's cutlass, and stabbed him to death.

~

It was just after 10 am on Thursday 18 October, day three of case number 70094/00: Regina v Katherine Mary Knight. Dozens of prospective jurors who hadn't skipped their jury duty when given the opportunity by Justice O'Keefe the day before, were waiting to hear if they would get the chance to play Solomon and decide if Kathy Knight was guilty of murdering John Price. But something unusual was unfolding. Early the previous afternoon, the judge adjourned the hearing, asking the jury candidates to return at 9.30 am for court to start at ten. All he would say was that the prosecution counsel and Katherine Knight's Queen's Counsel had met with him. 'It is unusual, but the circumstances that have arisen are unusual as well,' Justice O'Keefe said, creating a frisson of mystery.

As instructed, all but five of the original potential jurors trundled back into the courthouse at 9.30 am on day three. They never heard if they had the right stuff to sit on the jury. At 10 am sharp, the accused was brought into the dock. She sat briefly, then was asked to stand. Justice O'Keefe's associate quickly read the arraignment. It was clumsy but according to form: 'For that Katherine Mary Knight on or about 29 February 2000 at Aberdeen in the State of New South Wales did murder John Charles Thomas Price,' the associate read, looking down her nose at the paper in front of her.

A plea was called for and Katherine Knight spoke for the first and nearly last time at her murder trial.

'Guilty,' she said.

Had they been allowed to, prosecutors Mark Macadam and Kylie Henry would have punched the air in exultation, but instead they let out a sigh of relief.

Justice O'Keefe spoke directly to the accused, who stood looking at him: 'You understand, Mrs Knight, do you, the effect of that plea?'

'Beg your pardon?' she said, her speech hard and clipped, finished with a rising inflection.

'You understand the effect of that plea – that is, that you are admitting to the charge of murder?' the judge said.

'Yes, your Honour.'

'You have taken counsel's advice, have you?'

'Yes, your Honour.'

'And I understand that you have had the opportunity to consider that matter overnight?'

'Yes, your Honour.'

'And you are content to lodge that plea, is that correct?'

'Yes, your Honour.'

And that was that. Katherine Knight sat down and with those sixteen words changed the course of her future.

The judge turned to the jury and, after a polite explanation, dismissed them. They were no longer needed because Katherine Knight's guilty plea had turned what was going to be a murder trial of an innocent woman accused of a horrible crime into a hearing to determine the appropriate sentence for the woman who had pleaded guilty to it. The jurors now didn't have to hear the grisly details of how she had killed John Price, and for that they could be thankful.

Katherine Knight was alone in the dock.

During the next hour, lawyers for the defendant and the Crown informed the court how they would proceed, who they would call as witnesses, and what evidence they would present to assist the judge, who would determine an appropriate sentence for Katherine Knight. The business end of the day was almost over. One last formality remained outstanding.

Katherine Knight had remained silent and solemn. She showed little emotion. Justice O'Keefe turned to her and asked her to stand up. She did. He looked her in the eye.

'Mrs Knight, you have pleaded guilty to a charge of murder and I have accepted that plea,' he said, mistakenly addressing the divorcee as Missus, something he would correct later when she said she preferred to be called Miss Knight, which was her maiden name. 'As a consequence, I judge you to be guilty of murder and a conviction for murder will be recorded accordingly. Do you understand?'

She used the same phrase she had uttered previously, nothing more, nothing less.

'Yes, your Honour.'

Katherine Knight admitted she was a killer. She never uttered another word publicly about what had happened.

1

In blue heeler country

Aberdeen is not Arcadia, nor is it the land of opportunity, even though it's close enough to the big smoke. And it's not much of a town. Once you've hit the city limits and slowed your car to the posted speed of 60 kilometres per hour, it takes a mere two minutes to enter and exit via the New England Highway.

Inside the city limits, the highway turns into MacQueen Street, and heading north up the first slow hill on the right stands a copse of shops called the Aberdeen Valley Fair, from where the locals can buy groceries and rent videos. A block away is the white Bogas station, which has been there for decades, with the same set of pumps selling petrol, leaded, unleaded and superior, and a separate one for gas.

On the left-hand side, modest houses run down and up a gentle hill until they get to the corner of Bedford Street and the first of only a handful of double-storey buildings on the street, the Aberdeen Hotel, an imposing structure that recalls the glory days of when it was built. Next to it is a bakery which sells fine meat pies and pastries to truckers and contractors who can always find a parking spot on the gravel shoulder outside. Then, more houses.

Further down the road, still on the left, is the first of two shops that lay claim to the name of the General Store. It belongs to Lorna Driscoll, a woman with shoulder-length grey hair who sells discount petrol from a single petrol pump, its rounded corners giving away its age like a woman who still wears hairnets. On the opposite side of the highway is the Aberdeen railway station – hidden down a slope, it's easy to miss. St Paul's Uniting Church, a pretty little box-like structure with a picture-book steeple, is next on the left, followed immediately by the police station, home to a uniformed officer who is traditionally known as the lock-up keeper.

From there, zigzagging between both sides of the street, is the rest of Aberdeen; the RSL club with its own bowling green, Barton's newsagency, the little rose garden with an Aberdeen township map, the craft shop, the old bank that has been turned into the Possum Pottery store, a hardware store, the Shell petrol station, the coin-operated laundry, the Commercial Hotel, the Segenhoe Inn and, finally, the second General Store, this one owned by Gerri Edwards, a tall blonde with the body of a thoroughbred.

Ironically, Aberdeen is memorable precisely because, unlike other country towns, there is nothing much to remember it by. It has a library, a fire station, a post office, two primary schools, a kindergarten, and three churches (Catholic, Uniting and Anglican), but it has no core. There is no Avenue of Honour announcing you've arrived. No clock tower in the middle of a divided road dedicated to lost servicemen and women. There is no main shopping strip holding it together and no common intersection that marks the heart and soul of the community's commerce. There is not one corner that everyone crosses to get to somewhere else.

MacQueen Street feeds and divides the town, but it divides it by asphalt only. Aberdeen is one hundred per cent working class, mostly white, mostly Australian born and bred, and as homogeneous as it gets in the bush. It is a geographical halfway house, unceremoniously plonked in the middle of the more affluent Scone to the north and, to the south, Muswellbrook, a larger city just 'bursting with energy', according to its welcome sign. Aberdeen, on the other hand, is bursting with nothing.

With a population of 1750 and located 266 kilometres north and slightly west of Sydney, it is without industry and minus purpose since the abattoir closed its doors on 16 April 1999 after 107 years of operation. Australia Meat Holdings, which owned the abattoir in its final years, pulled the pin on the Moray Street meatworks which, for all its life, had been the only game in town, employment wise. Generation after generation worked at the old plant which sat at the foot of a hill on the high side of town. It was successful, processing six hundred head of cattle a day, five days a week. But changing circumstances and newer meatworks elsewhere, improved by technology and modernity, meant that four hundred and twenty loyal employees, many of them locals, lost their jobs when the doors slammed shut.

Humble towns are allowed one boast and Aberdeen's is a beaut, cementing her place in Australia's iconography: it is the birthplace of the blue heeler cattle dog. Back in the early nineteenth century English drover George Hall and his wife Mary set sail from Ireland with their four children. The family thrived in the colony and in 1808, in a place then called Portland Head in New South Wales, Mary Hall gave birth to her seventh child, a boy she named Thomas. By the 1830s, Thomas Hall had established Dartbrook in the Upper Hunter Valley, a rich successful grazing property that was, at the time, better known in the region than one of the nation's oldest and most respected pioneer and pastoralist families, the Whites, who settled the magnificent Belltrees property on the Gundy Road in 1831 and are still there today.

Like his father, Thomas was a brilliant farmer. Necessity, he discovered, is the mother of invention. Hall ran free-range cattle on his fenceless property, so he needed a feisty, strong dog that could adapt to both the harsh climate and difficult landscape of the Hunter Valley to control his roaming cattle. The dogs then being used by farmers yapped incessantly and sent the cattle into a frenzy. Other canines were tested and failed when their ferret-like bite damaged the stock.

Hall imported two smooth-haired merle Scotch collies from his parents' native Northumberland, and in 1840, he crossed dingoes – silent, sneaky and fast – with the litter of the two dogs he had imported. The resulting pups were a stocky, salt and pepper flecked heeler known initially as Hall's heelers. It was another Hall success, and the breed came to be known as the blue heeler for its flinty colour.

~

Katherine's father Ken Knight's people had settled in Aberdeen in the 1800s, planting their roots in the district and digging in deep. They were a part of the community. Ken was raised in a tiny wooden cottage that sat bang on top of a lump of earth known as the Needles, a foothill in the shadow of the Barrington Tops Mountains. The view was spectacular any way you looked. In the distance to the north, halfway to the horizon, was the elegant township of Scone, its main road lined with lovely old sandstone buildings the colour of dusty gold. It sat at the end of lush green fields that rolled into each other like slow moving waves, their boundaries marked by fairytale fences that mapped out thoroughbred horse studs, revealing the riches of the land's owners. Looking east, down into the valley of the mountain range, one could see the freshwater Lake Glenbawn, home to the wedge-tailed eagle and kestrel, and stocked with trout and Murray cod. Further west and south were the flatlands of dairy farms and manicured vineyards, the sharp wedges of open cut mines and the dark hills of their haul.

If the view was grand, the Knight house itself wasn't much. In fact it looked like an imposter amid the majesty of the surrounding environment. There was no electricity, and on windy days, which were often, a chill swept through the cracks in the planks that had been knocked together by hand. In late June and early July, the morning frosts would bite hard and the temperature would fall well below zero, chilling a body to the bone and keeping it that way all day. Seen from a distance, the hut cut a lonely image, but it was home.

Ken Knight's parents raised six children there, Richard (or Dick), Keith, James (who was known as Jimmy), Ted and Elizabeth (who was born mute and is known locally as Deaf Betty). And of course Ken. As was custom in the Australia of the 1940s, children could leave school at the age of fourteen, and that suited

Ken fine. For a working-class teenager in the 1940s, having a job was a ticket to freedom and it was freedom rather than books that Ken was interested in.

The Australian Chilling and Freezing Company owned by the Nelson Brothers had opened its doors in 1892 after the art of freezing had been perfected, and it became the first Australian abattoir to export frozen beef and lamb to appreciative foreign markets. It was also the biggest local employer. There was no shortage of work in Aberdeen for those who weren't born lazy or didn't think themselves a cut above a job in the meatworks. Not long after Ken turned fourteen, the tall, skinny teenager joined the slaughter-floor.

Barbara Knight, Katherine's mother, was born Barbara Claire Thorley in a family of eight children. The Thorleys were Muswellbrook people. The young Barbara Thorley was something of a local beauty when she met Jack Roughan in the early 1940s. After a short courtship, they were married. In 1945 she gave birth to Patrick, quickly followed by Martin. Then came Neville on 10 January 1950 and, exactly one year and eleven days later, Barry. But the young Roughan marriage was already in trouble by the time Barry was born and when he was just six months old, Barbara took off.

You had to understand the place and time to understand how unusual it was. World War II had ended six years before. Australian boys who left as young and naive soldiers to fight on foreign soil returned as worldly men, but they returned to a nation that had lost none of its restrictive, conservative values. In small towns, women were expected to be dutifully domesticated and generally, at least outwardly so, were rarely asked their opinions. They promised to honour and obey.

Wives and mothers were not expected to do what Barbara Roughan did. They didn't just leave the family home. You made your bed, you lay in it: But Barbara marched to her own beat and she left.

Under family law in the 1950s, the father routinely won custody if families faltered when the mother left, and Patrick and Martin Roughan were considered old enough to live with their father. Their younger brothers, Neville and Barry, were both under eighteen months old and too little to be cared for by their father, who had to work to make a living to pay for their upkeep. So the two little Roughan tykes were shipped off to live with their aunt on their father's side, Margaret Ann Tanner, known as Nan, in Granville. 'She was the ants pants,' Barry Roughan remembered fondly nearly fifty years later.

Within the year, Barbara met Kenneth Charles Knight and in 1952 they were married. By 1953 Barb was pregnant with Kenneth Charles Knight the second, who would become known as Charlie so as not to confuse matters, and the honeymoon was over.

At that time the Australian economy was riding high on the sheep's back, and the cow and the pig carried a heavy load too. If a farmer was raising cattle, sheep or pigs and a population was eating them, a slaughterman could always find work. All he needed were his knives and a work ethic. Ken Knight took his family to Wallangarra, a small border town in Queensland.

Wallangarra had a meatworks and the first pub across state lines, but it didn't have a hospital. When Barbara Knight was ready to give birth for the sixth time in October 1955, she headed south into her home state of New South Wales to Tenterfield, travelling 18 kilometres on tired country roads with a belly swollen to bursting with two unborn girls. If another hospital had been closer, she would have gone there.

Ken Knight was not at the hospital when the girls were born. A tall, lean man with a hook of a nose and light blue eyes that shone like glass, and hands as raspy as Sydney sandstone, he was in the middle of another twelve-hour shift of back-breaking labour 'dressing' cattle carcasses on the slaughter-floor at the Wallangarra meatworks.

The word 'dressing' is a misnomer, one of many anodyne euphemisms the meat industry employs to describe jobs so bloody and brutal that calling them by their true name would be macabre. The language is like a little inside joke. Slaughtermen, similarly, are ill-named. To slaughter is to kill, but these men, and they are 99.9 per cent men, don't kill anything. That's left to a bloke they call the 'knocker'. The knocker works in a 'knock box' and kills the livestock using a captive bolt gun fired square between the eyes where the brain is closest to the skull. The animal is walked single file into a confined race. A gate closes behind it. Its head is raised and fully extended by a jaw lock. The knocker lines up the bolt gun loaded with a 75 mm bolt, and fires. Bang, instant death. Decades ago, death was more intimate. A knocker used naked force and speared the beast through the back of the neck, cutting the spinal cord. Death was gruesome and sometimes it was neither instant nor easy. The introduction of the bolt gun marked the meeting of humanity, technology and efficiency.

Once the animal is 'stunned', or dead, its corpse is turned over, literally, to an army of skilled slaughtermen lined up at various points on the slaughter-floor. Their job is to 'dress' the beast, which is the opposite of what they do. They strip it of everything that made it a living, breathing animal.

Depending on the abattoir, the dead animal is hung by either its front or hind leg from a chain attached to an overhead pulley. Under international regulations, a slaughterman has to 'stick' the beast within sixty seconds of its death. Sticking the beast means draining it of blood in preparation for what follows – a gruesome but precise and artful choreography by dozens of blokes carving knives through flesh and bone. Standing in position around the slaughter-floor in their bright white overalls and galumphing white rubber boots, the slaughtermen look like a brutish chorus line in a macabre ballet, glints of light bouncing off their steel blades.

With a 15 centimetre curved knife a slaughterman rips into the two jugular veins with a sharp, fast downward cut about 300–400 millimetres long. Then he swings his knife in a deliberate upward thrust into the veins that only a minute earlier had been pumping life through a beast that can weigh up to three tonnes. There is no room for error. Hot blood floods from the gaping hole over a grate in the floor into the tank below. It spurts out fast enough to fill a four-gallon bucket in seconds. If the beast hasn't been swung in the right direction, angled away from the slaughterman, the stuck vein will spew sticky, iron-smelling blood over his boots and overalls like a tap with its spigot opened at full force.

And that's just the beginning. Slaughtermen then skin the animal. They eviscerate it, splitting it open down the centre and cutting out its guts, lungs, heart and offal. The smell of exposed guts is overwhelming and seeps into every pore, but the slaughtermen get used to it, just as they get used to their white overalls turning red from flesh and blood. They flank it, skin the anus, remove its head, and cut it into presentable sides of raw meat like those you see swinging from meat-hooks in old-fashioned butcher shops.

Slaughtermen are at their best after they've had about fourteen years of experience in the industry, and Ken Knight was nearing the top of his game, but the work can be cyclical. Meatworks have down-times, when slaughtermen and labourers pack up their knives and hit the bitumen in search of work elsewhere. Ken Knight never minded moving, and after a few years at Wallangarra, he crossed the border into New South Wales and took a job on the slaughter-floor at the Gunnedah meatworks.

Gunnedah is a workers' town, pure Australia, and if anyone ever thought otherwise, they need only read 'My Country', the poem written by the town's most famous 'adopted' daughter, Dorothea Mackellar, as a homage to her nation and the region. Some even claimed the poem's most recognised lines were inspired by the town in central northeast New South Wales. And who could argue? Gunnedah *was* a land of sweeping plains and it was a perfect place for country kids to spread their wings.

Ken and Barbara Knight arrived in Gunnedah in 1957 with their three children Charlie, Joy and Kath. Within eighteen months, Barb's ex-husband Jack Roughan died and Barbara scrambled to get her four eldest boys back. She succeeded with the teenagers Patrick and Martin, who had been living with their father, but Neville and Barry were happy with the only mother they had ever known, their beloved Nan.

At seven and eight years old, the two younger boys were as thick as thieves. They were in school in Sydney and had made their own little circle of friends. Nan had also provided a home for one of the boys' cousins whose parents couldn't look after him. Nan refused to let Neville and Barry go, protesting that no good could come from disrupting their little lives again. She treated them as though they were her own boys, and loved them. As family folklore goes, Nan called on the Catholic Church to help mount her case that Neville and Barry should stay with her and their cousin, a family unit of its own. Ultimately, the younger boys stayed in Sydney and Barry and Neville had little to do with their mother until they were reunited with her years later, after Nan died when they were in their late teens.

By 1959, then, Barbara and Ken Knight had five children to raise. Ken was at the meatworks, putting in long hours on rotating shifts to bring in enough money to feed, clothe and educate the children. The Knights weren't rich, Ken had to work, but they weren't on the poverty line either. They lived in a rented house in town and enrolled all five children in the local public schools.

Barbara Knight could be a bit of a hothead, and was known to swear. She was a tough disciplinarian and neighbours remembered her for her short-fused temper and obscene language which she rarely censored. Like most couples, Barbara and Ken had their moments during their marriage but they stayed together, through the good times and bad.

By the time Barb had settled her extended family, she was pregnant again with her eighth and final child. On 12 December 1961, Shane Knight was born in Gunnedah hospital. Finally, an exhausted Barb's child-bearing years were done. She was in her thirties.

Five years later, they returned to Aberdeen for a few months before travelling north up the Newell Highway to Moree, where Ken Knight was offered work in yet another abattoir. He never had to worry – he was good at his job, and he was respected. And in the country, respect is a powerful thing. The Knights lived in Moree for nearly three years, and Shane had his first days in kindergarten there.

~

In 1966 the world was in the middle of a cultural revolution. Australian Prime Minister Robert Gordon Menzies resigned from office after thirty-two years and Harold Holt took his place, quickly declaring 'All the way with LBJ' in support of the US war against Vietnam. The Holden Motor Company stopped production of its bestseller, the EH Holden. Percy Sledge had a hit with the Motown song 'When A Man Loves A Woman'. Brian

Henderson was turning the first baby-boomers into a nation of rockers with his top-rating television music show 'Bandstand', and their parents had fallen in love with an American import called 'Peyton Place'. Outside Australia, evil was given two names: Ian Brady and Myra Hindley. The English thrill-killers were jailed for life for murdering three teenagers in a chilling sex and mutilation crime spree the likes of which had not been seen before.

The times they were a'changing and the revolution was as much about sex and gender politics as it was about culture. Women were burning their bras and experimenting with free love and empowerment. Simone de Beauvoir's groundbreaking book *The Second Sex* had been in bookstores for fifteen years, and the third wave of feminists were mobilising in the war for equal rights. Germaine Greer was at Sydney University studying her way up to *The Female Eunuch*. Britain appointed the first female judge. And President John F. Kennedy's Commission on the Status of Women was knee-deep investigating the lives of female workers. Women were tapping at the glass ceiling and they were hellbent on hearing it shatter sometime soon.

If women's lib got within cooee of the bush, Barbara Knight didn't hear its call. Feminism was just a fancy-sounding word from educated, middle-class womenfolk from the city. It didn't apply to her, thank you very much. And it wasn't going to change her life, not one iota. Barbara Knight already *was* a working mother. Seven days a week, twenty-four hours a day. The role of parenting fell completely to her, there was no talk of dividing household chores. It was all women's work.

In the bush, women didn't work outside of the home, and if they did, it was a shame, an embarrassment. Barbara didn't need to. Ken took care of that. He often worked two double shifts on the weekends. After finishing his butchering, he'd join the loading gang, filling train carriages with expertly packed meat bound for export to Japan and the United States. As he said later, 'She didn't need to work. I did.'

And anyway, with six children at home, Barbara had enough on her plate. Not only did she have to deal with energetic and rambunctious boys scrambling for her attention, she was, in the parlance of her class, chief cook and bottle washer. Ken's wage had to stretch to feed eight people seven days a week. Every meal had to count. Last night's roast turned into today's shepherd's pie, and leftover veggies became bubble and squeak. Corned beef could be Sunday's lunch and Tuesday's sandwich meat. There were no electric dishwashers, washing machines or dryers. A vacuum cleaner was a luxury she couldn't even conceive of. She cooked, cleaned, sewed and raised children. But Barbara didn't complain. There was nothing to complain about. She had no choice. She just did it.

Ken and Barbara ran a strict household. There was no mucking about and the kids did what they were told. 'Just fairly, not over strict, but just fairly,' Ken would say later. They had dinner at the family table each night when Ken arrived home from work. Meat and three veg. Afterwards, the kids chipped in with cleaning up.

'Just [an] ordinary upbringing. Not like today, they didn't run the streets everywhere like today,' Ken said. 'Today they don't know where their kids are. See, them days people spent more time together. Not like now with TV and whatever. TV spoiled everything, it has. It's ruined the world, I reckon.'

In 1969, Ken decided to return to his hometown of Aberdeen. This time, it was for good.

2

At last, girls

Katherine Mary Knight came in to this world in second place. Her feisty twin, Joy Gwendoline, pushed ahead and forced her way out of her mother's birth canal thirty minutes before her sister, hungrily drawing her first gasp of air into a pair of tiny lungs. It was 24 October 1955, and Joy was the sixth child – and, auspiciously, the first daughter – of Barbara Knight.

As the first girl, it was a cause for celebration but there was no champagne. When Katherine Mary arrived half an hour later, Barbara's brood numbered seven, but it's fair to say she was probably too exhausted to celebrate again. Six years later there would be an eighth child, another boy, Shane, making it six boys and two girls neatly divided between two fathers, four apiece. Katherine's four half-brothers – Patrick, Martin, Neville and Barry – were Roughan boys, but there was no mistaking the maternal connection. They were all capped by the same fiery red hair, a gift from their mother's side.

Joy and Katherine were born in the historic town of Tenterfield, known as the 'Birthplace of the Nation'. Serendipity shined on them but they didn't know it. The girls had the honour of sharing their birth date with the young country's ambitious push to nationhood. On the very same day sixty-six years earlier, a bear of a man by the name of Sir Henry Parkes strode into the main hall at the Tenterfield School of Arts and declared that Australia's six independent colonies should unite to form a Federation. Seven decades later, Tenterfield found another kind of popular fame when a saddler named George Woolnough was immortalised by his grandson, Peter Allen, in the song 'The Tenterfield Saddler'. But Barbara Knight didn't choose Tenterfield for its history. She was there by necessity. The Prince Albert Memorial Hospital had been serving the Tenterfield community since 1862, and that's where Barbara went to give birth to her only girls.

Joy and Katherine brought to the family the double delights of twinship and daughters. Barbara knew what it was like to raise boys – rough and tumble terrors loaded with testosterone, sorting each other out as they grew up, each finding his own natural place in the family. Joy and Katherine were something new, and they were a pair.

Like most infant twins, they were rarely apart. They were fed together, slept together, bathed together and, generally, changed together. Twins often develop a special language that only they can understand, and most entertain each other in their cots. Initially their closeness was as much for their mother's convenience as for anything else, but the bond Joy and Katherine developed as infants deepened as the girls grew up, bringing them closer. They were often together and, eventually, they would work and socialise with each other.

But just as they were close, they were also different. Joy and Katherine are fraternal twins, not identical, and even though they shared their mother's womb, they shared the same percentage of genetic coding as their other siblings. Joy was the more outgoing of the girls, her youngest brother Shane recalled. As a child she had more friends than Katherine, and was more of a leader. Katherine was more feminine, more girly, the one who helped out around the house, played with her dolls, and made things. She also had a maternal streak which she displayed in her early years, mothering her baby brother. 'She was kind of like a mother. She would look after me and that. Help with the cooking and cleaning and that,' Shane said of Katherine. 'I suppose you'd call it family oriented. Joy was more like the tomboy. Joy was the tough one, she wouldn't take no shit from nobody.'

After their half-brother Barry Roughan was reunited with his family and got to know them better, Joy would be the one he turned to when he needed to share confidences or seek advice: 'The one person I trusted with my life. If [there was] anyone I could tell a secret to, it was Joy,' Barry said. 'She was the one member of the family everyone looked up to. Joy can do no wrong. Joy was the ants pants. She was Mum's favourite . . . Joy was calm. She wasn't like Katherine. Katherine has always been a bit fiery.'

Katherine had only one or two friends and generally kept to herself and played with her dolls. She also loved animals but wasn't allowed to keep pets because their father had greyhounds. But Katherine found a way around the no-pet edict by picking up injured strays and bringing them home.

'Anything she found that was hurt or something, she'd bring it home and want someone to fix it for her, and then she'd want to keep it,' her brother Shane said. 'Wasn't allowed to keep dogs or cats. If she found a bird with a broken wing she could keep it till it was better, but nothing big. We had greyhounds when we were younger and any pets would have been eaten [by the dogs].'

The phenomenon of twins has captured the popular imagination for centuries. Do they think alike? Why do they look alike? Why don't they look more alike? Why do some mirror each other almost perfectly and yet others are polar opposites? Do they share a magical telepathy, unexplained by any science?

In the nineteenth century, an Englishman named Sir Francis Galton turned his attention to the study of twins, believing they could shed some light on the theories of nurture and nature. Galton, an explorer, meteorologist and the man who discovered the innate uniqueness of fingerprints, had a pedigree. He was a cousin of the famous evolutionary theorist Charles Darwin. Galton wanted to know if biology shaped destiny. Did genes determine behaviour? Was genius inherited? There was no better social and biological laboratory than that provided by twins.

Identical twins are nature's clones and occur when a single fertilised egg splits in two around the time it is implanted in the womb, usually by the twelfth day after conception. Dizygotic twins, as fraternal twins such as Katherine and Joy are scientifically known, are conceived when two separate sperm fertilise two separate eggs. They are no more genetically alike than any two siblings – male or female – with the same biological parents. While they share 25 per cent of their genes and may share the same tastes and interests, they are not identical nor will they necessarily act and behave identically.

Katherine's and Joy's differences didn't end with their personalities but, in part, were probably a result of them. Katherine's school life wasn't as blessed as her sister's. Academic achievement was not her strong point. She repeated Grade 5 and was always in the lowest or second lowest class. By the time she left school at the age of fifteen, Katherine had achieved only minimal reading and writing skills. 'She wasn't the smartest pencil in the box, but she was alright,' Shane remembered. Despite her lack of academic achievement, Katherine rarely missed school and was 'just a normal kid growing up, I suppose', her father Ken said.

By high school, though, Katherine was already showing signs of being an angry young girl with disciplinary problems. In 1968, a year before Ken Knight moved the family back to Aberdeen, a thirteen-year-old Katherine was hauled before the Children's Court and received a good behaviour bond for an offence. As required by law, the records are sealed and the charge is not known. Surprisingly, for all that would follow, it was the first and only time Katherine was ever before the court – until March 2000. More than thirty years later, Crown prosecutor Mark Macadam would tell the New South Wales Supreme Court that it could not take the juvenile matter into account at Katherine Knight's sentencing for murder.

Barbara and Ken Knight were strict disciplinarians, and Barbara was known for her language and fiery temper. There was no modern-day 'tough love' discipline or 'time out' or considered reasoning with the Knight children.

'It all stems from her mum. The language that'd come out of her mouth was unreal, and that's how those kids grew up,' one neighbour recalled years later. 'Every second word was eff this and eff that, and all the rest of it, and that is how they grew up.

You wouldn't want her [Barbara Knight] for your best friend, put it that way. But on the other hand, if you wanted anything done or you needed help she'd be there to help you, sort of a split personality.'

When Katherine was eleven, her mother gave her an old-fashioned pram with a curved hood that reached over the carriage like a protective canopy. Katherine loved the pram and pushed her dolls around in it. She kept it all her life. In the hours before she committed murder, the pram would take on a more symbolic meaning.

Shane only ever saw Katherine as a kind, caring sister who always looked out for his welfare. It wasn't until years later, when she was a young woman and involved with men, that her problems started. She was never violent, he said. 'No, not like they reckon in the paper, that she used to go around bullying all the schoolkids. Nah, not true, she'd rather help ya than hurt ya.

'Actually I've never seen her lose her temper or that. Never. She was always a good kid, that I knew of. I never seen her beating anyone or giving them a hard time or anything. She's always nice to everybody. But, um, that's only my opinion, other people say different things. I think a lot of 'em don't worry about the truth as long as it's a good story. Well, that's what I've found in the last four or five months, anyway,' Shane said, slipping into the present and referring to the press coverage about his sister's crime.

Shane Knight is a solid man who shaves his head bald and wears a full beard that has turned white. He has his father's blue eyes and he speaks in slow, deliberate sentences, weighing his words carefully, while rolling his cigarettes to an anorexic thinness. He worked in the hide-room at the Aberdeen meatworks curing and preparing the cattle skins for sale, but has been unemployed since he was diagnosed with diabetes in 1996. 'You just feel as weak as a lamb,' Shane said. 'When I found out I had it, I wouldn't have been able to wrestle a five year old.'

Shane believes in family and the cohesiveness of the family as a unit. He lives with his father at the small family farmhouse about 10 kilometres outside Aberdeen on an unmarked road with rough edges opposite a picturesque horse stud. From the eastern side of the house they can see the tiny outline of the hut on the Needles where Ken grew up. Ken Knight moved the family to the weatherboard farmhouse in 1979. Set on a couple of acres of land, they keep sheep in a field off to one side of the house and have a working dog. There was a time when they kept cattle, and would gather as a family every four months or so to butcher a cow.

'When we bought this place, we got a couple of cows and some pigs and sheep and chooks and we'd knock a cow every six months or something. It would usually take about an hour to do, that's if everyone pitched in and helped,' Shane said.

Katherine and Joy, both married by the time Ken bought the house, would also help out, but Katherine 'would never do the knife work'. Ken, a trained slaughterman, was the butcher. The closest Katherine got to the livestock was when it was dead stock, or plucking the chooks when they were being prepared for the kitchen.

'Usually we would kill 'em and dress 'em and they [the girls] would do the hose work and bring the bucket with the heart and liver and whatever else we're going to eat off it. But their job didn't come into it until a week later. That was boning it and slicing it up into steaks and that. Because you have to put them in a fridge for a week to let it set or they come out all wrong. So they were the slicers, and Joy's husband was the boner.

'It was a big event for us. It would take three or four hours to bone one out and dress it up – cutting it into chops and steak and mincemeat and all that stuff.

'We used to quarter it up. Me and the old fella'd keep a quarter, Joy and John'd keep a quarter, Katherine'd get a quarter and Charlie'd get a quarter. But they never get nothing if they never helped do it. It's been a while since we done one, but. It's been about ten years since we had a cow. The old fella is getting pretty old and he was the main skinner. The others could do it but they couldn't do as good a job as what he could. That makes a lot of difference. Yes, it can ruin the whole body if you don't do it properly. We still do the odd sheep and that.'

When the family moved back to Aberdeen in 1969, Katherine and Joy were thirteen and enrolled in the first form of Muswellbrook High. They lived in town, in Mount Street, and were surrounded by cousins and aunts and uncles at every turn. This was, after all, Knight country. The girls took the bus to and from school each day, getting dropped off near the railway station on the main road. Katherine was still a bit of a loner, but she was never a timid outcast. She wore glasses and was tall for her age. Her flame-coloured hair made her stand out even more. She couldn't be inconspicuous no matter how much she wanted to or how hard she tried.

Childhood can be tribal, and it's often brutal and cruel. Loners and misfits fall to the bottom of the adolescent social heap and are frequently targeted by boys and girls eager to assert their dominance and enjoy the rewards of popularity that come with it.

Sharon Turner* went to the same high school and remembered Katherine as being an easy mark for the boys on the bus. But she knew how to look after herself, probably a result of growing up with four brothers at home.

The bus trip from Muswellbrook to Aberdeen took about forty-five minutes with various stops on the way. By the time it turned left off the New England Highway to let the Knight twins off, Kath would have endured an entire journey's worth of insults from boys with bum-fluff on their face and spots ready to explode. Kath wasn't a natural beauty, and the boys made sure she knew it. As the bus moved off, Sharon would say, 'Oh, here we go,' and press her face to the window to watch while Kath took on her tormentors.

'She wasn't what you'd call the nicest looking of the twins. And I can remember the bus used to go around the top hotel there, and they'd get off the bus, and Kathy's favourite saying was, "Here, Joy, hold my glasses". She used to bash the boys up because they tormented her,' Sharon said.

'"Here, Joy, here are my glasses", and she'd get in a fist fight with the boys. They'd call her names, anything obscene. She could bash 'em, don't worry about that. She wouldn't take any crap . . . she could look after herself. I used to say . . . Katherine could look after herself in jail. Oh yeah, don't worry about that, she wasn't frightened of anybody. If she had something to say, she'd say it.'

Donna Dixon* grew up in Aberdeen and lived on the same block as the Knights when they returned to town in 1969. Donna is a few years younger than Katherine and Joy, but the girls were friendly. As teenagers, they got on well and, to Donna's mind, Katherine never really stood out all that much. Donna remembered once watching with ghoulish fascination when Katherine gouged a witchetty grub out of a tree stump and ate it.

'I nearly dropped dead when she did,' Donna said, laughing. 'Well, I don't know whether she really ate it or whether she was pretending. She just pulled one out of the log at her house, "Have you tried these? These are really nice". I remember saying, "No" but she said, "Oh no, they're beautiful". But I can't really remember whether she ate it or not.

'When we were kids her and her sister were very good to my older sister in high school. My older sister actually was getting bullied. And they were really good to her. They stuck up for her with these other girls because she used to get belted around fairly often and kicked in the legs and money taken off her – they were total bitches,' Donna said.

'And Katherine and Joy must have found out about it, and I can remember Mum and Dad always talking about it. They just looked after her which was good, especially coming from a small country town. And coming from a small country town you wouldn't think that anybody would be capable of doing what she did,' Donna said, shifting into the present. 'But you hear people say that when she worked at the meatworks she was fabulous with a knife and things like that.'

When she met Kathy, Robin Smith* was a pretty and petite thirteen year old who liked to hang out with the new twins in town. There's not much for teenagers to do in tiny country towns and things can grow pretty stale pretty quickly. The twins' newness gave them an added frisson.

Now in her forties and still petite, Robin remembered once walking along MacQueen Street, past Barton's newsagency, with Kathy and a couple of other girlfriends on a summer night, just on dusk. A bunch of boys were on the other side of the road, in a park where the rose garden now stands. Things change at a glacial pace in small towns, and the sameness helps the memory.

Anyway, the boys started howling their mating rituals, a typical if inelegant teenaged song of sledging accompanied by wolf whistles. The girls were happy for the attention and giggled. All except Kathy.

'We didn't know she had this long-bladed knife . . . and that day she pulled out the knife and said, "Come on, if you want to have a go at us, come on" . . . They only walked halfway across the road and bolted, but you can't blame them . . . wouldn't you?' Robin said. 'We just all looked at each other, I think we were all in shock actually . . . I'll never forget that.'

None of the girls ever told their parents, knowing that carrying a knife was bound to get them into trouble – big time – and they would be guilty by association.

'We just all looked at each other and still couldn't believe it the next day. Well, you don't expect someone of that age to have knives, and particularly back then because things were quite calm and harmless . . . not like it is today. But that's how she was . . . That was the last time we ever went out.'

3

Inside the abattoir

As a child Katherine Knight knew what she wanted to do and where she wanted to work when she grew up. She wanted to join the abattoir like her old man. For her, the romance of work was locked behind the walls of the old blonde brick building on Moray Street in Aberdeen where her father Ken Knight worked as a slaughterman. And, for reasons even she probably couldn't understand, she wanted to follow in his footsteps.

Kathy had grown up surrounded by the industry and had moved from town to country town following her father as he took his knives to meatworks around the state and across the border. Her older brother Charlie worked at the Aberdeen meatworks, as did her sister Joy, and for one brief moment even her mother had donned the apron and lined up in the slicers' room. A few years later, her youngest brother would follow the family tradition and go into the hide-room curing skins – salting them down and drying them out.

Kathy didn't put a lot of thought into her future, she didn't need to. Aberdeen had an abattoir, so Aberdeen had employment. It was a natural progression from school to work, as if it had all been carefully mapped out for her. 'Most people when they left school went to the meatworks, there wasn't much else,' Kathy's father said.

At the age of fifteen Kathy could legally leave school and that was good enough for her and her parents. School wasn't a social event like it was for other girls her age. With an easy exit on offer, she didn't even bother sweating on the final few months to finish Year 8 at Muswellbrook High School. Her reading and writing weren't the best – in fact, they were appalling – but perfect penmanship and Shakespearean sonnets were not going to help anyone clean out intestines in the offal room at the meatworks.

At first, Kathy's application for a job at the abattoir was unsuccessful, so she reluctantly got a job with a clothing company down the highway from Aberdeen. Her fortunes changed when, in 1971, she applied to the abattoir again, and this time she got in. She was sixteen and about to enter the bloody world of animal slaughter. 'They were in the boning room, the two girls, Shane was in the hidehouse,' Ken said.

Slaughterhouses are historically male-only environments, and have changed little despite the increase in women workers over the years. When Kathy started more than thirty years ago, the Aberdeen abattoir was rough and rugged, and proud to be so. The blokes who worked there didn't give a tinker's cuss about propriety in front of the ladies. It was *their* workspace, and if a woman didn't like it, she could lump it or leave it. They spoke in sentences that were rarely more than a dozen words long and spiced with language that could turn the air blue.

The Aberdeen abattoir, which had separate floors for beef, sheep and pork, had an unofficial and primitive hierarchy. At the top of the social order were the slaughtermen. Next came the all-male boner gangs, then the mixed-sex army of slicers. At the bottom of the social totem pole were the labourers – men and women – and the juniors, scraping up the rear. The labourers cleaned the blood and animal flesh from the floor and benches, and worked in the offal or pre-trim rooms. They also worked in the rendering department where all the waste from the abattoir – *all* of it – was cooked, pressed and pushed into tallow. If the wind wasn't blowing across the Upper Hunter Valley hills on the days the cookers were processing 70 tonnes per hour, a rancid smell would hang in the air over Aberdeen.

Women's work was confined to the slicers' floor, and the pre-trim and offal rooms, or with the clean-up gang.

The kill floor was populated exclusively by men – the experts who did the slaughtering, the bloodletting and the butchering. After stunning a bull or cow with a bolt gun fired between the eyes, they shackled the beasts with chains around either one of the fore or hind legs so they could be dragged upside down at just the right height to have their throats cut. Their stomachs would be sliced open so their insides could be removed. At the peak of production, sixty-seven syncopated men would be capable of processing sixty-five head of cattle hanging from the chains at any one time.

On the pig floor, the knocker used an electric device with two sharp prongs about 7 centimetres apart to zap the hog into unconsciousness as it came through a race on a conveyor belt. The stun gun, which was attached to the top of the arm by a glove, was applied behind the pig's ears and knocked the animal out so it could be shackled and hoisted up onto the rail before being 'stuck' and bled out. The dead pig was then dropped into a tank of boiling water to help remove the bristles from its skin.

A few years later when she was married, Kathy Knight's husband David Kellett worked at the abattoir with her. He was a slicer and had also worked on the pig floor, stunning the animals. Occasionally she would watch him work. 'They would shake and rattle and roll and drop down unconscious,' David Kellett said. 'She'd come and watch me sometimes. I'd think nothing of it. Why would you? Just a job.' In the New South Wales Supreme Court years later a psychiatrist would testify that Kathy had revealed to him that she loved talking to an older man who worked as a sticker on the pig floor. She said she would regularly visit and talk with him.

Once the animal carcass had been dressed, it would be refrigerated overnight so the flesh would set. The next day it was turned over to the all-male boner gangs who stripped the quarter sides of meat using steel hooks and straight knives in vicious downward cutting motions. The boners wore mesh gloves to prevent injuries and stood about a metre apart as the carcasses swung in front of them from chains. It was dangerous work. If the honeycombed mesh glove filled with cold fat and grease, a boner could drop a knife or lose their grip on a hook. Accidents happened, people were stabbed or cut or sliced.

When they were finished, the raw chunks of beef, pork, lamb or mutton went to the slicers, who were lined up shoulder to shoulder at waist-high work benches a few steps below them. Brandishing razor-sharp curved knives with a blade about 15 centimetres long, the slicers trimmed the excess fat and imperfections off the lumps of meat, making them presentable for market and the butcher's shop. Sharp knives were a part of the trade and slicers and boners had to buy their own tools and keep them in first-class condition in order to do their jobs efficiently.

Like all juniors, Katherine Knight started at the bottom of the slaughterhouse food chain when she went to work at the Aberdeen abattoir in 1971 as a general labourer. After getting the standard introduction to the plant operations, she was taken to the offal room where she worked on the animal carcasses in the final stages of cleaning. Later she would say that she enjoyed getting the blood out of the bone marrow and cleaning it out. 'She enjoyed slicing, she enjoyed that work,' a psychiatrist testified in court later.

Joy, Kathy's sister, was a slicer. They were better paid than the labourers, their jobs were cleaner, and their shifts often finished earlier. Soon Kathy was working in the boners' room as a slicer alongside Joy, and she would use the skills she learnt at Aberdeen during the better part of the next fourteen years in one abattoir or another in New South Wales and Queensland.

Robin Smith spent fifteen years working at meatworks in country New South Wales and said the atmosphere was rough and ready.

The boners and the slicers, she said, spoke to the lesser paid labourers 'like a mongrel dog in the street' but would leave them alone if the labourers dished out as good as they got. It was a dog eat dog world, and to survive you had to be tough. 'They'd leave you alone as long as you spoke to them the same way they spoke to you,' Robin said.

Robin had known Kathy for years. She was good at her job, Robin said. Efficient and swift with a knife. Her movements were economical and precise. 'She was good in that respect. She did her job and everything and she was good at it, and good at handling the knives and sharpening them and keeping them sharp,' Robin said. But she wouldn't take any of the boners' crap. Showing an early feistiness, Kathy Knight refused to put up with their taunts. She could match them word for profane word, but by crikey, they weren't going to get away with sledging her personally. Robin remembered Kathy flying off the handle during one shift when a couple of the boners started to make fun of her. She dropped the chunk of beef she was working with on the bench and raced up the stairs to confront them.

'She went after them and grabbed them by their throat and had her knife out – that was one incident – and then it happened again but the leading hand and the foreman in the plant stepped in and apparently pulled her off,' Robin said.

'She wasn't afraid of going after them . . . I mean to say, I've got a bad temper but going to that extreme? I'd never think of going to that extreme regardless of what it was over, I wouldn't.'

Robin was in the back room and heard the commotion. The incident was the talk of the abattoir for days.

'I knew her to say hello, there were a lot of people from the meatworks who worked with her and back then there used to be a little bit of playful things that would go on, but people said you never ever played with Kath,' remembered Aberdeen local Ronnie Wilton, who was a good mate of one of Kathy's later boyfriends, Dave Saunders. 'I remember [one bloke] who used to work at the meatworks, and one particular day, I don't know whether [he] had thrown a bit of meat or fat at her, you know, that sort of thing when you're working, and she's just turned around and then she's caught him and she said to [him], waving the knife, she said, "If you ever do that again, I will rip this through you", and [he] said, "The look in her eye . . . I never, ever done it again".'

4

The pillion passenger groom

As a young man, David Stanford Kellett was a beer drinker and a bit of a bad boy – not bad bad, but mischievous bad. Nicknamed Shorty for obvious reasons, he was young, foolhardy and foolish, and if there was trouble to be had, David Kellett was the one to have it. He didn't live life by the book. At the age of sixteen he had already moved from his hometown of Coffs Harbour to Kempsey, where he was living with his girlfriend, an older woman who had just turned eighteen.

He'd ride to his job at the New South Wales government railways on his Ariel motorbike, a beautiful machine that growled when you gave it some throttle then softened into a steady purr as it cruised along. The bike was a perfect accessory for Kellett. He was a bodgie, one of thousands of dissolute Australian teenagers who, with their female counterparts the widgies, had been at the vanguard of rock 'n' roll. As a vast counter-conformist group, they threw a big pebble in the social pond which had, until then, been relatively sedate. They eschewed the post-war fashions of their parents and adopted their own strict dress code: tight stovepipe pants that finished just above the ankle, pointy shoes with a semi-Cuban heel, and black leather jackets that zipped up with menacing-looking metal teeth. They wore their hair greased into pompadours or ducktails. They looked different, they dressed different and they were different. It was a conservative era and they were seen as a threat. In some cities they were even banned from town hall dances. They were more larrikin than thug, but their new clannishness gave cause for concern.

Even the bodgie dress code was occasionally considered dangerous. In the late sixties David Kellett had even been hauled before the local courts in Kempsey and fined $50 for wearing an offensive weapon – a black leather jacket. The garment was adorned with silver studs on the collar, elbows and sleeve cuffs. A magistrate gave him twenty-four hours to have the offending studs removed or the jacket would be confiscated. David Kellett complied. It was his second brush with the law. A year or so earlier, when he was still sixteen, he'd been busted for underage drinking – a schooner of Tooheys Old – at the Wauchope Hotel where he'd gone after a mate who worked with him on the railway was killed in a train accident.

Soon after, he was involved in rescuing a busload of school children whose vehicle had been collected by the 3.10 Daylight Express at the Kempsey railway crossing. Kellett had just been relieved from his shift as a junior porter and was walking away down the line when he heard the sickening, screeching sound of metal on metal as a train ploughed into the bus. Six children were killed.

'I was pulling bodies out . . . that sort of devastated me,' Kellett said. He started drinking.

In 1966 David Kellett had joined the railways at the age of fifteen years and nine months, as a junior porter working at Macksville on the north coast, a spit away from the oyster-growing coastal town of Nambucca Heads. Almost four full decades ago, it was another era in railways, before electricity revolutionised transportation. As part of his duties, David Kellett would ride a three-wheeler trike out to the signal box, fill the lamps with kerosene and wipe the dirt and soot from the red and green lenses. He'd help stow luggage and open and close the gates to let the trains through.

Every fortnight he'd collect $67 pay for two weeks work, unless he copped a $20 bung, railway terminology for a fine. And there were a few times that he did, especially after he'd started drinking following the two fatal incidents. By then, he had progressed to signalman and the working day was divided into three shifts, morning, afternoon and night – the latter being known as the graveyard shift. Kellett split his days between stations at Grafton, Taree and Kempsey.

If Kellett worked the graveyard, he would sometimes load his crib with dinner and a six-pack of Tooheys Old. Sometimes the end result would not make for efficient running of the New South Wales railways. Occasionally Kellett would fall asleep at the signals from one too many Tooheys, and miss changing the tracks – a manual job in those days – causing a delay. After dozing off one too many times, his bosses told him he was being transferred and gave him a choice of three destinations. Kellett wasn't going to be their problem anymore.

He chose Muswellbrook in the Upper Hunter Valley. It sounded good to the boy from Coffs Harbour, if only because he'd never been there. He packed his swag, hopped in his green Mark 3 Ford Zephyr, which had replaced his motorbike, and headed south. It was 1969 and Kellett was eighteen. He was put up at the railway barracks, half a stubby's walk from the Muswellbrook train station, and went to work shunting the coal trains at the Liddell Power Station. Every morning the rail car would pick the crew up at the station in town and they'd ride out to Liddell. It brought them back at the close of the shift each night.

Kellett had moved on from the eighteen year old and met another young lady, Maxine*, with whom he fell madly in love. But he was drinking too much and getting into trouble. The second of six children, he was brought up the right way, with good solid values and a full understanding of right and wrong. His mother Jean Dodson* rarely touched a shandy and his step-father Mack* was not a big drinker. David just fell in with the wrong crowd. Most Friday nights he would get hammered in one of Muswellbrook's four hotels – the Royal, the Railway, the Muswellbrook or the Prince of Wales. Saturday nights he'd usually get done by the local wallopers for drunk and disorderly and spend the night in the cells at the Muswellbrook police station.

The next morning, the coppers would send him out to buy the Sunday papers and hamburgers – the breakfast of champions – then get him to wash their cars before sending him on his way.

When the Muswellbrook magistrate next convened his court, Shorty would shuffle in to face the music. He'd be fined and warned to straighten up and fly right. It didn't happen just once or twice. 'I was mad. I was mixed up with the wrong crowd in town, and if anything'd go, I would do it. If they wanted the car on the side of the road that was broken down, I'd go and steal it for 'em, things like that. No violence,' David Kellett said, '[it was] more mischievous bad shit.'

He was sacked from the railways when he was caught committing a break and enter and stealing hardware from the Muswellbrook rail yards. A few weeks earlier, he'd been nicked for getting into a fight with a man who gate-crashed a party he was throwing. The crasher king-hit Kellett on the back of the head when he was asked to leave. Kellett retaliated. Noses were bloodied, cheekbones broken. The bloke who hit Kellett came off second best, but Kellett drove his opponent to hospital. Kellett fled when the police arrived and led them on a car chase around the streets of Muswellbrook.

When Kellett presented in court for the assault and the subsequent break and enter, the judge, not surprisingly, did not take his list of priors lightly and sentenced him to five years hard labour in B-Block at East Maitland prison. David Kellett appealed and won, and was released on a five-year conditional bond after serving three months. As part of his release conditions he had to report to Muswellbrook police station three times a week. And he had to keep out of trouble, otherwise it was back to the pokey. Which is how David Kellett found himself stuck in the Upper Hunter region. He needed a job, and like a lot of people in the area, the meatworks in Aberdeen provided one. Kellett was hired as a slicer.

It was there, in 1973, that he met Charlie Knight, Katherine Knight's older brother, and the two quickly became drinking mates. David was still going out with Maxine, but it was about to end. Charlie told David he had a younger sister, Katherine, who was also working as a slicer at the abattoir, and Charlie introduced them to each other. One thing led to another, and pretty soon David Kellett had a new girlfriend.

David Kellett was on the rebound after breaking up with Maxine, and Katherine Knight filled the void. To David, Katherine was tall and slim, quiet and shy, withdrawn even. She'd only had one boyfriend before him, she didn't smoke or drink and was loyal and generous. It made for a nice balance. 'When I first met her she was attractive, she had glasses, and she did have the most wonderful smile,' David said. 'Sort of tilt her head to the side a bit, butter wouldn't melt in her mouth.'

Katherine fell for the rascal in David Kellett, and from day one she addressed him by his surname, Kellett. He couldn't remember Kathy calling him David once throughout the nine years they would be together. Even her family called him Kellett. David got on well with Kathy's mother Barbara, which was just as well because when she turned eighteen, he was her ticket out of home, with Barbara's approval.

Moving out of home the first time is an important step, and Kathy couldn't do it fast enough. She had a rocky relationship with her father, and even though she and her mother got on well, they still argued, and her mother used corporal punishment on Kathy. 'Kathy used to get flogged with the jug cord, more than anyone,' David said, adding that she was headstrong. Barbara Knight warned David to watch out for Kathy if he ever did anything wrong by her. She'll go off, Barbara said. David just laughed it off.

The young couple rented a farmhouse on the road leading out to Rouchel and settled down. Kathy loved her independence but she still used her parents as a benchmark for her relationship with Kellett, comparing her household to the way her mother did things. David remembered Barbara's foul language – the effs and the c's spicing every sentence – and Kathy used it too. Still, the first year things were great for Kathy and Kellett, as they were dubbed. 'She started off really wonderful . . . as good as gold,' David remembered. 'Started off perfect.'

It helped that David got on famously with Joy, Katherine's twin. Kathy and Joy were as close as twins can be, and for a young woman in love, having your sister or friend approve of your new boyfriend carried significant weight. Wherever Joy was, David was and vice versa. Katherine was always there too, but David said he and Joy used to love making tongues wag by holding hands in public. Hell, it broke up the monotony of country town life, but there was never anything in it, other than a friendship.

Kellett, as cavalier as ever, was still up to his antics. 'I was just rough and wild, anything goes, anyone said, "I dare ya", I'd do it,' he said.

About a year into the relationship, the couple threw a party at their place. Kellett decided the festivities wouldn't be complete without a barbecue so he took his .303 rifle and a chainsaw and went hunting. Because they lived on a working farm, he didn't have to go far. The weapon, a Lee-Enfield bolt-action gun with a 10-round magazine, was one that had been used by the Australian Defence Forces from World War I through to 1959. Kellett had picked it up for $50 in a second-hand gun shop. The chainsaw came from the shed. Kellett picked a steer from the farm and shot it. He used the chainsaw to cut it into rudimentary steaks. Voilà! Barbecue.

Kellett's days as a cattle rustler didn't last long, though. He was busted for castle rustling when scavenging dingoes dug up the carcass, leaving it strewn over the property. The farmer, noticing a missing head from his stock, had found it and reported it to police.

Kellett was in breach of his bond, which could have landed him back in East Maitland prison for five years, but he was in luck. Kellett was likeable enough – a crook, yes, but likeable just the same – and the local police prosecutor was feeling generous. Whether he was sick of seeing Kellett in the system, or maybe because he liked him, the detective gave Kellett the benefit of the doubt and said he wouldn't remind the judge that this David Stanford Kellett was the same man who had been before him previously. In return, he said Kellett had to promise to break away from his rambunctious Muswellbrook crew. It was that or spend the next five years in jail.

For Kellett, it was a no-brainer. For a man in his twenties, five years was a long time, and he'd already done three months of a five-year hard labour stint. He knew that 'hard labour' wasn't an exaggeration. He'd previously shared a cell with two tough crooks who were on the way to making Her Majesty the Queen their lifelong hostess. There was no television, no video, no nothing. Morning roll calls were deliberately humiliating, meant to strip away the arrogance of the criminal. Inmates lined up behind a white line – not on it or over it – and had to answer with a salute when their numbers were called. David Kellett hated the salute.

In court, the prosecutor kept his word and protected Kellett when the judge showed a hint of recognition. Maybe he could see the hidden promise in the brash young man. Kellett was fined $50 for rustling steer, ordered to pay restitution to the farmer and placed on a three-month bond. Kellett kept his end of the bargain. In the thirty years since, he's kept his nose clean, repaying the trust the policeman placed in him.

Katherine was with him every step of the way. 'We were only living together at that time, we weren't married, and she stood by me one hundred per cent . . . she stood by me, side by side,' David Kellett remembered. Some girls are like that, irrevocably drawn to bad boys like a compass needle is drawn to true north. And so it was with Katherine Knight. She kept a photo album of press clippings chronicling David's waywardness, and there were quite a few items in it. 'She used to keep everything like that,' he said.

Katherine Mary Knight became Mrs David Stanford Kellett before her nineteenth birthday in 1974. David hadn't intended to marry Kathy right there and then – he was only twenty-three and still had some living to do. Looking back on it now, he thinks Kathy may even have asked him to marry her, he can't be sure, but he believes Kathy got married to spite her parents. They weren't invited to the ceremony, which is probably just as well.

That Saturday, David started drinking at home around 7 am. Kathy was in charge. She got on her motorbike, instructed Kellett to get behind her and hold on. By the time they rode from Aberdeen down the New England Highway to Muswellbrook, he was six sheets to the wind. They dropped into the Royal Hotel for a heart-starter before walking across the road to the Muswellbrook courthouse – a place David was more than familiar with.

It was the seventies and David and Kathy were dressed for the times. She wore a gold mini dress, the same one she would wear at her twenty-first birthday, and didn't carry flowers. It is impossible to hold them when you're steering a motorbike and have a drunken groom as a pillion passenger with his arms wrapped around your waist. David wore a purple paisley shirt with purple bell-bottoms. Kathy's brother Charlie stood by her side and Kellett's best man, Neville, had to help him stand up. David didn't tell his mother and stepfather, or his five siblings, that he was getting married. His mother wouldn't meet Katherine for another few months.

David paid $20 for the marriage licence and twenty minutes later – $20 for twenty minutes – the celebrant pronounced them man and wife. David had made an honest woman of Katherine Knight. They dropped in to Kathy's parents' house and told Ken and Barbara Knight their good news, and continued partying. David kept drinking and got drunker and drunker. They went home and consummated the marriage but before the night was out, David got his first real taste of the dark side of Katherine's nature

'You see, I kept on passing out, I'd had that much to drink. The first thing we did when we got to the place we had, was have sex – first thing we did. And I was pretty drunk because I kept on drinking all day and all night,' David said. 'And she woke me up through the night and that was it again, and that was okay.'

The next time Katherine woke her new husband, she had her hands wrapped around his throat, squeezing. She wasn't happy and yet she appeared calm as she dug her fingers into his flesh and accused him of a less than stellar sexual performance.

'I remember she said her parents did it five times on their wedding night – she used to compare everything to her parents,' David Kellett said.

David was drunk, and he went back to sleep, putting the incident out of his mind.

Jean and Mack Dodson met their new daughter-in-law a few months after David and Kathy had tied the knot. They drove down highway number 1 from their house on the north coast to Aberdeen. Jean was impressed by Kathy's honesty, especially when she confided in her that she couldn't cook, something that her mother also confirmed. 'Her mother said to me, "I don't know how they are going to go in married life, she can't cook",' Jean said. In those days, girls from the country usually came to a marriage with a certain level of culinary skill, and Kathy's admission was charming. She was also clean and tidy, and her house was spotless – little things that mothers-in-law notice.

Kathy was quiet but Jean quickly found she was well and truly in charge of the financial side of the marriage. It didn't surprise Jean. All her boys let their wives control the family purse strings. But with Kathy, it was a little more obsessive: 'When we first knew her she would walk across from one shop to another, for example, to see what a packet of Weet-Bix cost . . . if she could save a cent here or there, she would willingly do it,' Jean said.

Jean and Mack gave the newlyweds $2000 for a deposit on a home and returned to the north coast. They kept in touch by phone but, being so far away, Jean was not privy to the day-to-day events of her son's marriage. Had they been closer, she might have detected a creeping worry forming in her son's mind.

Things had started out beautifully, but a year into the marriage they had started to sour and David felt as if a noose had been tightened around his neck. He got on well with Barbara Knight but she was always present in the little home they bought opposite the wheat silos in Short Street, even if she wasn't physically there. 'We had a lot of big fights when we first got married because her mother said I should do this and I should do that, she shouldn't have to do this and, in this marriage, I should have to do that,' David said. 'And I told her one day, I do remember telling her that one of these days I will just piss off, because I'm not married to your mother, I'm married to you.'

David was at a loss to explain why Katherine was always comparing her marriage to that of her parents, especially when she didn't think it was perfect. And he couldn't fathom Kathy's hair-trigger temper, her mood swings and the way she started dishing out backhanders over nothing: 'I'd hang clothes on the line, if I hung a shirt on the wrong way, she'd come behind me, started swinging, and I'd just push her out the road and laugh at her,' David said. 'Her knickers had to be hung on the inside line, close to the middle with towels, sheets, whatever, around them so no one could see them. She was obsessed with that. If I hung the washing out and she happened to be looking out and see me hanging a shirt upside down, she'd rave and rant and carry on and scream, and I'd just sort of wave to her, blow her a kiss, give her the finger or something, or just laugh at her.'

'If I didn't even answer her it would make it worse. I'd just walk around the back yard, tip the washing basket upside down on the grass and say, "Do it yourself".'

By the middle of 1975, David was fed up with Kathy's moods but she fell pregnant with their first child. They got through Christmas but within a couple of months David had had enough of Kathy's moodiness and started an affair with another Aberdeen woman, Susan*.

Kathy gave birth to Melissa Ann on 11 May 1976, but by then the marriage was as fragile as it could be. David shot through with Susan, who was also pregnant with his child, and headed to Queensland. Kathy was equal parts devastated and furious. She called the police, and David was stopped at the border of New South Wales and Queensland, coincidentally at Wallangarra, the town where Kathy had spent her first few years. Police tore the car apart searching for drugs – at Kathy's suggestion – but found nothing. David and Susan went to Nambour but their relationship was doomed from the start and ended soon after. Susan gave birth to a son a couple of months after Melissa was born.

Kathy was crushed by David's desertion. One well-told story in Aberdeen was that she took out her anger on baby Melissa, who she blamed for Kellett's negative feelings towards her. Melissa was not the problem, but Kathy needed someone to blame. What she did next would become intricately woven into the fabric of Aberdeen folklore.

As the story has it, Kathy walked down the embankment to the train tracks holding her two-month-old baby in her arms. She put Melissa in the middle of the parallel rails and left her there. Ted Abrahams, a pensioner who lived in a small room on the ground floor of the Aberdeen Hotel which has now been turned into a poker machine alcove, was foraging along the top of the tracks and saw the baby. He scurried down and picked her up, taking her to safety. Lorna Driscoll, the owner of the Aberdeen general store which was directly opposite the tracks, saw Ted holding baby Melissa in his arms.

Later that day at a house up on Graeme Street, Kathy grabbed an axe from a woodpile and started swinging it above her head threatening people, including an old man. One woman who witnessed it said Kathy was hysterical and her strength was unbelievable. Katherine was apprehended by police, who took her to St Elmo's hospital in Tamworth. Years later, Katherine Knight told police that she suffered post-natal depression after the births of her four children. Her ex-husband David said she never mentioned the train track incident after they got back together and it was several years before he heard about it. He still doesn't know if it's true, but said if it was, then Kathy would have been doing it to get back at him.

On Tuesday 3 August 1976, Katherine Knight walked out the front door of her home in Short Street, across the main road that divided Aberdeen in two, and down to Molly Perry's house. Molly, who had worked with Kathy at the meatworks, lived on the western side of the street, opposite the Bogas petrol station, just a few minutes by foot from where Kathy and David Kellett bought their first house. Molly was at home with her children Margaret and Henry when Kathy knocked on the front door asking for help because her baby Melissa was sick. Kathy asked Molly to drive her and Melissa to the doctor's. Molly said of course she would.

Margaret, who was sixteen at the time, went to help with her mother and her younger brother went with them. When they arrived Kathy pulled a butcher's knife on Margaret and slashed her on the left cheek just below the eye. It was chaos. It had all happened so fast. Their hearts would have been pounding. According to a newspaper report Kathy forced them into the car and demanded they take her to David Kellett. Molly drove into the Bogas petrol station for petrol and they ran free.

Lloyd Lyne was the sergeant of police at Aberdeen in 1976, having moved there with his wife from Bowraville as part of a promotion eight years earlier. Aberdeen was a two-man station and Sergeant Lyne knew just about everyone in town. Serious crime wasn't a problem in Aberdeen, but the police were kept busy with petty matters like theft and drunk and disorderly. At the end of a long day and after a few too many beers, the meat workers could get a bit bloody at the pubs in town. Lyne and his offsider, Constable Daryll Mackell, also had to keep an eye on the drifters who passed through, carrying their secrets and past lives with them.

Sergeant Lyne was on duty that Tuesday with Constable Mackell, who had been involved in the incident a few days earlier when Kathy had been taken to the hospital in Tamworth. Mackell was filling Sergeant Lyne in on Kathy's threats when she went by the station. Cripes, Mackell said, there she goes now. Not long after, Lyne and Mackell received a phone call from the manager of the Bogas, who said that Katherine Kellett, as she was known then, was out of control, waving a knife around, and had hold of a boy by the shirt.

Officers Lyne and Mackell ran outside, jumped in the police car, turned the siren on and raced the 500 or so metres up the road to the petrol station. Kathy was in the main office threatening the manager behind the counter. She was holding Henry Perry with one hand and a knife with the other.

'She had the knife in her hand – in her left hand – and she was holding on to the little boy . . . She got hold of a little kid somehow or other and she got him by the front of his shirt and was waving the knife,' remembered the now-retired Sergeant Lyne. 'The poor little bugger, his eyes were sticking out and we got him away from her . . . he was too frightened to cry. I think he just bolted and took off across the road straight home and never looked back.'

Lyne and Mackell grabbed a couple of broomsticks to try to knock the knife out of Kathy's hand. They surrounded her and told her to drop the knife: 'We didn't have a lot of trouble. We got a broom each and attacked her. When I say attacked, we prodded her from both sides and she dropped the knife and let the kid go,' Lyne said. In the scuffle, the sergeant received a minor cut on the arm but it didn't register until later when he saw blood. 'It was not from her attacking or coming at me, but from the scuffle with her,' Lyne said later, dispelling the local myth that Kathy had stabbed a policeman and gotten away with it.

Lyne and Mackell took Kathy to a doctor in Muswellbrook who issued a Schedule 2 under the Mental Health Act and they drove her to Morisset hospital where she was admitted for psychiatric treatment.

'We never really used to find out why [people] did those things, really, we just had to deal with it. I don't think there was any special motive. She just got a bit of a bee in her bonnet and away she went,' Lyne said. 'She was assessed and they kept her there for a while. And she was treated, of course. And I don't know what happened after that. That was the end of it as far as I was concerned. I didn't think it was a big deal at the time.'

It turned out later that Katherine Knight had tried to car-jack Molly Perry because she wanted Molly to drive her to Coffs Harbour where David Kellett's mother lived. She wanted to ask Jean why David had left her. She wanted to kill herself and Jean.

'It happened a long time ago and I have had to see her about town ever since. After the incident Kathy just acted as if nothing happened and the whole thing has been pretty hard on everyone,' Margaret told *The Newcastle Herald*'s Donna Page.

Twenty-five years later in the New South Wales Supreme Court, forensic psychiatrist Dr Robert Delaforce, who spent almost nine hours interviewing Katherine Knight in Mulawa Women's Correctional Centre in June 2000, testified that Katherine had told him that she planned to kill Jean Dodson and herself after she concluded David was having an affair. Justice O'Keefe asked him why Katherine would pick on David's mother as the object of murder.

'To me that was an out-of-control, impulsive personality disordered woman with post traumatic stress disorder; unpremeditated, no planning of it, disorganised chaotic behaviour that is characteristic of that disorder,' Dr Delaforce answered. Years later, it would be the same person and the same personality disorder, but the events would be so much less chaotic and out of control.

While Katherine Knight was in Morisset hospital her three-month-old baby daughter Melissa was looked after by her maternal grandparents, Barbara and Ken Knight.

When she was discharged her diagnosis was 'personality disorder'.

Personality disorder is one of the most controversial and elastic areas in psychiatry, so vast and changing that it is often difficult to diagnose specifically and accurately. Mental health professionals rely on the American Psychiatric Association's Diagnostic and Statistical Manual, Fourth Edition (DSM-IV) in making a diagnosis. It describes personality disorder as 'an enduring pattern of inner experience and behaviour that deviates markedly from the expectations of the individual's culture, is pervasive and inflexible, has an onset in adolescence or early adulthood, is stable over time, and leads to distress or impairment'.

Currently, the DSM-IV has identified ten specific personality disorders, including borderline personality disorder (BPD), which is characterised by impulsive, dramatic, erratic and emotional behaviour. People who are diagnosed with BPD have an extreme fear of being abandoned and make frantic efforts to avoid it. They express inappropriate and intense anger, and are prone to verbal outbursts and enduring bitterness. They also experience extreme mood swings tracing the arc from total adoration to abject hate within minutes. BPD is extraordinarily hard to treat because the person who has it is so predictably unpredictable.

It is the layman's paradox. People with BPD can be so much in love one minute but the next, they lose control and are capable of dangerous behaviour, striking out at the very one they love. The medical analogy often used to describe people with this condition is that it is like having measles. The person has a lot of 'good' skin, but there are some bad spots too. The difference is, measles goes away. A personality disorder, on the other hand, is pervasive throughout a person's life.

~

David Kellett was still in Queensland, driving trucks and living on his own in a little flat beside the famed Story Bridge Hotel (which still holds cockroach races each Australia Day) in the heart of Brisbane, when he received a telephone call from the Aberdeen police informing him that his wife had been committed to a psychiatric hospital. David rang his mother and together they drove several hundred kilometres to visit her. It was heartbreaking. Kathy was locked in a ward and heavily sedated. She said she still loved David.

After six days a medical tribunal was convened at Morisset hospital to determine if Kathy was mentally well enough to be discharged. David Kellett and his mother were at the hearing. Kathy told Jean that she was the only one who had ever loved her or showed her what love meant but she had wanted to kill her. 'She did say at that courthouse . . . that I was the only one that ever showed her what love meant, because she didn't understand,' Jean said.

Jean offered to take Katherine home with her and David: 'I offered, because she said she loved David and David thought he loved her.'

Kathy was released into Jean's care and custody on 9 August 1976. Before leaving the hospital, the doctor gave Jean strict instructions to ensure Kathy took her medication.

Aberdeen is 200 kilometres from Morisset, and not en route to Coffs Harbour, but David and his mother had to pick up Melissa from her grandparents, Ken and Barbara Knight. While Kathy went inside to get the baby, her mother Barbara came out to the car to see David. Some of Kathy's family were standing on the front verandah.

As soon as Barbara got to the driver's window, she attacked David. She leaned through and grabbed him around the throat and started to swear at him and blame him for Kathy's break-down and for her being locked up in Morisset hospital. David sat there with his hands on the steering wheel, not game to make a move, and Jean ran next door shouting for someone to ring the police. No one answered the door. Jean was terrified and felt powerless to do anything. David was being choked.

'Kathy came out and she seemed to grab her mother – I can see it as clearly as if it was today – and she grabbed her with the left hand and she swung a punch and she knocked her mother down,' Jean said, getting upset at the memory. 'Her mother just buckled at the knees and went down . . . and it was just one king hit and her mother went down. She didn't expect it, she didn't see it coming, she had two arms back through the window. She possibly hit her mother on the side of the head. I remember her knees just buckled and she went straight to the ground.'

Kathy yelled at her mother to never touch David again, and Jean feared the fight would erupt into a full-on brawl. Kathy's family remained on the verandah.

'I don't remember what happened to the mother, she was just on the ground. I suppose she got herself up, I don't know, I can't remember, I was too upset, and I couldn't get out of the place quick enough. The way she did it, wow.'

It was the first time Jean had seen Kathy's capacity for violence. And it was only the beginning.

David Kellett took his wife and daughter to his mother's house where they stayed for two weeks while Kathy recovered, taking the medication the doctor gave Jean for her. Jean remembered Kathy was quiet and kept to herself but later when she went to David's sister's house, she would blow off steam. After that, they settled in Woodridge in Queensland, in a rented house in Pamela Crescent. Kathy got a job as a slicer at the Dinmore meatworks in Ipswich, west Brisbane, and rode her motorbike to work. She liked her job and asked David to specially mount her two slicers' knives on a board and attach it to the wall above her pillow. 'She liked the knives, knives were her security blanket. I had to sharpen them for her,' David Kellett said. 'They are sharp, they'd shave you. They had to be sharp.'

David kept on trucking. He adored his baby daughter and desperately wanted to make his marriage work for Melissa's sake. So did Kathy. Whatever had happened in the past was kept in the past, or at least that's what David thought. 'Most perfect mother and wife you'd ever wish for. It started off well,' David said.

It didn't last. She was irascible and her moodiness had crept back into the marriage, informing everything she did. She was demanding and controlling and had not forgotten or forgiven David's affair with Susan. Katherine Knight was fury full strength, followed by a violence chaser. 'There was a lot of things that used to fly around that house sometimes. Oh yeah. I'd throw them and deliberately miss. I never, ever raised a finger or a hand to her. Never. Never hit her. I've never hit a woman in me life. I never raised a hand in anger to her,' David Kellett said. 'It was Kathy who did all the bashing.'

Jean Dodson kept in touch by phone and each time she rang, she could measure Katherine's mood by the tone of her voice. Kathy would insult Jean's son and abuse him. Each call was incrementally worse. 'They were very bad days when they lived at Woodridge, and it was impossible, when we'd go there, Dad and myself. She would go into tirades, terrible rages over anything and nothing,' Jean remembered. 'It took nothing . . . the pepper and salt wasn't right or the pegs weren't right or the kettle didn't have enough water in to boil. It wouldn't take anything for her to turn the air blue.'

The rages were one thing, but when Jean saw the knives in the bedroom, she was stunned. Katherine told Jean she kept them at the bottom of the bed, between the sheets. 'I did ask her on one occasion, "Why do you keep the knives in the bed? I would have thought that was strange". "Just in case I need them". And she had a petulant look on her face and the eyes went down, the head went down, and I couldn't think why she would need them,' Jean said.

'Oh, she was a mixture of a girl, she was a Jekyll and Hyde. She could be one thing one minute and stark raving the next.'

Years before David and Kathy married, Barbara Knight had warned her future son-in-law about her daughter's short fuse. David used to laugh it off. Back then, she was great fun to be with and he saw none of the things Barbara counselled him to be cautious of. But when the violence started, Kathy would always go for David's head, giving him a swift backhander when he didn't do what she wanted.

'Her mother always did say to me, "You better watch that, don't play up on her, she'll kill you",' David remembered. 'Her mother even warned me before we were married, "You better watch this one, she's crazy . . . Don't do the wrong thing by her". And I just laughed it off.'

David found out how right Barbara Knight was. One day he came home from work and caught Kathy in bed with a meat worker. David was enraged, and made the bloke jump out of the window. 'He's not coming down, walking down my bloody steps,' he said.

Katherine's affair was a 'payback' – tit for tat – but again, the couple decided they wanted to resuscitate the marriage and did what so many warring spouses do: they had another baby. Natasha Maree Kellett was born in Nambour on 6 March 1980. David and Kathy bought a house in Landsborough and moved their family again, hoping against hope that this time it would work.

David Kellett played competition darts. It was an easy sport and a sociable one at that. You could play with a schooner in one hand and the dart in the other, and sometimes the booze helped to get a bullseye. After the Kelletts moved to Landsborough, David played at the Maleny Club Hotel. Kathy was a paradox to him. She'd tell him to go and have a few beers and play some darts, and then she'd get all antsy that he wasn't home. David considered the couple of hours he spent at darts a welcome relief from Kathy's moods, but it wasn't an escape.

Kathy rang the pub one night at five past ten, David remembered.

'Get your arse home,' she said.

'I'm on me last game, I'll be home when I'm ready,' he replied.

'I come home from the pub, twenty past ten, after playing competition darts, and she's sconed me as I come through the door. I woke up in Nambour hospital. Hit me on the side of the head or back of the head, or somewhere, with that much force it blackened both me eyes,' David remembered. 'Could've been a fry-pan, Besser block, I don't know, two tonne of steel or a block of concrete, I wouldn't have a clue. I know it was big and heavy and hard.'

Asked why Katherine attacked him, he said, 'because I defied her . . . You just didn't defy her.'

David was in hospital for four days and the police were involved, but he didn't want to press charges because of the children. 'She was very remorseful, all that type of thing, and not long after she put a knife to me throat,' he said.

He remembered the day with crystal clear clarity. He had his truck loaded and parked out the front of the Landsborough house ready for a short haul the following day to the Tarong Power Station, about 130 kilometres away and just south of Sir Joh Bjelke-Petersen country in Kingaroy. 'I woke up and she was straddled across me chest with one of her bloody meatwork knives across me throat and she said, "Is that right that truck drivers have got girlfriends in every town?",' David Kellett said. 'She straddled across me chest and held the knife actually on me throat. She only had to reach a foot and grab it . . . I wouldn't want to give her the shits, I can tell you. I could feel it.

'I was asleep and woke up and thought, "What's going on here?". I had to practically beg and plead [with] her, and said, "No, that's bullshit".'

The look on Katherine Knight's face was cold and savage. 'See how easy it is?' Kathy said. David Kellett doesn't mince words. 'I was shit scared,' he said. It was the most terrifying moment in his marriage.

The Kellett marriage continued to be as volatile as ever. At some point Kathy had moved out and lived in a caravan park at Churchill, but she returned to their Landsborough home after a couple of weeks. That's when Kathy's suspicions started eating away at her. She believed David was having an affair with the next-door neighbour, a seventeen-year-old schoolgirl, and she could barely conceal her rages. It was the last thing on his mind, especially with a wife like Kathy. Who knows what she'd do?

Another night David was playing darts at the pub when Kathy rang, ordering him home. She thought he was there with a woman. It was almost an exact repeat of the earlier incident.

'Why don't you go to the pub and play darts for a while,' Kathy said early in the night.

'I'll see you at half past ten,' he replied, telling the story as if it were happening now.

'Okay, I'll put tea in the oven.'

'And then ten o'clock on the dot she rings, "Get home now". Just snapped like that. You know, darts don't finish exactly on time, I've played darts all me life, and she went bloody berko, burned me clothes,' David said. 'She actually rang me up, said, "The clothes are in the bathtub burning", and I thought, oh, I better go home and see what the sick bitch is doing. And, yep, there's all me clothes in the bathtub, all on fire, because I defied her. She said come home now, and I said I'll be home very shortly.'

Kathy had taken everything in her husband's wardrobe, dumped it in the bath, doused it with kerosene and put a match to it. Whoomph! Up it went. Smoke filled the house. All he had left were the clothes he was wearing – the purple bell-bottoms and the purple paisley shirt he had worn to his wedding. Kellett was no clotheshorse, but the irony of what he was left standing in wasn't lost on him.

The final incident came in 1983. David came home from one too many drinks at the pub and Kathy hit him on the head with a Dick sharpening steel. She hit him so hard that skin from his scalp stuck to the steel.

'I'd come home from the pub after a few too many, and I'd known then not to give her the shits, and she opened me head up. She opened me up,' David said.

He was treated by the ambulance and taken to Nambour hospital. He didn't press charges against Katherine because he was too afraid of what she might do to Melissa and Natasha. In 2000 after she had been charged with murder Katherine Knight claimed that David had been physically violent towards her, claims Justice Barry O'Keefe later rejected. David, the judge wrote in his sentencing of Knight, had said, 'I never raised a finger against her, not even in self-defence'. It was Kathy who was unpredictably violent, David said. 'I accept Mr Kellett's evidence as the more correct version of what occurred,' Justice O'Keefe said. 'In particular the evidence establishes violent, vindictive, vengeful acts on the part of the prisoner directed at her spouse.'

The end of the marriage was as sudden and unexpected as Kathy's violence. David had been away on a trucking trip and came home in the middle of the night to find the house empty. He walked in the front door and turned on the light-switch only to be met with darkness. He flicked on his cigarette lighter and discovered in the dim glow that Kathy had cleaned out the house, taking everything, from the curtains to the light bulbs. All she left was an old couch that David's sister had given him and some Tupperware. She even took his power tools from the shed. Kathy moved back home to her parents' farm in Aberdeen with the two little girls.

'When I came home and found out she [had] actually gone and took everything, I thought, jeez, there is a God somewhere,' he said.

5

Pricey comes to town

John Price was twenty-six when he breezed into Aberdeen in 1981, a young man chiselled by years of hard manual labour with a mutually agreeable easy-going nature and strict work ethic. He brought with him his wife of eight years, Colleen, and two little children, eight-year-old Johnathon, and seven-year-old Rosemary Kay. For almost all of their married life, Pricey and Colleen had been on the move, towing a 22-foot white Viscount caravan from one place to another for work and adventure, from Wee Waa where the Price family had settled on the banks of the Namoi River in northwestern New South Wales, to Queensland and back again, with various stops along the way. Colleen loved the travelling lifestyle. She loved Pricey even more. He was fun and he completely adored her, making her the cornerstone of their new young family. He earned the money and she managed it.

The ease with which she found herself building a family resulted from her own need to fill a personal void and correct the familial flaws in her past. Colleen's mother, Gwendoline, had left home when Colleen was a young girl, leaving her and her four younger brothers in the care of their father Miles Jones, a shearer. When he went off to work, which was often, and often hundreds of miles away, the children would be split between four paternal aunts who lived near each other in the district around Walgett, another country town with little more to offer than the people who lived there.

Colleen would be with one aunt for a few months, and when she tired of her, the young girl would be shipped off to another aunt for a few months. Her brothers were treated the same way, with one eventually landing in a home for young boys in Sydney. She had little stability as a youngster and it wasn't until she was eleven that she went to school for the first time. She felt like she'd been pushed from pillar to post her whole life. Later she discovered that her mother had moved to Sydney and remarried, having five more children, but Colleen never saw her half-brothers and sister. It was as if a part of her life died when Gwendoline upped and left and she could never reclaim it. With John Price, Colleen had the chance to make her own family, and she did.

John Charles Thomas Price was born in Gunnedah on 4 April 1955, the eldest of six children and the only one not born in Queensland. His parents, Cynthia Ann Orthon and Percy Harold Price, who was known by all and sundry as John White, never married. They were cotton chipping contractors from Wee Waa, the cotton capital of Australia. The industry turned around the small town of Wee Waa, doubling its population from 1000 to more than 2000 in two decades from the early 1960s, making New South Wales the biggest cotton exporter in Australia, producing 70 per cent of the country's output.

When the seasons were good, Cynthia and John ran a gang of up to forty cotton chippers – men and women including local Aborigines, seasonal farm workers and tourists eager to make a solid buck. They moved from cotton farm to cotton farm owned by private families in the northwestern part of the state, most of which had to be irrigated because the heavens frequently failed them.

Chipping is hard, unforgiving work and takes place during the summer growing season plus a month either side, from November through to March. Temperatures in the bush in January and February can be brutal, often racing into the high 30s before noon. Sometimes it soars into the low 40s, the extra couple of degrees enough to cause a grown man or woman to faint. Chippers rise before dawn to beat the heat and from 5 am to 2 pm they walk up and down rows of rich, black fertile soil removing weeds and burrs from the cotton plants, swinging their hoes by hand, checking their paths to make sure they don't tread on a venomous king brown or pale-headed snake idly wrapped around a cotton boll warming its cold-blooded coil.

It was a harsh environment in which to start a family, but Cynthia Orthon had lost none of the romance that most young women have. She named her first-born John, after a singer, John Charles Thomas, an American recording star and matinee idol on Broadway who hit the big time during the Roaring Twenties and went on to become one of the world's most popular opera singers until his death in 1960. His voice, scratchy on the old 78 rpm lacquer records, would come through the static-filled wireless speakers, spilling over the rugged Australian outback and filling the Price caravan with a mellifluous, creamy voice and dreams of a glitzy life on Broadway and beyond.

The origins of his name were glamorous but in a way that is uniquely Australian, John Price of Gunnedah was quickly given a nickname. His family called him 'Tom', which he hated but repeatedly failed to shake until later in his teenage years when he became universally known as Pricey. He mightn't have liked his nickname, but Pricey was tickled with the history of his namesake and was quick to reveal who he was named after when in new company.

'Named after a world famous singer, I am,' he'd say with pride and a glint in his eye.

With their first offspring still in a baby carriage, Cynthia, who was part Aboriginal, and John White followed the work and moved to southern Queensland for a few years, living in their caravan in campsites around Dirranbandi on the Bekhara River, chipping cotton fields. Over the next few years, Cynthia gave birth to five more children in quick succession, Raymond, Judith, Robert Edward, Cynthia Ann and Shane.

Eventually the family returned to Wee Waa and lived in a caravan on the banks of the Namoi River on Cudgewa, a 7000-acre cotton-growing property they worked on down Doreen's Lane, a dirt track that turns off the Kamilaroi Highway and loops back around to Narrabri. Later they would move to Collarenebri, setting up camp on Collymongle Station, less than 100 kilometres from Lightning Ridge.

Cynthia loved all her children but she developed a unique bond with her first-born in a way that many mothers do. Pricey's education was brief, and not very successful. By the time he was fifteen, he could neither read nor write well but he was driving dozers and graders and scrapers and learning how to lay irrigation pipes and build dams. He had a natural aptitude for it and easily developed the level eye needed to construct intricate and complex irrigation systems. As well, he was a natural with the heavy machinery and was quickly able to master a variety of trucks and earth moving equipment. He had a good job and, to tell the truth, he was living every boy's childhood dream.

In the summer of 1972, a striking, sweet and shy Colleen Jones moved in with her uncle in Wee Waa. Her life until then had been tough. For the previous seven years she had lived with her four aunties in a string of humpies around Walgett and Uralla, going to school when she could and teaching herself to read and write along the way. When she got to Wee Waa she was sixteen. Colleen heard about cotton chipping jobs going on the Cudgewa property. She wasn't afraid of hard work and signed up. She didn't need an education and the money was good even though the work was back-breakingly monotonous and hot.

One late summer afternoon at the end of a long day in the field, Colleen went into town for a milkshake. Wee Waa's population was growing slowly, as was the town centre, but back then it wasn't that flash. A string of shops lined Rose Street, the main road through town, and its greatest attractions, depending on your sobriety or your patriotism, were either the Imperial Hotel, the Royal Hotel or the clock tower that was erected in 1938 to the memory of lost servicemen bearing the words 'Lest We Forget'. Colleen was leaning up against the front of the little milk bar when John Price rode up on his Honda 500 motorbike with a couple of mates.

Pricey was exactly six months older than Colleen and, at seventeen, was youthfully handsome and cocky. His round face was highlighted by dark brown eyes that twinkled as if they held secrets he promised to share. He had thick curly hair and was tanned from the summer sun. Colleen thought he wasn't half bad looking. With flashing hazel eyes that turned a piercing green when the sun hit them and long hair that she kept gathered in a ponytail she wore down her back, Colleen was petite and pretty, if a bit of a tomboy. She preferred jeans and jumpers to the flowing cheesecloth skirts and tie-dyed hippie gear of the seventies. Impressed, John Price nudged one of his mates, who introduced him as 'Tom', a name that would stick with Colleen.

'We just clicked as friends. I was sixteen and a half, he was seventeen. One thing led to another and we went for motorbike rides and we just got together,' Colleen said, sitting in her lounge-room with photographs of Elvis Presley on the walls and collectables and picture frames on every bench-top, her long hair still held neatly behind her head in a braided bun.

'He just liked his motorbikes and he was an easy-going, cheeky-faced person. He was never actually a show-off, he always had a cheeky grin and he was the type of person who was always drawing people to him.'

There wasn't much to do in Wee Waa and Colleen and Pricey spent every spare moment they could roaring through the countryside on his motorbike, a couple of teenagers falling in love fast. Soon they were talking about getting married. They were young and crazy for each other. Why wait? Colleen was only sixteen and had to ask her father for permission. Her dad, Miles Jones, liked Pricey. He had no problem with the shortish young bloke on the motorbike who clearly adored his daughter. Pricey was well mannered and likeable, his family were hard workers and well known in the community and, besides, it was just a formality as far as he was concerned. Colleen had effectively been looking after herself since her mum took off when she was little and Miles saw no reason to deny his daughter what she wanted. She'd had it tough enough as it was. But the teenagers still had a problem. Pricey was only seventeen and, according to the law, had to wait until he was of legal age to get married.

For teenagers anxious to get on with their lives, the wait was excruciating but there was nothing they could do, except, well, what comes naturally. Carelessly. That Christmas, Colleen fell pregnant. She had not long turned seventeen. It was unexpected but it didn't matter to either of them. All they had to do now was get married as soon as they could. On Saturday 7 April, exactly three days after Pricey turned eighteen, and with Colleen's pregnancy not yet showing, they walked out of St Augustine's Church of England as man and radiant wife, grinning from ear to ear.

The wedding was a big affair, and had already started a few days earlier on Pricey's birthday with a doozy of a barbecue. As the guests kept arriving, the party kept on going, right up to the ceremony. Following tradition, Colleen was walked down the aisle by her father, wearing a long white dress with a lace overlay bodice and a long veil trailing behind her. Pricey wore a suit, pleased as punch and neat as a pin, his usually untamable hair held in check for the day by some potion he picked up in town.

After the confetti was thrown and the bride and groom had kissed for the cameras to the teasing whoops of his bushie mates, a convoy of cars, trucks and four-wheel drives took off for the Cudgewa property and a wedding breakfast. Trestle tables had been set up in a long corrugated iron shed for the celebration and nearly everyone who worked on the property was present, as well as friends from Wee Waa.

'It was a big do,' Colleen remembered, smiling.

Colleen and Pricey bought a small caravan soon after and moved onto the Cudgewa property with his parents, Cynthia and John. They set up at a little place not named on any map called Pian Pumps on the Pian River. It was rustic and rudimentary. They had to fetch water from the river in 44-gallon drums, but they loved it. Pricey kept working and Col's belly grew. On 7 September, Johnathon was born in Wee Waa, and early the next year, wanting to be on their own, they moved into town, towing their caravan to the local caravan park where they set up house and stumbled along learning to be parents as they went. With the optimism of youth, Col and Pricey were unstoppable and in love.

Within months, Col was pregnant again, and the next December she gave birth to her second child, Rosemary Kay, in the Wee Waa hospital. They stayed put in Wee Waa for a few more years, but before Johnathon and Rosemary were five, the couple decided to hit the road in their caravan, heading north looking for work. Pricey was working for an earth moving and trucking company called Chaplins, operating heavy machinery at dam construction sites. The bosses said they needed him at Mungindi on the border of Queensland, and Pricey and Col were keen for adventure.

En route, Chaplins diverted Pricey to Stradbroke Island, just off the coast of Queensland near Brisbane, where he worked driving an earth-mover and shifting mineral sands. It was a veritable tropical paradise for the bushie couple but the job only lasted a month and they headed inland again. They got as far north as Bundaberg where little Johnathon, now five, started school, but they were soon on the road again heading down to Mungindi, via Dalby. Johnathon continued his education via correspondence. Rosemary was still too young to go to school.

They stayed in Mungindi for nearly two years. Pricey built dams and Col raised the children. They lived in a 22-foot Viscount caravan and had a ball. Col learnt how to work on car engines and qualified for an articulated truck licence. For the kids, as well as Pricey, life was an adventure, and things occasionally went wrong.

'I remember when we first went up there he actually burnt out a bloody dozer,' Col remembered over a cup of tea in her living room. 'He drove it across a bloody paddock, and a fire came and the wind changed.'

She recalled another time when Pricey was building a dam near Dalby. Col and the kids dropped him off at the site and Pricey got in the scraper. While waving goodbye to the kids in the car, he started the scraper and it tipped over the side of the dam. It took about a week trying to get it back up and out.

Pricey never worried too much about anything. He had a carefree nature and was easily liked by just about everyone he ever met. Col, who has clairvoyant skills and is sometimes able to see things before they happen, believed his spirit of generosity and his giving nature were the reasons he was put on earth, so engaging was his personality. No matter where they went, Pricey would quickly develop an entourage of blokes who liked to sit around and shoot the breeze while knocking back a few beers at the end of the day.

'I have known people who met him in a pub and stayed two days,' Colleen said. 'He got on so good with other people. He was such an easy-going person and he just didn't have enough time – even though he had his family, he still had all his friends as well. There was never enough of him to go around for everyone. He would do anything for you and never expect anything in return, that's just how he was.'

By the end of the seventies, Chaplins had been taken over by the international transport company Brambles. The dams around Mungindi had been built and Pricey and Col returned to Wee Waa looking for work. It was what a lot of non-farming country folk were doing, going to where the work was, and for Col and Pricey it had one singular advantage: they were going home. Pricey's mum and dad still lived in the scrub and their cotton chipping business was a going concern. Col also liked the idea of her two young children being closer to their grandparents.

Things were going perfectly for Pricey. Then his life was shattered by a single shot from a .22 calibre rifle.

It happened a few hours after the sun had gone down on 26 June 1980. Nine-thirty, to be precise. Pricey and Colleen were living at a caravan park in Wee Waa, having returned from Queensland. His parents John White and Cynthia, his younger brother Bob and Bob's de facto Glenda and their seven-year-old daughter were camped at Clarkes Dam on Collymongle Station where they were working, 40 kilometres from Collarenebri, which is about 100 kilometres northwest of Wee Waa. Each had their own caravan set amid bone-dry scrubland, with a communal campfire between the two.

Cynthia, John and Bob knocked off work about ten past four. They opened a few beers and John cooked tea. After dinner, Bob and his parents decided to go kangaroo shooting, leaving Glenda and their daughter at the camp. John White was handy with a weapon. He owned a .22 Magnum Winchester rifle, a second .22 rifle, and a 410 shotgun. So when he sighted a 'roo, he lined up his aim and fired. Bob retrieved the dead 'roo but couldn't see a bullet hole and reckoned it died of a heart attack.

Since the age of fifteen Bob had been in trouble with the law and was known, police said at the time, as 'an associate of the criminal element'. Back at the camp and getting stuck into the beer, John asked his son about the whereabouts of another crook and the arguing started.

When Bob got in his truck to leave, his father grabbed a .22 rifle and fired it into the air after him. Bob didn't need a bullet to stop him, the old truck broke down only a couple of hundred metres along the track. When Bob came back to the camp, he whacked his dad across the face and disarmed him.

John went to his caravan and started loading the 410 shotgun he kept in a rifle bag in the cupboard. Cynthia, wearing a pink nightie and blue dressing gown, her Escort cigarettes tucked into the pocket, went to disarm her husband but before she got there, Bob snuck up and grabbed his father's .22 Winchester rifle from inside the caravan door, and crept back several metres to the truck where he loaded it with three .22 calibre super speed hollow point bullets. Bob could see his father through the open door, urgently trying to load the 410, and figured if he shot the light out, his father would put the weapon down. Bob aimed the .22 at the Tilly kerosene lamp on the table inside the caravan.

He fired, but the bullet missed its mark and hit his mum in the head, piercing her skull with a perfectly round and neat hole above the left ear.

'Bob, Bob, you've shot your mother,' John cried out.

Both men dropped their rifles and Bob rushed over to his wounded mother, lying on the mat outside the door to the caravan. Bob tried to pick her up and she said, 'Bobby, oh Bobby.' They carried Cynthia to the Toyota HiLux ute and Bob drove like mad to Collarenebri hospital, but she died in his arms as he lifted her out of the truck and was pronounced dead at 10.10 pm by Dr Ak Beng Kwa. She was forty-three.

Everyone, including Bob's father, the police and a later judge, put the fatal shooting down to an accident, fuelled by the two dozen cans of beer the adults drank that night. But the law is the law and someone had to be responsible.

The way Colleen remembered it more than twenty years later was that Bob never meant the gun to go off – 'it was an accidental shooting' – but it did, and Cynthia was dead, killed by her own son as in a Greek tragedy.

'We were living in the caravan park in Wee Waa – the kids were young. We were in bed, actually, because Pricey had to go to work. And just before there was a knock on the door, I "heard" the gun go off,' Colleen said referring to her gift of clairvoyancy.

The policeman said he had bad news and told Colleen that *her* mother had been shot dead. She hadn't seen her mother for nearly two decades and shook her head. For a split second she wondered how anyone from a part of her life she'd long since buried would even know where to find her. Colleen told the officer he was wrong, and when he said the dead woman was named 'Cynthia', it all fell into place.

Colleen was in shock. Cynthia and Colleen were close: 'She was the mother I never had.' She got Pricey out of bed and followed him to the door as the policeman told him what happened. Pricey was shattered.

'I think I lost a lot of Pricey when his mum did die. She loved all her kids but there was a spark between him and his mum. It was just a part of him that died and no one really understood it and we never spoke about it really, because there was never a time,' Colleen said.

'Pricey was never a person to speak about how he actually felt. Pricey was still a happy-go-lucky person but you could look at him and see a part of him gone because he lost his mum. It was understandable. And he had his own family as well, and trying to deal with that and knowing that your own brother did it as well, it was a lot for him to take on. Pricey never forgave him [Bob] and I don't think he ever will. And I know it breaks his mum's heart too, because he can't forgive him.'

Robert Edward Price was charged with one count of feloniously slaying his mother Cynthia Ann Orthon. On 5 November 1980 he went before Justice Cantor at the Central Criminal Court on St James Road, Sydney, where he pleaded guilty to manslaughter. On 20 November, in Court 13A, he was sentenced to seven years imprisonment with a three-year non-parole period that expired on 27 June 1983.

'It is difficult to understand the primitive behaviour pattern of both the prisoner and his father,' Justice Cantor said in his sentence. 'However, I am mindful of the fact that it was the prisoner's father who first picked up a firearm after arguing with the prisoner. Not only did he pick it up, he discharged it several times. The prisoner disarmed his father who immediately armed himself with, and commenced to load, a shotgun.

'On the material before me, it was the prisoner's father who was threatening to use a firearm.

'I should observe that whatever provocation may have been offered by the prisoner and his father it in no way justified or excused the use of firearms by either of them. However, it is to be remembered that it is not alleged that the prisoner was trying to shoot his father when he fired the shot which killed his mother. The prisoner will have to live with the knowledge that he, in discharging this rifle, is responsible for her death.

'Such a punishment far exceeds the penalty I now impose.'

John White and his children buried Cynthia in the Wee Waa cemetery, but for Pricey, the country town he called home had lost its charm. He heard the Howick Coal Company just outside of Muswellbrook was looking for miners. Pricey and Col discussed it. Miners earned a steady quid. Sure, the work was dangerous, more so if the mine was underground and not an open cut pit, and yes, the shifts were long, but it paid well and the benefits were good. They packed the kids off to Pricey's father for the day, and went to Aberdeen for an interview. The mine is located at Pike's Gully on the New England Highway, halfway between Muswellbrook and Singleton.

Pricey couldn't read or write well but he could sign his name, and when it came to operating heavy duty machinery, he was one of the best. He'd been working with machinery so long he knew by heart what the signs meant, even if he couldn't read them. He knew his way around a grader, a dozer and a scraper with his eyes closed. And he was a careful operator. He didn't take risks. Pricey made an impression and scored the job on the basis that he serve a three-week probation. If he didn't mess up, he'd have the job full-time.

Col and Pricey were elated. They went back to Wee Waa, hooked the ball joint of the caravan to the back of their old truck, packed up the kids, and moved to Aberdeen for the next chapter in their lives. At the end of the three-week trial period when Pricey was told he had a permanent job if he wanted it, he and Col moved into the Willow Grove Caravan Park on the banks of the Hunter River, and set up their recently upgraded 30-foot Millard mobile home. They stayed there for the next five years, enrolling the kids in the local primary school, building friendships and becoming part of the social fabric of the small, close-knit town.

'We got on well with everyone wherever we went. That was the thing with Pricey, he was such an easy-going person, we were always having a barbecue with people,' Colleen said. 'There was never a weekend that went by that we didn't have a get-together with a barbecue. Living in a caravan park is like a big family and you know who not to mix with and who to mix with. He was just a very well-liked person.

'He was never an aggressive person. I can honestly say I think in all the years I've known Pricey, I think we had three arguments at the most. They were just words – if I have something to say I'll say it. You didn't need to get in an argument with him. He just wasn't that type of person.'

In 1981 the heart of Aberdeen was the meatworks, which employed about four hundred people, at least half of them locals. Most lived on the western side of the railway tracks, but as the Hunter Valley region's mining industry grew, so too did Aberdeen, which spread further up the hills on the eastern side of the tracks, on the abattoir side of the New England Highway. Miners and workers from the Liddell and Bayswater power stations forty minutes down the road moved in and many, like the Prices, settled temporarily at the Willow Grove Caravan Park.

'It was good times. I used to buy him a carton of beer and a carton of smokes every week and he had his money to go down for a few beers with the boys,' Colleen remembered.

Pricey met Laurie Lewis, a fellow miner from the Howick mine, during the first three weeks he was in town. He was having a drink at the Commercial Hotel about a hundred metres up the road from the caravan park. Pricey hadn't been in town long enough to make the top pub his home-base yet, but that would come. A mutual miner friend introduced them over a Tooheys

New and they became instant mates. Laurie was a few years older than Pricey but they got on like a house on fire. Their friendship deepened when they realised their lives had run on parallel paths.

Both were married young, Laurie to Fran; both had two young children; both were out-of-towners from the bush – Laurie was from Emmaville, just north of Glen Innes – and both were living a few vans away from each other at Willow Grove. Over the next two decades, Pricey and Laurie became best mates, seeing each other through the tough times, going on fishing trips, chopping firewood and drinking at the pub. Pricey eventually made Laurie the sole executor of his will.

Pricey and Laurie weren't too dissimilar in personality, although in looks Laurie weighed in leaner than Pricey and was a good few inches taller. These days he wears his grey hair in a bit of a rockabilly squiff, which works well when he's playing a guitar around a campfire, singing songs. But back then, before it started going grey, he wore it longer in the back. Laurie Lewis is a direct bloke. He calls a spade a shovel and is fiercely loyal. He's a man's man who laughs with an infectious chuckle. Loves his fishing and frequently led trips away with the boys – no sheilas allowed – to Deepwater or Bonshaw or Ballina. A core crew would head up for a few days of fishing, occasionally they'd go for a week, all loaded with rod, baits, sleeping and cooking equipment, and plenty of beer, wine and spirits to last the requisite time. Pricey was a regular.

'Loved his beer. Aaaaah, loved his beer,' Laurie said, sipping an orange juice and declining Fran's offer of a slice of Boston bun. 'Yeah, lived for his grog.' Chuckle. 'Just an ordinary everyday Australian scrubber. Worked to make a quid and have a beer and that's it. Buy a few clothes, a car or something, that's all he was happy with. That's all he wanted. And he wanted to leave the kids something.

'He was pretty rough. He was as rough as guts but as a friend, you wouldn't find a more stand-by bloke. Stand up for you or help you out any time. He was always lending money to someone else. Giving money away all the time. At his funeral I said there wouldn't be a person out there who wouldn't owe Pricey a favour or money of some sort, and I wasn't exaggerating. He was that sort of fella. He would give you his last two bob. And a lot of people used that, his character. It cost him a lot in terms of money and a few things that he lost because he loaned things and never got it back, loaned money and never got it back.'

The early days in Aberdeen were fun. The kids went to school and the young families built something of an extended family at the caravan park, mostly a result of proximity. They'd drink at the Aberdeen RSL, just a short walk up the hill on the corner of Moray and MacQueen streets, or go to the Sunday raffles at the Aberdeen bowling club in Jefferson Park, near the nine-hole golf course, the local Tigers football club and the tennis courts. Whenever the local clubs held a dance, Pricey and Col, Laurie and Fran, and a few other young couples from Willow Grove put on their finery and headed out for a night.

'He'd join in anything for fun. He loved dancing, "jiving" he used to call it – "jiiiiiiivin",' Laurie said, drawing out the 'i' the way Pricey used to. 'He'd get anyone up, even a chair. He just loved dancin'. He'd come around and ask everyone for a dance, anyone, doesn't matter who it was, from sixteen to eighty. Oh, he loved his dancin', Pricey.'

On the weekends Colleen took the kids to sport. Pricey wasn't into that type of thing with the kids – fishing and horse riding he could handle, but not the sports.

For Laurie Lewis, Pricey's lack of enthusiasm for his kids' sport was the one thing he and his best mate argued about. Laurie couldn't think of anything better than watching his kids' sporting victories and thought Pricey was missing the best part of being a dad. He thought Pricey was depriving himself of something special with his son, Johnathon, who played football for the local rugby team.

'He loved his kids, no doubt about that. The one thing that I didn't like about him was that he wouldn't go and watch the sports. I'd say, "Why don't you go and watch them play football or basketball or whatever they play?",' Laurie said, shaking his head. 'Ah, they don't want me there,' he recalled Pricey saying. 'I said you can have a beer while you watch them, it doesn't matter, as long as you don't get drunk and go driving them home drunk. "Ah, they don't want me. I'd go crook, getting up at them if they don't score". He just wouldn't go. Which was a shame.'

After five years at Willow Grove, Pricey decided it was time to set down his roots permanently in Aberdeen. His job at Howick was as safe as houses, and the family felt at home in the town. On 2 May 1985 Col and Pricey's second daughter, Jackie, was born and their family was complete. And Aberdeen wasn't far from his birthplace. Pricey and Col started shopping for land and decided on a block in St Andrews Street.

Col was happy at the caravan park, and didn't necessarily want to move. 'It's a good life. I missed it actually. It was John's idea to buy the house and I was happy to stay in the van. His mum always wanted him to have a home and we ended up buying a block and building a house.'

But the property was perfect and it was on the high side of the street, where it caught the rising sun. They bought the land for a few thousand dollars and employed local carpenter John Cooper to build a three-bedroom, red brick veneer house with a brown-tiled verandah that ran along the front. The house was built close to the eastern edge of the block and faced south on to St Andrews Street. A Hills Hoist went up in the middle of the back yard. Later, Pricey added two galvanised steel garden sheds – for secret men's business – and a brick barbecue along the eastern fence. The back yard was huge, giving Johnathon and Rosemary plenty of room to run about in. Col improvised with furnishings when they first moved in and, like all young families in a new house, hung sheets as curtains and fussed over turning the house into a home.

6

Another baby, another breakup

In 1984 when Katherine Knight left Kellett in Queensland she moved back home to her parents' property on the road that ran out to Rouchel. It would have been the last place she wanted to be. She couldn't wait to get out of home when she was eighteen and now, ten years later, she was back. To make matters worse, she was back with a failed marriage to her name and two little girls to raise.

It wasn't easy. Melissa was enrolled at Aberdeen primary school and Natasha went to the local preschool until she followed her big sister into primary. Kathy was trying to get over the breakup. She also had to get a job and once again found herself at the Aberdeen meatworks as a slicer. Not much had changed. Things were working out, but life at home was far from perfect. Finally, Kathy got jack of it. She packed up and moved out with the kids. They shifted into a rented property at McCullys Gap, just outside of Muswellbrook.

Kathy wasn't yet thirty and was dating again, but the first few fellas didn't last long. Katherine was a protective mother who put her daughters first and wanted them to be happy and safe. But she didn't like being on her own.

'She was a good mother, a real good mother,' her brother Shane said. But she picked the wrong men. 'That was most of her trouble, she hung around and got on with the wrong people,' he said. Shane didn't like most of the men his sister would date.

'She was a good mum and there is no doubt about that. I couldn't have asked for a better mother. I used to get smacked hard – Mum grew up that way, so that is the way things were,' Kathy's second daughter Natasha told *The Newcastle Herald*'s Donna Page in an interview. 'With the younger kids she started to change. Mum started learning as we got older that things were different in terms of discipline and punishment. We are from the country and Mum has always been a bush girl. She loved to go camping and doing outdoor things.'

Kathy worked and she was able to provide for her girls but the same year she was re-employed at the abattoir, she hurt her back. Back injuries are shockers, and Kathy's was giving her grief. In 1985 it flared up. Her doctor gave her a couple of weeks off but when she returned she aggravated it again and took more time off. It got so bad that she couldn't return to the abattoir and her employment was officially terminated in August.

The following year, Katherine moved the kids to a Housing Commission house in Segenhoe Street in Aberdeen. It was a better location and meant that the girls could walk to school a few blocks down the road. Living in Aberdeen was also an improvement for Kathy's social life. There were a couple of clubs and, at that time, three pubs where she could meet men. She was young, tall and slim, and she was comfortable in her own skin. She didn't mind going up to the bowling club or the RSL on her own, and in a small town like Aberdeen, you were always bound to run into someone to have a chat with. Two degrees of separation.

That was how, around November 1986, she met her next boyfriend, David Saunders, born and bred in Scone, and the second of four children. David Saunders is a true blue Aussie bloke – he doesn't mind hard work, loves his beer and is honest enough to tell you he's a 'pisspot'. He's the kind of fella who happily drives his mates a couple of hundred clicks to pick up a new truck or lending them his car when theirs is getting repaired. 'I'm Dave and no one is going to change Dave,' he said over a beer at his local, the Thoroughbred Hotel, in Scone.

He was a miner at the Hunter Valley No. 1 Colliery on the western side of the New England Highway near Ravensworth and had been through his own divorce when he met Katherine Knight. He was at the Aberdeen bowling club knocking back a couple of Tooheys and having a yarn with a mate when Kath came in. She was seven years younger than him, she was on her own, and his mate knew her. That was all the invitation anyone needed in the country where civility is a prized commodity. She joined them and the threesome sat down and played cards.

Sharon Turner, the girl who used to ride home to Aberdeen on the school bus from Muswellbrook High School with the Knight sisters, said it was easy for people to like Kathy because she was a nice person and would do anything for you: 'She was kind-hearted and she was fun to be with. She'd laugh, she'd joke . . . If you didn't know her from way back, you wouldn't think she was capable of it,' said Sharon years later, in reference to the murder.

'She was genuinely a kind person. We were cutting down trees one day . . . and she brought a chainsaw down and started it up and started helping. She would do it for you and not think twice about it. Kind-natured. Helpful. Would help anybody. But in a relationship, no one would believe what she could do. You had to have known her from way back to realise,' said Sharon. 'She wasn't stupid either, you know. She was – how can I put it? – quite cunning. It's hard to explain. She was no bloody idiot . . . if she knew she was right, she would pursue that. She wasn't stupid. She'd know if someone was pulling the wool over her eyes.'

David Saunders didn't know a thing about Kathy's background and he found her exactly as Sharon described her – kind-hearted and great fun to be with. When it came to romance, David was a slow mover but he and Kathy dated a few times over the next couple of weeks. David had offered to take a mate and his wife to the airport in Sydney for a holiday they were taking to Singapore, and he asked Kathy if she'd like to go with him. They'd stay in the city for the night, see a few sights, and drive back the following day. Kathy said yes and asked her mother to baby-sit her grandchildren. Dave and Kathy took the picturesque

Putty Road route there and back, and the weekend away marked the real beginning of their relationship.

On 6 December 1986, Kathy's mother died suddenly. Barbara Knight was fifty-nine years old and Kathy was devastated. They were as close as could be and had developed a nice friendship in which they would discuss everything. There was even a time when Barbara briefly moved into the McCullys Gap house with Kathy and her grandchildren – three generations of women under the same roof.

Things went smoothly for Kathy and David for the first couple of months of their relationship. They got on well and had a healthy sex life. David kept his flat in Scone but spent more and more time with Kathy at her house in Segenhoe Street and eventually moved in. He liked her little girls and, being a father himself, knew all about the commitments of parenting. Melissa and Natasha seemed to like him and called him Dave.

But then, suddenly, it went downhill. David Saunders has no idea why, but Kathy went 'off her bean'. She was the jealous type. She started accusing him of sleeping with other women and would verbally abuse him, screaming and shouting and calling him everything under the sun. Then one night towards the middle of January Kathy and David had a blue. David Saunders moved back to his flat in Scone, but Kathy was soon banging on his door asking him to come back. He did. When she was good she was great. Things would be going fine but then she'd lock him out again. Dave could never predict when Kathy might do it but he knew she would.

And so began a pattern of behaviour that repeated itself during the next three years of their relationship. Up, then down.

'She was alright but she used to go right off the bean every now and then, you know,' David said.

Why?

'I used to look at the moon,' he said with a shrug, meaning he had no idea what would set her off. 'If I was up here [Scone] and there was a blue, she would be chasing me all the time. She'd kick me out one minute and she'd be there an hour later trying to find me.'

David Saunders, who is a good few inches shorter than Katherine, said he never hit her or initiated their fights, but, he said, he would defend himself against her when she lashed out at him, which was frequently: 'I have never, ever done anything wrong. I mean, if Katherine hit me, she would get one back. I am talking about – I'm there to protect myself. I wouldn't go and belt into her or anything like that,' he said.

The relationship was 'basically good', but Kathy was erratic and violent.

Katherine Knight marched to the beat of her own drum and didn't care who could hear it. She was that type of person but she also had a certain guilelessness about her. Her dress sense was uniquely hers and was often the subject of snide remarks. She was a clever seamstress and good at crafts, but it was the way she put things together that would have people talking.

'This didn't go with that – not your Sussan ad, that's for sure. None of Kath's clothes went together. She was like a bit of a hill-billy but she liked that, and that's the way she was,' said her friend Cheryl Sullivan. 'She didn't give a bugger about what anyone else thought about her. She dressed for her. She didn't dress to please people. That was her motto and that was the way she thought, which was good.

'She didn't have a problem with any of that. A few people used to laugh at her down the street and that, what she was wearing and pick at her, but I just took Kath for Kath, that's probably why we got on.'

Cheryl and her late husband Richard lived in St Andrews Street for several years and first met Kathy at the Segenhoe Inn when it was still a pub. Kathy was easy to talk to, and they hit it off. Cheryl also knew Kathy's sister-in-law Val Roughan, who was married to Kathy's half-brother Barry. The women would play bingo together at the Muswellbrook District Workers' Club and occasionally Kathy and Cheryl would go to the movies, but Cheryl would avoid the film if a horror movie was playing. Kathy was serious about her horror films, Cheryl said.

'I had no qualms against Kathy at all. I've had none whatso-ever, she was really nice to me and my children. We would joke around, go power walking, to the pictures, to town. She would baby-sit my kids. I have never seen a bad side to her actually, not at all, not once. I never did,' said Cheryl. 'I was told about a few things – how she attacked her ex-boyfriend with an axe, put her child under a semi-trailer when it was a baby in a pram and that. I didn't know if they were true. But I didn't see that side of Kathy. Kathy was a happy person . . . I never seen a bad side to Kathy, she never did anything wrong to me and half the time I just put down the rumours as just to be rumours.'

Still, for all of Kathy's good points, Cheryl sometimes detected a darker side and she knew better than to push things or ask Kathy questions that she didn't want to answer. 'Sometimes she'd get cranky or something like that with you. If you asked her a question about – oh, I don't know, certain things, she'd get cranky with you and she would click,' said Cheryl. 'You could see anger in her, coming into her and then you turn around and realise you're best just to leave things alone.'

As their relationship progressed, David Saunders and Kathy Knight found their own rhythm. When she'd kick him out of the house, he'd retreat to his flat in Scone for a couple of days until Kathy came and asked him to come back to Segenhoe Street. One night in May 1987, Dave was over at his mate's house having a few beers after she'd given him his marching orders yet again. After a few too many brews, he walked home, leaving his car parked at his mate's, not wanting to risk driving under the influence. Not long after he got inside, there was a knock on the front door and it was Kathy, asking Dave to come home to Aberdeen with her. She said she wanted to talk about their fractured relationship. Her two daughters were at their grandfather's. What could he do?

He went back to Aberdeen but within minutes, Kathy was at him, accusing Dave of sleeping with another woman. He wasn't but Kathy was winding herself tighter and tighter, and started to push Dave. He pushed back, to get away from her. As Kathy kept pushing and shoving, she screamed that she was pregnant. Then she started yelling that Dave had kicked her in the stomach. She kept screaming, 'You kicked me in the stomach', over and over.

'I got accused of kicking her in the guts. I didn't do that. I didn't do it,' he said. 'I got accused of kicking her, I've never ever kicked her. She said she was pregnant, right, when we got back to her place she accused me of kicking her and I didn't kick her and I didn't hit her and I didn't do anything.'

The argument was spiralling out of control.

'Anyway we're out there and we're arguing . . . and she said, "I'll show you what I'm going to do with you", and she went and picked up the knife, and I didn't even think twice about it – a carving knife – and she went out [to the back yard]. I didn't see her do it, I'm telling you I didn't see her do it, but there was blood all over her, blood dripping down everywhere. And she says, "There's your dog out there, that's what I think of you". I said, "What are you talking about?" and I went out and here's the dog, dead.'

Dave had an eight-week-old pure-bred dingo and Katherine had sliced its throat open and dropped it on the ground. It was a clean cut, David said, slicing an imaginary knife through the air across an imaginary puppy's throat. Kathy went inside, covered in blood, still with the knife in her hand, and she called the police.

Kathy wasn't calm, Dave said, but 'she wasn't off her head – she could go off her head a lot worse than that'.

The police took no action, and once again David Saunders returned to his flat in Scone. The next morning he discovered that the wipers and aerial on his car that he left parked outside his mate's house had been bent out of shape, and the interior rear-view mirror was broken. Kathy later told him that she had done it. She also wasn't pregnant.

Years later, in the only interview she gave police following the murder of John Price, Katherine was asked about the relationship with David Saunders. She told Detective Bob Wells that there was violence on his part: 'I just kept calling the police every time he hit me.' When asked about killing the dog, she said she had done it.

'Can you tell me about that incident?' Detective Wells asked Katherine as the video cameras recorded the interview, which was later played at her sentencing hearing.

'He laid his steel-cap boots into me one day when I told him I was pregnant. I went out and cut his dog's throat,' she replied.

'Did it go any further or did, did you see –'

'I ended up having my nerves treated, but at that stage I just lost Mother . . .'

'When you cut the dog's throat, did the dog, was the dog dead?'

'It was a clean cut, they said.'

'Did you say anything to David at the time that you did that?'

'He said to me to kill him, and I threw the knife away and picked up a frying pan and hit him in the head with it.'

'Do you recall saying anything to him though about it?' Detective Wells asked.

'The dog, he seen it.'

It was reported years later that she had told psychiatrists that she killed the dog to pay him back for kicking her; which he denies. Soon after the puppy incident, Katherine and Dave were driving from Wingen, a little town about forty minutes north up the highway, to Aberdeen and stopped along the way to pick up a mate in Scone. As they were travelling back, Kathy started abusing Dave. He's forgotten the details in the years since – it was just another time Kathy went off – but he remembered she tried to jump out of the car as it was moving, and his mate Wayne had to hold her until Dave stopped the car and calmed her down.

Once home, Dave took the children to the neighbours and when he got back, Kathy was sprawled on the floor with pills scattered around her. Dave ran back to the neighbours' and they drove her to the outpatients department at the Scott Memorial Hospital in Scone. Kathy had taken an overdose and was unconscious overnight. She was admitted for a few days around May, during which time her family and David Saunders visited. She was also still grieving the death of her mum just before Christmas.

With Kathy recovering in hospital, her half-brother Neville Roughan told Dave that Kathy said there was violence in the relationship because of his drinking, but Dave told Neville that the only violence was from Kathy.

In one interview in prison with a forensic psychiatrist Katherine said she couldn't actually remember killing the dog. Some years after the incident, she told her next-door neighbour Gerri Edwards that she hit David Saunders over the head with a frypan and slit his dog's throat. It would take fourteen years before the incident was officially addressed again. In sentencing Katherine Knight for murder the judge referred to her slicing the dog's throat as 'an act of revenge'.

Before Kathy was home from hospital, the story was around Aberdeen. Some said that Kathy cut the dog's throat and then knocked Dave out with a frying pan, others that she dumped the dog on his chest for good measure, for when he came to. Katherine Knight went home and was referred to a psychiatrist in Tamworth. She also got back together with Dave Saunders.

One of Kathy's daughters would later say Dave was violent towards her mother, allegations he denied. Indeed, he said, according to Justice O'Keefe, 'it was me that was being assaulted.' Even though Katherine had claimed that Dave had mistreated her, the judge said he could not resolve whether Dave had been an 'aggressor' in the relationship. He said it was clear that Kathy had acted with violence, vengeance, malice and revenge towards her lover. But back then, none of that mattered.

In October that year, Kathy fell pregnant with her third child. The following June she gave birth to a little girl she named Sarah. Dave was there for the birth and said he was over the moon the moment he first held his perfect, redheaded baby in his arms.

'I had a smile out of [her] when she would have been – and everyone tells me I'm wrong – when she wouldn't even be two hours old and I had a smile. Everyone reckons it was wind, it wasn't wind, I've had three other kids,' he said.

Things were good for a while. Katherine was a good mother and looked after the girls. Dave bought the little wooden house on MacQueen Street, which meant he had somewhere to stay when Kathy booted him out of Segenhoe Street. It had become part of the routine. About six months after the baby was born, Dave, Kathy and the three girls moved into MacQueen Street. In 1989 Kathy finally received the compensation payout from hurting her back at the abattoir and she used the money to pay off the $15 000 loan on the house, effectively making it hers.

Katherine's compensation payout gave her a financial independence that spelled freedom. She mightn't have had a stable relationship but at least now she had a home to call her own. It wasn't much, but it was hers. The cream-coloured weatherboard was blunt up against the footpath of MacQueen Street. The white timber door, which was tired and in need of a new coat of paint, opened directly onto the gravel and dirt footpath and if the wind was blowing in the wrong direction, an eddy of dust blew into the house, settling on the floor. An ugly power box sat smack in the middle of the front façade and was battered and scratched, and the pitched green corrugated iron roof had the occasional rust spot. A low-slung awning reached to the road and was propped up by four wooden posts painted fire-engine red to give them a bit of pizzazz.

During the following decade, the inside of the house became a showcase for Kathy's eccentricities. Walls were decorated with leather coats and motorbike jackets. She stretched a cow hide over the paintwork, and hung the treated horns of a water buffalo and steer, and antlers from a deer, on the lounge-room wall. She had a stuffed baby deer and a peacock, and mounted cow and sheep skulls on the walls, along with old animal traps and fur wraps. She loved sitting in her lounge-room and looking at her walls and taking in all the dead animals and the remnants of life now extinguished.

It was a trove of trash and treasure but to Kathy, it was her dream home. A giant wooden fork and spoon were mounted on one wall, an old rake and pitchfork were strung from the ceiling. She hammered patty cake tins and cooking utensils, meat cutters and farm equipment into the walls, and had a cabinet covered with crockery and figurines. She didn't ride but had a riding boot and crop on the wall, as well as a saddle.

The rafters in the ceiling were chock-a-block with old newspapers, books and clothes. Her video collection included a long list of horror movies with titles like *Expect No Mercy*; *Freeway – The Traffic is Murder*; *Jason Goes To Hell – Final Friday*; *Silent Night, Deadly Night 4*; *Resurrection*; *Idle Hands*; *Oxygen*; and *The Patriot*.

In court during her sentencing hearing for murder, Dr Robert Delaforce said Katherine Knight's house was a significant pointer to her personality: 'It is a place to me of death, of destruction. She is not in the garden and growing things. I am not aware there is a pet budgie there or something like that,' he said during cross-examination by Knight's QC, Peter Thraves. 'It is a theme of death, and some writers in psychiatry have made a lot of significance of this, they have given it a term, in fact, of necrophilis, and it literally means a love of death. She is surrounded by it, all of these dead things. She enjoyed her work at the abattoirs . . . why does someone enjoy their work so much at the abattoir? Why do they keep going to him who kills the pigs . . . These are all important signs. And back to the wall hangings, the theme of death, necrophilis – these things are all just so significant.'

'You would be aware, doctor, that many country houses in Europe would have very similar hangings on their walls; people who are into hunting, shooting and fishing . . . that would be the case, wouldn't it?' said Mr Thraves.

'But how many of them would murder? How many of them would cut a dog's throat?' Dr Delaforce answered.

Justice Barry O'Keefe spoke from the bench: 'They might be more likely to cut the throat of somebody who injured one of their hunting dogs?'

'That is in fact right,' concurred Dr Delaforce.

It was after she paid off the house that the problems between Katherine and Dave really fired up. Dave said the arguments increased and Kathy took out a couple of Apprehended Domestic Violence Orders against him, mainly for damage he would do to the home or property when they had a blue. But, he said, she was the one doing all the hitting, and he would just defend himself.

Dave travelled to work at the coal mine in a car crew with four or five other blokes from Aberdeen, and before too long, his injuries had become a running joke among his colleagues. None of the scratches or bruises or cuts were work injuries, and Dave told them it was the missus giving him a hiding. It's not the type of thing a tough, working-class bloke from the bush likes to admit. Things would get worse.

One weekend Dave, together with Kathy's cousin Brian Conlon, who was up from Sydney, took Melissa and Natasha fishing at Lake Glenbawn. They'd been out casting for bass for a good six or seven hours, and on the way back, they dropped into the RSL club for a quick ale and a six-pack. It was a Saturday evening and Dave remembered that he was at the bar for about ten minutes. When they got back to MacQueen Street, Kathy was ironing and started in on Dave about not being home in time for tea.

'I will never forget that night,' Dave recalled, 'because she's swinging me around, right, she's got me by the arms right out the front of the place, and as I'm going around I'm trying to get these beers to Brian, I'm saying, "Catch them". That was the night I got ironed out. She hit me with the iron. That was another time I had to go.'

Kathy was well and truly fired up. She was yelling and screaming and out of control. Kathy then turned on Brian and knocked him to the ground, and both men fled out the front door, too frightened to go back in. Brian left and Dave spent the next two nights with a mate in Scone. He returned to Aberdeen on the Monday morning and waited for his car crew to swing by to pick him up for the lift to work.

Ronnie Wilton was the designated driver who arrived at Mac-Queen Street that morning. He found Dave standing a few doors up and across the road from his house, decked out in the gear he'd been wearing the previous two days. He didn't have his work clothes and wasn't carrying his lunch. Dave's face had so many cuts and bruises that Ron thought he'd been through a war.

'It was a Monday morning and we were going to work and it was my turn to drive and I left home here and I was going down to pick up Dave,' said Ronnie. 'And what they call the old bank corner, which is opposite the paper shop, he was there and he was flagging me down, so I pulled up, and he hopped in and I just took one look at him and I said "Jesus Christ, Dave, you've been through World War Three, what the bloody hell happened to you?" . . . He didn't want to talk about it.'

He also didn't want to go inside his house to get anything and just told Ron to get going, so Ron drove to work, picking up the other blokes on the way and stopping at the old Esso garage in Muswellbrook where Dave bought a packet of orange slice biscuits for lunch. That afternoon on the way home in the car, Ronnie asked Dave again what happened and he told his mates what Kathy had done.

'I said, "Saundo, listen, you are going to tell us what happened because if anything, it's going to come out", because in Aberdeen it's pretty hard to keep a secret,' Ronnie said. 'He said, "Have you ever been ironed out?" I said, "Depends what you mean", and he said, "I mean ironed out, with a bloody iron".'

Dave told Ronnie that after taking Kathy's kids swimming at Lake Glenbawn to give her a break, he went and had a few drinks at the club and when he came home Kathy attacked him. Apparently, she wanted to go to the Saturday night raffles at the bowling club but he was late. 'He's walked in the door and . . . she was there with the iron on, and she's just gone bang, and [Dave said], "The first one hit me, and Christ . . . I tried to get up but she was just laying into me with the bloody iron" and he said, "I couldn't get to my feet . . . and I got to the front door and she was laying into me with the iron".'

Ronnie said that whenever he saw the couple at the club together he could tell if Kathy was getting angry by her complexion. 'I had seen her riled up, wild, and her face goes very red . . . And she could go very red in the face. And when you see the redness in the face, you knew to keep out of her road more or less.' Ronnie, like a few of Dave's other mates, knew that Dave was afraid of Kathy when she went into her rages, and that he would stay away from her for a few days. But he always went back. She would come and find him, and charm him into moving back in with her. One morning she turned up at 7 am. Her tactics never failed.

'With Kath she could be so violent and then you give her a couple of days to cool down and she is as nice as pie, and naturally Dave goes back to pick up some clothes and she is all over him like a – as if nothing had happened, and he is the most loveliest man in the world,' said Ronnie. 'And that was the way it more or less always happened, every time they had a major blue, you let her cool down for a couple of days and then you go back and she is as nice as pie, but in the end he knew that he had to get away from her . . . And she could just manipulate you – a man – and I could understand, coming from a man's point of view, you walk in the door and she is all over you. And that was the drawing point for him – that's why she could be so violent and then be so nice.'

Towards the end of 1988, Katherine and Dave were having yet another argument, this time in the kitchen, when Katherine grabbed a pair of scissors and stabbed him in the stomach. Dave fled to his mate's house. The injury was not serious enough to require medical attention, but it was a portent of what she would do years later in another kitchen a few blocks away.

'I got stabbed with scissors and ended up at John Kennedy's place. I said, "You'll have to put me up for a little bit, mate", I said, "I'm in trouble" . . . She used to go off about things at different times. I thought me dog was one thing, but the beer over me head [on another occasion] was another thing. There were that many times and that many things that happened I could tell you a lot more stuff but it'd take a day. All I remember . . . going to John Kennedy's and saying, "Can you help me get these out of me guts?"'

This time, Dave left, telling himself it would be the last time.

For most of the early part of 1989, David Saunders was living in Scone, having broken up with Katherine, but come September, they gave the relationship another chance. Not even Dave could explain why, but there they were again, locked in the familiarity of their own routine. It made no sense to anyone else who saw the arguments and cuts and bruises, but for some reason it made sense to Kathy and Dave.

'I'll never forget the day that I went to play bowls, this one really hurt, this one really hurt me,' said Dave, ready to launch into another story about Kathy's violence towards him.

He played a bit of lawn bowls, not very well, but good enough to get the black bowls close enough to the jack not to make a goose of himself. He was up at the Aberdeen RSL playing a few ends and Kathy was sitting on the benches watching and enjoying the afternoon sun. They looked like a happy couple. Dave's father had died of cancer not too long before and his mother had given most of his clothes and bowls gear to her son – father and son were the same size. Dave can be pretty sentimental, and it meant a lot to him.

Kathy left and went home and by the time Dave got home after a few cleansing ales at the bar, she had locked him out. He still hasn't worked out why – after all, she'd just been sitting there watching him play bowls as happy as Larry. He put his shoulder to the front door and pushed his way in.

'I did do something wrong,' said Dave. 'Well, I looked at it this way, it was my house, so I've got me shoulder to the door and went straight through the front door, didn't I? And she's belted into me and then she gets on the phone to me mother and my mother says, "I'll come and get Dave", and she comes down and I've got blood from arsehole to breakfast time.'

In the attack, Katherine cut his face. Dave changed out of his gear and went back to live with his mum at Scone for a week, but Kathy wanted him back.

'And I went back and I said, "Well, where's me clothes?" She said, "What clothes?" . . . She says, "There are no clothes". She'd cut them all up, she'd cut them all up. They were at the dump, I didn't see them, she cut them all up.'

In May they had another blue and before the week was out, Katherine and David had split up again.

For Dave Saunders, it was the end of the line. Nursing a beer at his local in Scone, a baseball cap pulled low over his forehead, as mates kept coming over and saying, 'G'day Saundo', Dave said he'd had enough and was out the door. He called his boss at the Hunter Valley mine and asked for long service leave. He cleared out of Scone and went down to Newcastle where he hid from Katherine Knight. Newcastle is a big enough city for any man to get lost in, and Dave did it well. He got a job as a panel beater – the first trade he learned on leaving school – and stayed well and truly clear of his former de facto. She rang his mates in Scone and Aberdeen wanting to know where to find him, but they all said they had no idea where he was. He'd gone to ground. She would look for him in his old watering holes in Scone, including The Thoroughbred and The Willow Tree, where he often drank in the front bar, but she had no luck. Later, when he finally returned, she had taken out another AVO against him and managed to stick the knife of revenge in again by keeping him away from his daughter. He said Kathy had actually told little Sarah he was dead.

'She said, "While ever your balls point to the ground you will never have that kid",' he said.

Ultimately, Dave did get access to his little girl, but years later when he gave her a puppy to take home to Aberdeen after a weekend visit, Kathy got nasty again and threatened to cut the dog's throat if Sarah kept it. Dave had already seen what Kathy could do to a dog. He took the pup away with him. 'That's why [Sarah] can have whatever she wants now,' he said.

~

While Kathy was going out with Dave Saunders, her estranged husband David Kellett had moved to Alice Springs where he was working as a trucker. Every year at Christmas he would send his girls presents and cards, and on their birthdays he sent flowers. They never received them. Kathy would intercept them and dispose of them before the girls got home from school.

'By then Kath would have them and destroy them and burn them and get rid of them and say, "No, the bastard never sent you anything",' David Kellett remembered. His girls' little faces would be crushed with disappointment. 'And I never knew. The girls just didn't communicate. I sent letters and I thought, "Oh well, they've wiped me". That was it.'

It wasn't until David Kellett was reunited with Melissa when she was sixteen that he found out the truth. Melissa told him that neither she nor Natasha ever received any birthday or Christmas presents, not even the big bunch of flowers he sent to mark her thirteenth birthday. Nor did they receive the letters that their dad frequently sent.

'When I saw Melissa when she was sixteen, she still had reservations but then she got to know me,' David Kellett said. Since then, they have rebuilt their relationship.

7

Empty promises and smashed teeth

John Chillingworth hopped off the train at Scone after its hour-long run from Newcastle one afternoon in May 1990. He had forty-three years on his hard-worn body and four cans of beer under his belt, maybe it was six, he can't really remember and he wasn't counting anyway. He had been working as a crane chaser until he was injured in a car crash, and every Friday, Chillingworth went home to spend the weekend with his mother in the same house she had lived in for nearly fifty years – the house where he grew up. Chillo, as he is known, didn't go directly home. Instead, he did what he always did. He headed straight for the main bar at the Willow Tree Hotel in the middle of Kelly Street, Scone's main drag, for a schooner of cold beer.

Chillo looks a bit like Paul Hogan did in the original Crocodile Dundee film. He's roguishly handsome, of average height with a lean build, and wears deep crevasses on his face like the Australian outback wears dry creek beds. His gravelly voice is the result of one too many whiskies and way too many cigarettes, but it has the resonance and gruffness of an old-time movie star. When amused, which is often, a laugh rumbles out of him.

The Willow Tree is a fine-looking two-storey red brick building. It doesn't have a prime corner position and isn't showy, but looks like it has lived with a self-imposed architectural modesty compared to the other hotels on Kelly Street.

Friday nights in country pubs are busy affairs, gateways to a long weekend of booze and partying. The main bar usually fills by five, five-thirty at the latest, and plays host to a mix of townies, farmers and occasional tourists who stand out because they don't fit in. Resting up against the bar, Chillo was exactly the type of wisecracking bloke that many women make a beeline for. He is charming but knows he can be a bit of a wiseguy, and with a few cans in him, his usual confidence was even bolder. 'I was a drinker back then, wasn't I?' he said, remembering that time eleven years later.

It was his cheeky larrikin streak that probably attracted Kathy Knight to Chillo. She'd just broken up with David Saunders after a three-year relationship that produced her third daughter, as well as lots of grief plus one dead dingo pup. She was thirty-five, living on a pension and looking for fun. And she didn't like wearing the title of single woman.

'She never ever wanted to be alone,' he said. 'She said, "If anything happens to you, you know I'll have another bloke within a day or two". She said, "I can't be alone, I've got to have someone with me". She told me that a few times.'

Spotting Chillo planted at the bar, Kathy moved quickly. Her idea of romance was a take-no-prisoners approach. Not for her the slow, shy two-step that usually marks the beginning of a relationship. Before the night was out, Kathy had taken him home. To Chillo, she was just a plain Jane but he was 'paaaara-lytic. I didn't even remember what she looked like the next day. My mate told me.' But the circumstances offended no one.

John Chillingworth was born and bred in Scone and was something of a local lad. He had a place in Newcastle, as well as a girlfriend and a job, but he'd half moved back to Scone near his beloved mum. He was married at twenty-two and divorced at twenty-six and was on the tail end of a long-term relationship that died a natural death the night he met Katherine Knight.

'She had a nice arse, and I was pissed. You want it straight, I'll give it to you straight, that's the only way. The drunker I got the prettier she looked,' he said. 'Anyhow, she came over and said, "Geez, you've got a cute arse", and I said, "Oh, thanks". And you're half whacked and a girl in a pub says that and you think, you're right here. And that's how it started. Unfortunately, that's the truth of it. There was no magic wand or anything . . . And I went back to Aberdeen – she took me back to Aberdeen in the car because I had no licence back then.

'Anyhow, I didn't see her for a week, a week and a half, and I was walking past her place one day and I thought, bugger it, I'll knock and say g'day. Just started from there.'

From then on they were an item, but they never lived together as husband and wife, or even as a more loosely defined de facto couple. He spent between three and five nights a week with Kathy Knight at her MacQueen Street house, and a couple of nights at his mum's. He eventually left Newcastle and got a job at the Aberdeen meatworks, where he had worked almost twenty years earlier.

For Chillo, the relationship was perfect and the early days were, he said, 'bloody beaut'. Kathy was terrific to be with; she was fun and liked to party, and that suited Chillo, who liked to drink and party. Because she wasn't a big drinker, Kathy was the designated driver as she was with just about everyone. She'd drop him off wherever he wanted to go and took him when he wanted to go somewhere else. She'd do anything for him, and even helped chop firewood for his mother and load topsoil into the back of a trailer for her garden. Kathy was as strong as any man.

It was a relationship of convenience, but it also went deeper. Chillo was drinking a lot back then, every day. Rockin' and rollin', getting into blues, as he called it. He was a man looking for an anchor and he thought Katherine Knight was it.

'It's just one of them things you do in life. I can't blame the booze for it, I done it, not that I blame anything, it's just one of those things that happen. You think this is the love of your life. Well, how could it be with everything that had happened? It couldn't last, I can say that now but I couldn't back then. Hindsight is a marvellous thing.

'You think you've found the perfect soul mate and it's only the piss telling you that. I thought I loved that woman more than I loved life. I did. I thought so.'

Chillingworth first knew Kathy Knight when he was at the Aberdeen meatworks and Kathy had just started working there. She was sixteen and already stood out, not just because of her red hair. He only knew her vaguely. She was several years younger than him and he was involved. 'She was always a bit of a keep-away-from girl. Always had that violent streak, that mean streak,' he recalled.

Chillo got married and left Scone and Kathy Knight never entered his thoughts until that night nearly twenty years later when she picked him up in the pub. While he'd been away, stories about Kathy Knight became legend in the Upper Hunter Valley district. He was unaware of her antics but his mates weren't and warned him that hooking up with her was bad news. He didn't care – and if he did, he wasn't going to let on. After all, he was a bloke.

'I didn't give a bugger what anyone else thought, see. I knew, in me heart, it probably wasn't right, not right. But it was none of their business to me. They thought I was too good for her. The blokes I used to work with and mates I've grown up with, played football with and all that stuff. I'd only been back a short time meself and they'd known her all their life. I'd met her years ago at the meatworks, many many years ago. She was always scatty then.'

He shook his head and inhaled on his Winfield Red. 'And a bloke got tangled up with her, didn't he?'

Within two months Kathy was pregnant with her fourth child. She was tickled pink and so was John Chillingworth who, at forty-three, had always wanted to be a father. His own dad took off when he was young and John's mother had raised him and his sister single-handedly before she remarried. For him, fatherhood was a dream come true. But Kathy hadn't quite put the past behind her, and the cracks were already starting to show in the relationship.

One night after several beers at the top pub in Aberdeen, Kath went ballistic. Chillo had had a skinful, and she drove off, leaving him stranded in town. He walked down to the little MacQueen Street house but she point-blank refused to let him in. He could get lost for all she cared. So he hitchhiked back to his mum's at Scone. Things were a bit strained for a few days, but then it was all back on again. It was how it would be from then on.

Soon after, they had another blue and Chillo went to Newcastle for a couple of days. Katherine Knight wasted no time and spent the weekend with her ex, David Saunders. When Chillo came back, she flaunted the fling and spat out that she wanted nothing more to do with him. For spiteful measure, she added that she wanted to get back with Saunders. He was shattered. She was having his baby. He pleaded with her for them to stay together. For Kathy, his reaction was a turn-up for the books. The men in Katherine Knight's life usually walked out on her.

It's possible she was moved at the novelty of a man begging her not to end the relationship, and she relented, but she wouldn't let him move into her little wooden house for fear she might lose her pension. Chillo forgave the affair with Saunders but, by then, the rot had set in and the relationship had begun to unravel.

Throughout the pregnancy, Kathy would tell Chillo the baby wasn't his. They'd have an argument and she'd taunt him, saying the baby was David Saunders' or someone else's. It was an absolute nonsense – just Kathy being her cruel, vindictive self.

John Chillingworth had another problem on his hands apart from a mercurial girlfriend. Her eldest daughter Melissa couldn't stand him. She'd just turned fourteen, a tricky time for most teenage girls but even more so when their mum takes up with a new bloke. Since her mother left her father, David Kellett, in 1984 amid bitterness and violence, her against him, Melissa and Natasha had witnessed a string of men pass in and out of their mother's life, and none of them were remembered fondly. Even though his and Kath's was really only a part-time relationship, Chillo had never been a surrogate father to a teenage girl before, and it wasn't long before he clashed with Melissa.

'Mum was always very sensitive, she always followed her heart, she fell in love fast,' Natasha later told the *Herald*'s Donna Page.

John Chillingworth is a hard-working straight man and lives by simple values. Be decent, treat others with respect and as you would have them treat you. He doesn't preach, but he points out that it says that in the Bible. Chillo hasn't always been that way but since going cold turkey and giving up the booze on 7 August 1991, he's tried to follow that basic rule every single day in every single way. He hasn't always succeeded, but then, he is human.

He denied ever hitting Kathy or Natasha but said his relationship with Melissa was fraught with difficulties. Yes, he admits he hit her once and he regrets it now. And he had no idea it would spark an act of revenge by Kathy, of the type he had only heard about. Sitting in his dining room in his neat, new house in a beachside suburb in Queensland, with the takings of his 3 am to 3 pm cabbie shift sorted on the table in front of him – minus a $30 fare that some mug passenger had skipped out on – Chillo recalled the fight: 'Melissa didn't like someone else coming in and taking over the roost. I think, probably, that's where it started,' he said. 'Her and I had a run-in very early in the piece and she never, ever [forgave] me. And I tried, and she tried at times, but that hatred was always there.

'I gave her a clip on the ear-hole one night for back-answering her mother, and her mother didn't like it. That's the night she smashed my false teeth. I probably had had a few to drink and I woke up the next morning and my teeth are all over the floor, smashed to pieces.'

Kathy told him that she smashed them as a payback because he hit Melissa. When he got angry over it, she smashed a second pair of dentures.

'I am sorry for it now, it should never have happened but it did. Unfortunately, it's just one of those things that did happen, probably through the booze. She took a dislike to me ever since,' he said. 'You can't turn back the clock, you'd like to be able to at times. I would definitely take that back, but you can't do that, that's why you have got to forget and forgive. It's not easy.'

If Chillo had any desire to see the future, he only needed to look at Kathy's past. It was all there in technicolour, some of it in black and blue and bloody red, but he didn't want to know about it. He was in love – well, he thought he was, and he was definitely in lust. She was also pregnant with their child. Still, it wasn't easy and their relationship danced over the same treacherous and shifting sands her previous ones had. One minute it was on, then it was off again. As the days rolled by, Kathy was increasingly ambivalent and hostile to him and her vindictiveness grew. There was never any physical violence, maybe a bit of pushing and shoving, but she'd do little things like lock him out of the house without warning. She'd yell and swear at him, call his family names, and say nasty things.

'That was Kathy. She'd get back at you no matter what you did. If you done something to her, she'd get you back tenfold. She was just that way. That's the type of lady she was,' he said, lighting up a cigarette. 'Revenge was her main – a weapon of hers. I've never seen a woman like her. I don't want to see another one.'

Chillo recognised in Katherine Knight a very complex personality. She was loving and caring – 'She would give you the shirt off her back' – but revenge and sex were her weapons.

'You never knew when you had Kathy. She had a saying, she'd say, "I love ya, I love ya, if I hate ya, I hate ya". And if Kathy hated ya, there was no limit to what she could do or would do to ya, in some way. It may not be personal. It might be the car or the house, your cat or your dog, or whatever,' he remembered. 'But if she loved ya, you'd have sex ten times a day, it comes back to that sexual thing.

'The violence a guy'd dish out Kathy, she'd give him back tenfold, oh yeah . . . I had no doubt she was going to maim somebody . . . Everyone who knew her knew she was going to do someone damage one day. I expected to read in the paper one day that she de-knackered someone. Bloody oath, that was always in the back of my mind, some bloke she'd get the shits with and slice them off. Yep, that thought, that was always there. But I never thought she'd go to the extent that she did, never. Not in my wildest dreams.'

In 1991, Kathy Knight gave birth to a boy she named Eric, and she made it known that she wanted him christened as quickly as possible. His delighted father agreed.

A month later, Chillo bought Kathy a second-hand Mitsubishi L300 van. With Kathy's youngest brother Shane, they went to Newcastle to pick it up. It was a Saturday. Shane drove the van home. Chillo and Kathy went in a separate car. They weren't far from MacQueen Street when she exploded and started in on him again about his drinking, yelling at him and calling his mother a 'whore'.

'We were coming between Aberdeen and Scone and she said, "I'm taking you home, you are not staying with me tonight". And

I said, "Oh bullshit",' he remembered. 'She said, "No, I've had enough of you", then she grabbed me glasses and crushed them. Then I give her a smack in the mouth and it blackened her eye.'

Kathy punched him in the face, and he gave her another backhander.

Kathy drove straight to the Scone police station, dropped him off out the front, and had him charged, he remembered.

Kathy took out an Apprehended Violence Order against him, which stopped him from coming near her or the house. After dealing with the police, Kathy went to Scone hospital and was treated for swelling of the left cheek and bruising under her left eye. A doctor put an icepack on her cheek and gave her some Panadol and sent her home.

She and Chillo split up but it lasted less than a week.

'Then Eric had to be christened and we got back together, didn't we . . .?' he said. 'Eric gets christened and things are rosy again.' Kathy went to the christening with a black eye.

Just as she had done with her ex-husband David Kellett and her former de-facto, David Saunders, Katherine would bad-mouth John Chillingworth nearly ten years after they split up. After being charged with murdering John Price in early 2000, she claimed to have been assaulted by Chillo on many occasions, but, as Justice Barry O'Keefe noted when sentencing her, 'the available records do not support her claims'. The judge could not be certain about Kath and Chillo's relationship but he said 'it is clear that she engaged in spiteful, vindictive and vengeful behaviour when she felt, whether with or without justification, that she had been slighted by her partner'.

Katherine Knight's ability to swing from loving her partner to hating him in minutes is one of the characteristics of borderline personality disorder. Those who have it can suddenly change their view of the person they have idealised. They are impulsive, dramatic, erratic and emotional. According to the American Psychiatric Association's Diagnostic and Statistical Manual, Fourth Edition (DSM-IV), people with the disorder can 'empathise with and nurture other people, but only with the expectation that the other person will "be there" in return to meet their own needs on demand'. They are also easily bored, express inappropriate and intense anger, and are prone to verbal outbursts and display enduring bitterness. All of which Kathy Knight did.

Inexplicably, and despite getting back together with Chillingworth, Kathy didn't withdraw the charges against him and when the matter went to court, she went with him. He said he was fined $619 for assault and placed on a two-year bond. Even more inexplicably, they went home together.

'Oh yeah, we went to court together, yeeeeah,' he said, disbelief drawing out the word. 'And then went home and had it off. Fair dinkum, and this is the type of thing, you know, that very day.'

The relationship wasn't getting better after the birth of Eric even though Chillo is a naturally good father who revelled in fatherhood. The tiny house at MacQueen was even more crowded. Two of the girls had to share a bedroom, and Chillo's relationship with Melissa hadn't improved. Kathy kept at him over his drinking and told him that if he didn't cut back, she'd leave him for good. He couldn't bear the thought of not having any contact with his son, and on 7 August, when the baby was just five months old, he stopped drinking. He credits Kathy with helping him sober up. He also went on to do a degree in drug and alcohol counselling and started helping out with the Salvation Army.

'I tried to get her interested in Al Anon because I believed that would have helped but she only went for the stories, other people's stories,' he said, sadness in his voice. 'She got a kick out of them, whether they had it good or bad or what, and she used to measure herself on it, my life ain't that bad. I said, Kathy, it's not good.'

His sobriety didn't save the relationship – 'deep down, she wanted the bloke she first met, and that bloke was a party-goer'. In early December 1993, Chillo was offered a two-week job with the Salvation Army's drug and alcohol counselling service in Queensland. He thought the change of scenery would do him good, and he took it, knowing he'd be back in Aberdeen in fourteen days. But he liked Queensland and decided to stay. He wanted to get a house for himself, Kathy and the four kids. Chillo moved into a caravan park at Nambour, and eventually found a job on the new highway being built at Noosa Heads.

Kathy came up for a two-week break just before Christmas. At the end of the first week, Chillo came home from a meeting and found her flirting with a fellow park resident, showing a bit of leg. He was furious and chipped her for it. Kathy flew off the handle, again, and claimed she'd done nothing wrong. She told him it was all over, packed her bags and left the next morning. It was the last time they were together. 'That broke my heart,' he said. He didn't know it at the time, but she'd already started seeing John Price back in Aberdeen.

'She was having an affair with him before she come up here. She come up just to see where the best side of the bed was to lie,' he said. 'I have no doubt that was going on, and had I not come back that night to the caravan park, ahhh, you'll never know. I know she screwed Dave Saunders when we were together, but we'd split up for a couple of days, that was okay. I suppose there would have been others but I was a bit naive at the time, I didn't want to know, I think that was a big thing . . . It was a weapon in her armoury.'

He was referring to sex and how she used it.

'She did with Pricey. The black negligee and the good sex before the murder.'

8

The man of her dreams

If Katherine Knight felt any shame about her behaviour, she kept it in a secret place only she knew how to find, well and truly hidden from everybody else. Hating to be alone and always looking for the next best thing, she went from man to man with the guiltless ease of a sailor coasting into another harbour. And like them, she had other ports in between and not a few wrecks cast in her stormy wake.

It wasn't as if she was a natural beauty or a compelling conversationalist gifted with the social charms and fine education of a city debutante or rich grazier's daughter from the surrounding district. She was undereducated, unemployed and frequently graceless. To top it off, she swore like a trooper, a personal habit that only hardened her already strong Australian accent.

While Katherine Knight was striking in that physically imperious way that many tall women are, unafraid of their height and refusing to stoop, she certainly was not beautiful. On paper, her long red hair, bright blue eyes and pale complexion were a description full of spectacular promise but in person, the promise was a cheat, somehow more hollow and the overall effect so much more plain. She wore glasses and was missing an eye tooth.

Katherine Knight also carried enough personal baggage to fill an ocean liner. She had four children to three fathers and hadn't worked since August 1985 when management at the Aberdeen abattoir terminated her employment with a handsome compensation payout because she had a crook back. Since then, she'd been receiving a fortnightly invalid pension and regular maintenance cheques from her children's fathers.

Already blessed with so little, Katherine Knight was further cursed with a roller-coaster personality. She was generous and giving, but that gentle side came with strings pulled taut. People knew of her ability to erupt in a rage, but they ignored it, putting it down to 'Kathy just being Kathy'.

'You wouldn't find a nicer person than her and she loved her sewing and embroidery, and all that. Fantastic at anything like that, she was,' said Robin Smith, who had worked with Katherine at the Aberdeen abattoir. 'But once you crossed her, that was it . . . I don't know whether you'd call it scatterbrained, but, you know, she was always hotheaded, and that type of thing. She was a nice person as long as you were nice to her and she thought you didn't do anything to hurt her, but then she could turn on you like anything.' That was just Kathy.

When women explode in a violent rage, society gives the rage a motive of its own as if it had manifested itself upon the unwitting, helpless woman. It doesn't suit the established view of women to believe that females can be violent in the same way that men can be, because to do so would mean having to accept that some women simply *are* violent *and* choose to be violent. It is easier to understand the rages and the violence as something beyond their control. Subsequently, when a woman explodes and does bad things, it is blamed on other causes that diminish or annul her culpability. She must have done it because she was coerced, or was menopausal or suffering premenstrual tension, or was the victim of battered wife syndrome. She might even have been temporarily insane or in a state of dissociation – not knowing what she was doing. Not bad, just a little bit mad. Not bad, just unable to help herself.

'Because we won't concede aggression and anger in women, the language we use to describe what they do is much more limited, and much more exonerative', writes Patricia Pearson in her book *When She Was Bad: How and Why Women Get Away With Murder*. Pearson continues:

> There exists perhaps three of four rationales for the whole, extraordinary diversity of violent acts women commit, and they all play into preexisting prejudices about female nature. The operative assumption is that the violent woman couldn't have wanted, deliberately, to cause harm. Therefore, if she says she was abused/coerced/insane, she probably was.
>
> The effect of cultural explanation for individual behaviour tilts women toward an interpretation of themselves as fundamentally innocent. What they do (what we all do) is to equate powerlessness with innocence. In acts of violence, this is not only an expedient, but a necessary, means of self-justification.

Katherine Knight was frequently violent and hot-tempered. People knew to expect it from her, but she never took responsibility for it. She could rationalise and justify her way out of any situation. She blamed the men in her life for the violence she perpetuated. After slashing the throat of an eight-week-old dingo pup, she blamed David Saunders, justifying the killing by alleging that he had kicked her in the stomach with steel-capped boots. The claim was not supported by evidence and he denies it. She justified slashing Margaret Perry's face in 1976 by saying she wanted her mother, Molly Perry, to drive her to Kathy's mother-in-law's house. She was twenty-one. Whenever she acted violently, she had an excuse. And people shrugged it off as 'just Kathy'.

Forensic psychiatrist Dr Rod Milton has more than thirty-five years experience investigating the human mind and fifteen of those have been spent peering inside the minds of some of Australia's most notorious criminals. Milton speaks with the reassuring cadence of a medical doctor and leans forward when talking, resting his head on his hand. He doesn't dress as one expects of a highly polished professional. Instead, he dresses like a country grandfather who is about to plop down in a rocking chair on the front verandah to enjoy the morning papers. He wears jeans held up by suspenders and has a fondness for crisp white shirts and comforting woolly cardigans.

His avuncular armour cleverly conceals the horrific nature of his work. Milton advised the chief police negotiator on how to handle serial killer Ivan Milat the day police arrested him in an early morning raid at his outer Sydney suburban house. He has frequently been called on by legal authorities around Australia to study crime scenes of unknown killers to determine the type of person responsible.

At the request of the New South Wales Director of Public Prosecutions, Milton spent three hours interviewing Katherine Knight in jail in October 2001. In his subsequent 55-page report that was tendered as evidence in her sentencing hearing and quoted by Justice Barry O'Keefe on 8 November 2001, he described her violence and rages as 'personality problems'. They 'are not in my view psychiatric disease', he wrote, 'they are her nature'.

'These personality problems did not stop her from knowing what she was doing, or whether it was right or wrong. Nor did they stop her from exercising control over her actions when she chose . . . The main effect of Ms Knight's personality problems was to cause difficulty for others. I question whether that should be regarded as an "abnormality of mind" and think, on balance, it is not.'

Oddly, and despite her personal shortcomings and tendency to violence, if the alchemy was right, and it mostly seemed to be when it came to men, Katherine Knight was able to snare the bloke she wanted. She was an accomplished lover. Perhaps more curiously, in the aftermath of her vengeance-fuelled rages as an aggressor armed with knives, scissors, fists and a wickedly sharp tongue, she was able to keep them. They stayed around for more.

David Kellett stayed with her after she wrapped her hands around his throat on their wedding night and burned all his clothes. David Saunders stayed with her after she slashed his dog's throat and stabbed him in the stomach. John Chillingworth was crushed when she walked out on him at the end of 1993, even though she had previously smashed his false teeth and ripped his glasses from his face. At the time he hoped she would come back.

~

It was no surprise that Katherine Knight met John Price in the top pub. It was, after all, the axis on which his social life spun. He didn't want to go far, nor did he need to. Pricey was a creature of habit and habits run deep in small towns and in men of few needs. He and Colleen separated in 1988 and even though his life was different, there was no real reason to change his routine.

It broke his heart when Col walked out of their new red brick house taking two-year-old Jackie and Rosemary, then thirteen, with her. Johnathon, who was fourteen years old, stayed with his father and never really understood why his mum left. Rosemary, who was still in school, soon moved back to live with her dad as well.

What made it harder for Pricey to understand was that their marriage had seemed so solid, and it was. They were married young and had three children. They hardly argued. Col didn't mind Pricey's drinking, and would buy him a case of Tooheys New at the start of each week. They built their new dream home in Aberdeen, and Col ran the household, taking care of the bills, the finances and the children's education. Pricey was an excellent and steady provider and had a good job with Howick Mines, which would eventually earn him $100 000 a year.

Their marriage didn't end with a heart-piercing bitterness because either one had cheated on the other. There were no third parties involved. They broke up, Col said, because there was never enough time for them as a couple. Pricey was so giving of himself that she started to feel short-changed, like she was missing something.

Col had married at eighteen, when all women are filled with notions of enduring romance, but fifteen years later, what she needed from her husband had deepened. Pricey still needed to have time with all his mates. He loved his beer and his fishing. They were on different wave-lengths.

'He gave his time to everyone and there was never enough time for him and me and I was young. I was married at eighteen and had two children by twenty-one . . . and I just got tired. I still had Pricey, but I never had him. I had his love but I didn't have him and we grew apart,' Colleen said. 'I felt guilty about leaving but I know that I did the right thing. When I left, it took me twelve months, it wasn't a spur of the moment thing. It took me twelve months to think about it and work everything out in my head – that it was the right thing.'

Pricey was devastated but there was never any animosity. They remained friends – more so than most married couples who split up after sharing so much of their lives at such a young and impressionable age. Pricey just didn't have it in him to be bitter, he wasn't a hater, and he still loved his wife. He adored her. In his eyes, they were a perfect match. He never gave up hope that she might come back, restoring their family to its unit of five. Pricey was an idealist even if he wasn't capable of giving Colleen what she needed from a husband.

'He had been asking me to come back to him for twelve years and I said, "Why, Pricey?" And he'd say, "Well, mate, you know how to handle the money", and he'd laugh at that. And I'd say, "But you and I, it wouldn't change, Pricey". And he'd say, "Maybe for a while".

'There would still be all his friends – I didn't mind all his friends – but I just wanted time for us, but he couldn't do that because it wasn't him. And like I said to him, you and I should never have been married because we are too different. I don't regret it, not at all . . . He gave his heart and soul to everyone. He was a kind person. He was a person who should never have been married because he had so much in him for other people, and to me that's what his life was on this earth, to spread himself around, he was such a giving person.'

Colleen was racked with guilt and didn't think it was right to take the house off Pricey – he built it and loved it. She moved into a nearby rented property. It was her decision to leave, and she did what she believed was the decent thing – she took nothing, just $6000 to buy a car. But Pricey was always there with a helping hand. His generosity hadn't shrivelled up when Colleen broke his heart. Years later, she asked Pricey if she could borrow $100 to fix her refrigerator. That very same afternoon Pricey, with son Johnathon in tow, drove from Aberdeen to Tamworth, where Col had ultimately settled with their youngest child Jackie, with a brand new fridge and deep freeze.

When she went on a holiday to Perth more than ten years after they had separated, he secretly slipped $500 into her bank account as spending money. When she asked him if he was the source of the bonus funds, he denied it. 'They were things that he did . . . He never asked for nothing back in return,' Colleen said.

Col remained the love of Pricey's life, and she loved him deeply, but she made it clear there was no chance of a reconciliation. She started a relationship with another fellow in Aberdeen, but when that ended, she moved to Tamworth. Pricey also started dating other women and had a couple of significant relationships. One woman moved into the St Andrews Street house with her children but it didn't last very long. Soon after, another girlfriend moved in while he was away on a fishing trip with Laurie Lewis and the boys. When Laurie dropped Pricey off at the house, they were surprised to see a woman waiting for him inside his front door. Pricey was not displeased, Laurie remembered. John Price was a man of few needs, and one of them was female company.

Katherine Knight met John Price in the top pub on a Friday night in 1993 – 8 October. She hadn't quite finished with John Chillingworth, but a little thing like that wasn't going to stop a woman like her. For Pricey, Fridays marked the beginning of another weekend of drinking intersected with family and friends, or whoever happened to be around. It could be a total stranger sometimes, given his extroverted nature.

Pricey and Kathy had known of each other for years even though they never socialised together. Pricey was friends with David Saunders, the father of Kathy's third child, Sarah, and had met her through David years earlier. Ironically, Pricey once took on the role of barroom counsellor to Saunders when he'd had a blue with Kathy. In the coming years, the role would be reversed, but neither man could ever have guessed that then. Colleen Price said: 'I would see her riding through town on her motorbike in her silver suit. I never had much to do with her, to be honest.'

There were other connections: Rosemary Price was school friends with Kathy's niece Tracey Knight and occasionally visited her at her grandparents' house on Rouchel Road.

Kathy was in the top pub that night with a girlfriend, having a drink, probably a Cadbury's chocolate liqueur or a Bailey's Irish Cream – it might even have been a beer, but usually she preferred a sweeter drop. The women spotted Pricey and, as bold as you like, started talking to him.

It was déjà vu. Had any of her exes been there they probably would have warned Pricey to steer clear, but they weren't. Katherine Knight's timing couldn't have been better, even if, technically, she wasn't quite single herself. Pricey liked the ladies and loved to go dancing. And he was single again, having recently broken up with another girlfriend.

They very quickly became an item. Once they were together, they often went dancing. It didn't matter to Pricey that she would tower over him on the dance floor. He was just happy for the company and the intimacy that might go with it.

The relationship really took off in early 1994 and those first few months went perfectly. The romantic in him surprised her with roses, and he quickly grew very fond of her children. 'He loved the kids, he told me himself, he said, "I love them little kids",' his best mate Laurie Lewis said. 'He'd take 'em for holidays and everything. He paid for [Eric's] glasses.'

Pricey referred to Sarah as 'my little mate' and he spoiled Eric, who was still too young for school. He bought him a fishing rod and taught him how to put the bait on the hook and cast the line, and one time had to rescue him from standing on an ant nest, Laurie recalled. Whenever Eric referred to Pricey, he did so like the big blokes did, calling him 'my mate'. Sarah thought he was nice too. If the kids did any household chores at Pricey's, he'd slip them some money. He also fixed Melissa's car, and worked on Kathy's house with Laurie at his side.

John Price's son Johnathon was still living at home with his dad, but Rosemary had moved out and started her own life in Muswellbrook. Kathy increasingly spent more time at the St Andrews Street house, often spending the night with Pricey in his queen sized bed while her two youngest children, Sarah and Eric, shared the bedroom that had once been the Price girls'.

Kathy was besotted with Pricey and she willingly sewed for him and cooked his meals, getting up at 5 am to prepare his breakfast and lunch. It wasn't long before she decided that he was her 'dream man'. They were in love. 'She dearly loved him, very much, I'm afraid. She was so wrapped up in him. That's what she used to tell me,' said Kathy's friend Cheryl Sullivan. Kathy's brothers Shane and Barry said the same thing: 'She loved him.'

Both Kathy Knight and John Price were big personalities but they didn't live a big life. They had expectations, but they kept them low. Kathy thought Pricey was an open person and when he'd had a few drinks in him, he'd get all touchy-feely, wrapping his arms around you or planting a big smacker on your cheek. She called him a 'pisspot'. Together they continued in the tradition of their first meeting and spent most Friday nights knocking about and knocking them back in the top pub.

Pricey introduced Kathy to rum and coke, and she took a liking to the taste but never turned into more than a social drinker. She didn't need to. She was outgoing enough, the life of the party. She'd have no inhibitions about hitting the dance floor in her skin tight black jeans and backless triangle-shaped Glomesh top. Sometimes she'd turn up at the pub in an Annie Get Your Gun ensemble, complete with cowboy hat and boots, much to the amusement of fellow drinkers. This was Aberdeen, meat workers and miners, not Tamworth with the showiness of its country and western music. But they'd grown used to Kathy's eccentricities.

'She was as mad as a wheel,' Laurie Lewis remembered. 'They went to me brother's wedding and she was up on the floor dancing with Pricey and my old man was there and he said, "Look at that redheaded thing there, if she keeps going she's going to shake herself completely to pieces".' At a Howick Mines Christmas party in 1996 held at the Singleton bowling club, Kathy 'rode him around the floor like a bloody horse', Laurie said.

Kathy Knight had few limitations but she knew that one of them was grog. When she had a bit of booze in her, she might explode quicker, she would later say in her police interview. 'I can build up a lot of, what do you call it, I can handle a lot without it, but when I've got it in me, I explode quicker,' she said. 'I let, like, you could, you can say things to me and say it and say it and say it and say it, when I haven't got alcohol in me. When I got alcohol in me I come back and say something back to you. You know what I mean?'

The policeman said he did.

Pricey's and Kath's lives went on, separate but together. They had small arguments typical of any relationship, but for the most part, they got on well. She bought him expensive gifts, including a $3000 barbecue and a $2000 stereo, but when they fought she would take them back. Pricey also insisted on some private time in the bar each weeknight after work and on Saturdays and Sundays. Some Sunday afternoons he would escort Kathy to Aberdeen bowling club where she took a chance on the weekly raffles. They also had an active and full sex life, and even when things started to sour between them, they still enjoyed a vigorous sexual relationship.

Kathy got used to the fact that Pricey was a joker and, with a few cans in him, was capable of cheeky behaviour in the bar, behaviour she complained of to her girlfriends. She put it down to Pricey being Pricey, in much the same way that he would eventually try to ignore her violent temper: Kathy just being Kathy.

About a year into the relationship they had their first big argument. It was a harbinger of what would follow. The golden days, it seemed, were done.

Johnathon Price was living at home with his dad. Initially, he had no worries about his father's relationship with Kathy Knight. As far as he could see, it was going along without any unusual problems. He later told Detective Senior Constable Vic Ford at Scone police station on what was the worst day of his life that his dad and Kathy argued.

Johnathon later told Michelle Coffey from *Who Weekly* magazine that Kathy was 'always a psycho'; 'she towered over Dad like all her other blokes, and she was incredibly jealous and aggressive. She hated me. When she threw a punch she was like a man. She was renowned all around Aberdeen as a bully from when she was a child.'

His sister Rosemary, now a married mother of three, also said she was not aware of any early problems between her father and Kath, even though they would have arguments. 'There was always something a little strange about her,' Rosemary told *The Newcastle Herald*. In another interview with Frances O'Shea in *The Daily Telegraph*, Rosemary said: 'My kids called her Nanny Kath. She was kind to them and me and sewed beautiful clothing for the kids. But I'd seen her go off at Dad and it was frightening. Over nothing she snapped. That's what Kath was like.'

'She dearly loved him . . . and then sometimes she'd just hate him. It was love hate, you know. Just the things he did; his drinking and that, and the way he used to treat her in front of people . . . it was an ongoing thing. That's the way they got on . . . they would just swear at each other but they still loved each other. It was just the communication thing they had going between them. I used to say to Richard, that's my ex, "I don't know why they bother",' said Kathy's friend Cheryl Sullivan. 'One minute they are together and then they broke up, then they are back together and then they broke up – and it just went on and on all the time. They'd break up, get back, break up, get back. And you would get to the point where someone would come up and say, "Did you hear about Kathy and John? They've broken up again". And I'd say, "In a couple of months they'll be back together", and sure enough, they were.'

9

True love travels on a gravel road

Katherine Knight may not have been the sharpest pencil in the box, but she was smart enough to know she had a problem. She was drinking more than she ever had and was getting into little niggly fights with Pricey. She hadn't even made it through a year with him and already his son Johnathon disliked her with a passion. The twenty-one year old's disdain for the speckled hen bordered on contempt, and that would come soon enough. He could barely bring himself to talk to her when she was in the house. Kathy was at St Andrews Street with increasing frequency and was being territorial, moving a few things in here and there to establish a sense of ownership.

It irked Johnathon and he'd be in his dad's ear about dumping Kathy, but Pricey chose the path of least resistance. Besides, he liked the company. When she really got under his skin, he would dismiss her with a few choice words that would have devastated most women and head to the top pub for a gripe with whoever was around – and, of course, a Tooheys New. To Katherine Knight, the language was nothing that she hadn't heard or used herself before and it meant nothing. She was still in the house and she was going nowhere.

But by the time the new year rolled around and another hot

summer was turning the land around Aberdeen a gentle golden brown, Kathy had started to worry about her future. She also had little faith in Pricey's fidelity for no good reason. Her paranoia was fired by his drinking and ebullient nature. Where he would gather people around them at the pub with his rambunctious yet entertaining personality – more booze, more volume – she would scare them off with her prickly nature. Especially women. Her first husband David Kellett had cheated on her and his infidelity was a source of exasperation, frustration and rage that descended into violence. Now she thought – wrongly – that Pricey was cheating on her too. The infatuation that buffers and protects tender emotions in the early days of romance had started to wear off by mid 1995.

Pricey, now eighteen months into a relationship, had been drinking and when he got home, he and Kathy engaged in another round of sex. Pricey called out another woman's name at the height of their love-making. She was stunned, then hurt – what woman wouldn't be?

In Katherine Knight's tortured mind, Pricey's mid-sex blunder was proof enough he played around. Pricey was probably too pissed to even remember, but the humiliation would have scorched her.

Everyone knew to expect trouble with Kathy, and so did she. She was already getting counselling when she took up with Pricey, according to his mate Laurie Lewis. She recognised the fault lines in her personality even if she didn't understand them. She would let things simmer inside until boiling point and then explode, screaming and yelling until the rage had blown itself out and she'd settle down again. Knowing herself, Katherine Knight packed up a few things, got three of her four kids together – Natasha, Sarah and Eric – and pointed the red van north to Ipswich in Queensland. She was going to get help, curiously, at Alcoholics Anonymous.

Kathy wasn't a sophisticated thinker nor was she a big drinker – if she'd have between two and six drinks a week, and if she consumed six in one session, she might get drunk. Why she chose AA when she wasn't an alcoholic, and why she chose an AA hundreds of kilometres away in Ipswich, is anyone's guess. AA has chapters much closer to Aberdeen, in Newcastle, Cessnock, Maitland and Dungog, to name just a few.

Maybe she just wanted to get out of the stifling closeness of her hometown where every move she made was faithfully and silently noted. That's the thing about living in rural districts: certain names come with certain expectations and Katherine had made sure what was expected of her was spectacular.

'I went to Brisbane to the alcoholic side of things, the only way I could get into it was saying I was an alcoholic, to get help for meself and for [my daughter], and Pricey come up there with me that time,' she would later tell Detective Bob Wells in the police interview that was played in court on the fifth day of her sentencing hearing on Tuesday 23 October 2001.

Kathy was out of the picture but she was in Pricey's head. He missed her. Even though she sometimes gave him hell, he loved her. 'Poor old Johnny, he had a bit of a weakness for women, he never had any luck with them,' one mate, Frank Heap, recalled. 'He sort of fell in love with them straightaway . . . he took them very serious, he wasn't just a fly-by-nighter, sort of thing. He treated all women with respect, that's right, he always did.'

Pricey took holidays from the mine and drove to Queensland to visit Kathy, which he would do a couple more times during her three-month stay there. Laurie said his younger brother Trevor even drove a car up for Pricey once. Pricey's mates couldn't understand the attraction, but there it was, larger than life.

'He used to come fishing with us, we used to go for seven or eight days, and one time, halfway through the week he said, "I've got to go home, I've got to go home". He was missing her, you know?' his best mate Laurie Lewis said. 'He really did think a lot of her, for a long time.'

Eventually, though, that changed. 'I think he was more in love with sex than anything else,' Laurie said. 'Because she was mad with sex, she'd do it anywhere, anytime, anyhow and with anyone too, but he loved that. It was a main part of his life . . . to have sex, and you know, he loved that more than her as a person.'

Towards the end of 1995, Kathy returned to Aberdeen, presumably having resolved whatever problems she thought she had. When Pricey asked her to move into his house, she conveniently forgot about their dramas and agreed. She told police that Pricey wouldn't let her live at her MacQueen Street house. Pricey had a guaranteed advantage: he was in a better financial position than Kathy and he had a bigger, nicer house. Natasha, who was fifteen, stayed in Ipswich and moved in with her dad, David Kellett. Johnathon Price had moved out and was sharing with a mate, which meant that Sarah and Eric could have a bedroom each.

'Johnathon had a lot of blues with him over this redheaded hen. He didn't want her in the house,' Laurie Lewis said. 'And Pricey said, "It's my house, I'll bring whoever I want in here", and then a blue would start. Johnathon did move out a couple of times but he did come back – it's a lot cheaper living at home, I suppose.'

Whatever it was, something wasn't quite right. Johnathon refused to put up with Kathy's ways, and knew how to push her buttons, his younger sister Jackie said, sitting at home with her mother.

Even so it couldn't have been more perfect for Katherine Knight. Pricey, she told her friends, was her 'dream man' and the new arrangements were an outward sign that their relationship was heading somewhere. Just where, no one really knew – this was one relationship that did not come with directions. But the move to St Andrews Street spoke of a degree of significance and a level of permanency between them as a couple. At least, that's what Kathy would have thought. Women analyse things like that.

Pricey's house was a big improvement on her little timber mausoleum at MacQueen Street, though she refused to give it up. She didn't want to move out lock, stock and barrel, but later told police that Pricey couldn't afford to keep her and the children. It was rubbish. By the mid 1990s, he was earning a six-figure salary at the mine. She stayed on her pension which she would lose if she moved in with Pricey.

No one really knows what goes on behind closed doors, but the people acquainted with Pricey and Kathy were aware that their relationship was highly flammable. No place was off limits if they were having an argument. Friends would see them at each other's throats in the top pub or outside on MacQueen Street, or inside Pricey's house in St Andrews Street. When they were good together, they were very good, egging each other on with their drinking and partying.

Amanda Pemberton met Kathy at the Commercial Hotel in Aberdeen in 1994 and spent most Thursday, Friday, and Saturday nights in the pub with her having a drink, a chat and a laugh. Even though there was almost a twenty-year age gap between them, the women became good friends. Amanda liked Kathy and for about eighteen months, before she left New South Wales, saw her almost every day.

'She was a really good person,' said Amanda. And, she was madly in love with Pricey. 'They were constantly, always doing something, whether it was going away for the weekend, weekend trips camping, going out to the raffles,' Amanda remembered. 'They were quite normal people. Both of them really happy people, very sociable . . . I'm not really sure about Kathy, but I know Pricey had quite a few friends that he associated with.

'Kathy, I don't know. Everybody used to say hello to her, but close friends, I'm not quite sure how many she had of them. But she was a very likeable person. But there were also some people who would more or less stay away from her because they knew that sometimes when she gets angry, she can get angry.'

Amanda could also identify Kathy's personality defects and had seen her yelling and swearing a couple of times.

'She had a temper and she could go off,' she said. 'You could get the feeling if you knew she wasn't in a good mood, you definitely wouldn't be on the wrong side of her. She had told me that she'd had arguments in the past with her ex . . . up in Queensland, and I know she said that she had stabbed him in prior years.'

Amanda was Kathy's friend, but she felt no divided loyalties in her affections for Pricey. He was, she said, a nice bloke who always made her feel welcome at his home whenever she visited Kathy there. 'He was constantly asking me to stay for tea. [He was] the joker, the normal joker, he had a joke with you, had a good talk with you and was a very nice person . . . John was a happy-go-lucky person.'

Most of the time the relationship was good, but still, Amanda saw the couple argue – sometimes Pricey would accuse Kathy of cheating when they were at the pub, and at other times, she'd get jealous and suspect he was playing up on her when he was up at the top pub.

'And I think they used to have a couple of arguments over the amount of alcohol he consumed. I have never actually seen him hit her or her hit him. I only ever heard verbally, verbal abuse, that's about all,' she said.

It was a story repeatedly told by most people who knew them. Katherine Knight later told police in her only interview with them that Pricey had said several times during their relationship that he wanted to end it and he wanted her out of the house. But then, he wouldn't follow through.

'Pricey tells me he loves me, and he's sorry, and things like that . . . he wanted me in the relationship with him, he just fires off every now and then,' Katherine told police.

Asked why Pricey would fire off, Kathy said: '. . . a bit of dust on the floor, you know, something's dropped on the floor, he'd go off.' It didn't sound like the easy-going Pricey everyone else knew – the bloke who would tell his kids to 'pull up a piece of carpet' and plonk on the floor when they were around. Colleen said Pricey's motto was, 'Just be happy'.

Laurie Lewis and Pricey worked together at Howick Mines and were as close as a couple of blokes in their forties could be after fourteen years of best-mateship. Laurie was in a perfect position to provide a window into Pricey's relationship with Katherine Knight. According to him, she was outgoing, enjoyed life and loved to dance, just like Pricey, and in the early days, it worked just fine. And Kathy was good to Pricey, Laurie said. But, over the years, Kathy wanted a greater hold on him. Pricey had never bothered to finalise his separation from Colleen, and had always hoped that she'd take him back again one day. Indeed Laurie said his mate blamed himself when Colleen left. Not surprisingly, his reluctance to get a divorce irritated Kathy. She also wanted him to spend more time with her and less with his mates. She was becoming more possessive, and it was showing. And so the arguments started.

'They were arguing . . . always arguing . . . They'd ring me up and I'd have to go down there and do the counselling,' Laurie recalled. 'I was their chief counsellor. They'd make up and would blue over something and away they'd go again. It was on and off, on and off all the time.'

If Kathy thought moving into Pricey's house would solve their problems and make him marry her, she was wrong. The house, according to Laurie, had become the reason they would argue. As executor of Pricey's will, Laurie knew that everything Pricey had worked for during his life was to be left to his three children. Hell, he'd even helped his mate write it out according to the letter of the law and witnessed it.

'That's what the blues were about, that house. He wouldn't marry her. She wanted to get married so she naturally could get half the house,' Laurie said, sitting at his kitchen table with photographs of Pricey scattered around him. 'And I said, "Boy, if you come at that, Pricey, make her sign a prenuptial agreement". "What's that?",' Laurie remembered Pricey asking him.

'I said, "You want the kids to have the house, don't you, and whatever you've got?" He said, "Yeah". I said, "That's the only way you can do it". "Aaaah, I'm not bloody marrying her, the redheaded . . ."

'He said, "I want my kids to have the house and whatever I've got. That's it".

' "He won't commit himself", she'd say. "He won't commit himself". I said, "What do you mean?" She'd say, "He won't marry me. I love him, he loves me, he won't get married".

'I said, I told her, "Kath, the only reason he won't marry you is he wants the kids to have his possessions". "I don't want his bloody house". I know different though. They never had an argument until that come up, it was always about the house.'

For a while, the arguments were limited to vicious verbal swipes. One would hurl abuse only to have the other return an equal serve by way of defence. Then they'd make up again. The language and antics would embarrass their friends, but most of them tried to ignore it, leaving Kathy and Pricey to sort themselves out the way they always did. Besides, it was none of their business. They were in love, if you could call it that, and they were consenting adults, old enough and ugly enough to look after themselves, as the saying goes.

Pricey finally asked Colleen for a divorce, and she gave it to him without any objection in March 1997. She understood the female perspective and knew Kathy needed to feel secure about her relationship with Pricey – or at least as secure as Kathy could be.

'It's like she wanted Pricey all to herself and she wanted to pull him away from his kids,' Colleen said. 'When he rang up and asked me [for the divorce], I said, "No problem, mate". It didn't matter, we'd still be mates. That was fine, but it was all her. She wanted it, and I can understand that, I didn't have a problem with that.

'It was like she really didn't want anyone else to have him. And that's how she done it. She wanted to start fights with everyone and blame his kids.'

The divorce didn't seem to make much difference.

The house was exactly how Col had left it – Pricey had changed nothing. The crockery, towels and linen were all as Col had arranged them years earlier, and the furniture was the same, and in the same places. It was as if Pricey didn't want to let the physical reminders of their marriage go.

Pricey's youngest daughter, Jackie, said that Kathy brought little to nothing to the house. 'She never had colourful things, like flowers and stuff.'

Later that year, the fighting escalated. It was around August and Laurie Lewis, 'chief counsellor' for Pricey and Kathy, got a phone call from his mate asking him to come down the road to help calm yet another argument. Kathy had launched herself at Pricey with either a pot or a pan and thumped him in the chest leaving a massive bruise the size of a man's fist. Pricey had grabbed hold of Kathy's wrists to stop her from hitting him, and bruised them. It was the only time Laurie had ever seen Kathy with any bruises caused by Pricey. He just wasn't the violent type. Years earlier, when Kathy was still with David Saunders, Laurie saw her 'run her claws down' Dave's face during an argument at the RSL.

The couple were still locked in their tortured dance, unable to figure it out, or possibly not really wanting to. Things that once seemed cute had lost their charm. Drunken moments they previously would have laughed off were turning toxic.

There were more blues over the next few months. One time, they were in Pricey's car – Kathy was behind the wheel because he'd lost his licence for driving under the influence – and they started arguing; about what, no one really knows.

'I don't know how much truth is in it now, but the story we got from her at the time was Pricey got nabbed for D.U.I. and went to court, and he blamed her . . . and she flipped her cool, didn't she?' Kathy's half-brother Barry Roughan remembered later. Yet another argument – this time Kathy was incandescent with rage, absolutely livid. This just added to what she saw as the cumulative insults – real or imagined – against her. In Katherine Knight's mind, enough was enough. She'd put up with David Kellett, David Saunders and John Chillingworth – she was not going to be putting up with John Price as well. A brooding anger more savage than anything she had experienced before began to ferment. It was the beginning of the end. 'That's when she cost him his job,' Barry said.

10

Kathy's revenge

Revenge is a powerfully toxic motive and it was all Katherine
Knight needed. In her mind, it turned her from a victim into
an avenger, giving her a chance, however slim, to claw back some
power by getting even with Pricey. That's what revenge does. In
the hands of an individual, victims become persecutors. It gives
the dispossessed a sense of power, the rudderless a promise of
control, and maniacs the hand of God. Not for nothing is it
written in the Testaments, Old and New, 'Vengeance is mine,
I shall repay, saith the Lord'.

But who does revenge belong to if not God? The jilted lover
hellbent on payback? The individual who feels wronged, rightly
or not? The gang member or Mafia hood who thinks he has been
disrespected or lost turf to a rival? The state that enacts lawful
capital punishment? Or borderless terrorists who kill thousands
of innocent people?

In some countries and cultures, revenge is sanctioned as an
ancient ritual – vengeance by rite, Biblical and barbaric. It is a
justifiable retaliation prescribed by religion, law and even
popular demand. There are places in the world where fathers and
sons commit vengeance-driven honour murders killing sisters and
daughters who have supposedly shamed them. In Athens, people

worship at the Temple of Vengeance. Palestinian organisations exact revenge by strapping nail-studded bomb packs to the waists of 21-year-old Palestinian women, ordinary florists and dress-makers, and sending them into crowded markets and restaurants with mass murder on their mind.

Cold-hearted or collective, furious or fanatical, revenge is never punishment. People who exact it may claim it makes them feel better and that it somehow restores their sense of justice and corrects a wrong done to them, but in the final analysis, does it? Revenge is a motive in and of itself just as profit, passion, hatred, power, domination, opportunism, desperation, compassion, ritual and fear are potent motivations for crime.

But revenge is different. It's as insidious as it gets, and it's darkly personal.

'A murder that is motivated by revenge is typically a crime of passion . . . Some revenge murders are carefully planned and carried out with startling calm and precision. Even though the victims of a person who is motivated by revenge may be numer-ous, the emotion itself is highly personalised,' wrote Michael D. Kelleher and C.L. Kelleher in their book *Murder Most Rare: The Female Serial Killer*. 'In response to this intense personal-isation, the revenge murderer will usually carry out her crimes alone . . . In the final analysis, this perpetrator is a victim of her own emotions and is often driven to murder by an overwhelming sense of rejection or abandonment.'

In *Women Who Kill*, Scottish writer Carol Anne Davis describes the female revenge killer as one who 'annihilates a lover who has scorned her, or she kills a rival. These women often operate under a strong level of neurosis so will see treachery and rivalry when there isn't any. Their rage can cause them to kill again and again.'

~

It was early 1998 and Katherine Knight had given up smoking. She was still living with Pricey, but since the incident in the car the previous October, things had never returned to the glory days of roses and romance. There were times when they barely toler-ated each other.

Pricey, typically, just got on with it. He was a man, he had a job, he had his mates and the top pub, and when he wanted it, he had sex with a willing and able partner. If he had to put up with a few temper tantrums and emotional brain damage along the way, he would. It was a complicated relationship. He loved Kathy but he'd already decided he wasn't going to marry her – his house was the sticking point – but he'd also decided that staying with her was easier than the alternative – for now. Besides, no relationship sails through life without its ups and downs, it just so happened that this one was stormy from the outset.

Katherine Knight was bitterly angry. She knew that what she had was deteriorating, and it was eating away at her. She hated that Pricey talked about other women and bought them drinks in the pub in front of her. She hated that she couldn't control the situation. And she hated most that Pricey wouldn't marry her.

She told her friend Sharon Turner that sometimes Pricey would wake up and call her 'Colleen', his ex-wife's name. When Kathy was angry with him, she'd say, 'Oh, I'm going to kill that bastard', Sharon remembered. 'But that's in jest, you know, like if they had a fight. "Oh, I'm going to kill that bastard", she used to say [that] all the time. But, I mean, a lot of people say that in jest, don't they?' Amanda Pemberton also once heard Kathy say to Pricey, 'If you leave me, I'll cut your balls out', but like Sharon, Amanda didn't think it was a serious threat.

It's no wonder her nerves were bad, Kathy was living a lie. On the outside, she was maintaining the charade of domestic bliss which, in her inimitable style, was occasionally bumpy. She cooked for Pricey, mended his clothes, bought his beer and picked him up from the pub. She went to bingo twice a week and took sewing classes. She power-walked around Aberdeen with her sister Joy, her aunty June and her brother Barry and his wife Val. She argued with Pricey and, as always, they kissed and made up. People just rolled their eyes.

But on the inside she was seething. With the same spiteful taste for revenge that she'd shown to her previous lovers, Katherine Knight launched herself on a destructive course. She was in payback mode.

~

Laurie Lewis lived one street away from Pricey in Aberdeen, higher up the hill and with long views to the northwest. Every morning, Laurie drove to Pricey's and picked him up for work. They had worked together for almost seventeen years at the Howick mine site and were a bit of an Oscar and Felix pair – their friendship was made of strong stuff. Laurie spent hours by Pricey's side rebuilding parts of Kathy's MacQueen Street home, tearing out the kitchen and bathroom and installing new ones, and working on the foundations to correct a lean. They complemented each other's personalities and riffed off each other, alternating between the straight man and the funny man, but if one could be said to be more responsible, it would have to be Laurie.

One perfect spring morning in September 1998, Laurie pulled up outside the St Andrews Street house. It was before 6.30 – they had a 7 am start time. Kathy was at the front door with Pricey. She had been up at 5.30 as usual, getting Pricey ready for work, cooking breakfast for him and making his lunch. Laurie watched as she gave him a kiss on the cheek, a pat on the back and a smile goodbye.

Everything seemed fine between them, Laurie silently registered to himself, knowing that 12 months earlier she had thumped Pricey so hard in the chest it left a black bruise the size of a fist. Laurie, who gave Kathy her nickname of the 'speckled hen', waved at her as they drove off. Only later would he realise how traitorous she had been in that moment, with her Judas kiss goodbye.

Laurie takes over the story, leaning forward, hands clasped together in front of him on the kitchen table, deeply serious. You have to go back three months before that day to truly understand the viciousness of what happened next, he said.

For the previous three months, Kathy had secretly videotaped things she alleged Pricey had stolen from the mine site. Kathy filmed two old vacuum cleaners that Pricey recovered from a drag-line. They had been dumped and were no good to anyone else, and Pricey figured he'd fix them up for Kathy. Besides, she liked old junk. Her joint was full of it. She also filmed household and kitchen items she reckoned he stole, including, ridiculously, a can of Mortein. As well, she accused him of stealing some oil, a couple of old drums and a discarded first aid kit that had been thrown out because the contents had expired.

In Kathy's intricate and insidious plan, she thought she could use the video to lord it over Pricey, to keep him in line after she said he hit her the previous October. 'I took that video so he wouldn't hit me again,' she later told police investigating his murder. Originally, Kathy said she had planned to show Pricey the video and warn him that if he touched her, she'd send it to his bosses, but before she got a chance to give him the warning, she claimed he hit her a second time so she sent the video. 'He was full of alcohol,' she told police.

Laurie continued: 'I was union shift representative on the job. We got to work that morning, they called him in. "Got to see you, it's pretty serious", and we didn't have a clue what it was about. And the next thing is, "We've got a film of ya, Pricey, thieving stuff from work and a video made of it". We asked to see the video, and we got to see the video, I did.'

With forensic reasoning, Laurie determined that Kathy had been working on her revenge by videotape (which had a commentary by Kathy) for at least three months because she accused Pricey of stealing the headlights on Pricey's old Land Rover and included them in her docu-theft video. He hadn't stolen them at all, but it was an important telltale sign. Pricey had sold the Land Rover about twelve weeks before Kathy sent the videotape, giving Laurie and him a timeline for her treachery.

'She set him up. They had a bit of an argument. And she had stuff on the video of spotlights on the front of his old Land Rover he had,' Laurie said, still seething with anger four years later. 'It was sold three months prior to that – that's how long she had been taking this video. Setting him up, lovey dovey all the time. They had a bit of a blue and he was going to kick her out of the house and so she sends it to the bosses.'

While management was interviewing Pricey with Laurie at his side, Kathy was at his home showing other mine executives through his house, pointing out things she said he'd nicked. It was a vulgar display of disloyalty and her coup de grace.

Katherine Knight was the smiling assassin – waving Pricey goodbye for work and then inviting the prosecution into his home. Pricey was in shock. He couldn't believe it. Laurie protested that she had no right to bring management into Pricey's house. But the damage had been done.

The first aid kit was Pricey's downfall. Pricey, who usually operated heavy machinery at the mine, had broken his leg earlier that year and had been placed on restricted duties during his recovery. He was working in the storeroom – 'hopping around', Laurie said – and while there, the storeman conducted a routine stocktake and tossed out the first aid kit.

'Pricey said, "Oh, I might take that home", and they said, "Yes, you can have it",' Laurie remembered. 'I had two witnesses plus the storeman, so I had three of them I found later that would stand up in court on Pricey's behalf,' Laurie said.

'So that's the only thing they really had to sack him on. The union would not back him because the first aid box is a standard . . . for the safety of the men. He was accused of that and he had no cover-up, even though it was old stock and it was proven to be old stock.'

With Laurie's help, Pricey negotiated the conditions of his termination. Because he was officially sacked, he would lose his entitlements from seventeen years of service, but instead the company agreed to deduct only his holiday pay and offered him counselling – he was respected for his work.

Pricey was devastated. He loved his job and was good at it. He was earning $100 000 a year, which is excellent money by anyone's standards, but even more so for an uneducated man.

Laurie Lewis drove Pricey home from the mine site in a company car the bosses had lent him for the trip, less than two hours after they arrived at work. That morning, Pricey kicked Katherine Knight out of his house. Kathy Knight had her half-brother Barry Roughan move her things out of Pricey's and back into the little house in MacQueen Street. The story was around Aberdeen in no time. No one could quite believe the viciousness of what she'd done, but really, no one was surprised either.

~

Geraldine Edwards has owned and run the Aberdeen General Store directly next door to Kathy Knight's since buying the shop and the house attached to it in 1995. Kathy was already living with Pricey when Gerri moved in, but she saw her every day when she popped in to the shop to buy cigarettes. Kathy was friendly and they developed a polite, neighbourly relationship.

Pricey also used Gerri's General Store to buy his smokes, and was the first in line to lend her tools if she needed any when she was setting up her shop. That September in 1998, Gerri spotted Kathy over the fence that runs between their houses and asked Kathy if she was moving back. Katherine said she'd had a fight with Pricey and he'd told her to get out.

Gerri Edwards didn't ask Kathy about her problems with Pricey, prudently preferring to keep her nose out of it. She was happy not knowing.

John Chillingworth, Kathy's last boyfriend before Pricey, kept up to date with Kathy's shenanigans whenever he dialled John Price's St Andrews Street home to talk to his and Kathy's son, Eric. Chillo and Pricey had known each other for years and Chillo wasn't dirty on being white-anted by him. After sorting out his life following the breakup with Kathy, Chillo thought Pricey had actually done him the favour he might never have been able to do for himself. There were no problems between them now, and the two blokes would chat on the phone, man to man, or in person when Chillingworth visited to pick up or drop off his son. They had something in common – and not all of it was pleasant.

Years later, John Chillingworth said that Kathy's act of vengeance with the Howick incident didn't stop when Pricey got fired. After Pricey kicked the speckled hen out, Kathy turfed all the meat from the deep freeze into the back yard. It was her parting shot at revenge, and this time it got two victims. The meat belonged to Pricey's son Johnathon, who by now openly hated her. It was eerily similar to what she would do eighteen months down the track with another piece of meat.

Cold, calculated and vengeful, that's how Chillo described her.

Three separate forensic psychiatrists would later spend a total of fifteen hours and thirty-six minutes interviewing Katherine Mary Knight for the purpose of her trial. Two were hired by the prosecution and agreed she was in full payback mode the day she sent the videotape to Pricey's bosses. The third, Dr Leonard

Lambeth, was acting for her legal defence team. Justice Barry O'Keefe noted in sentencing on 8 November 2001 that Katherine Knight had been untruthful about the content of the video to Dr Lambeth and others, making out that she had been a victim of assault by Pricey rather than him being a victim of her malice. Dr Rod Milton, for the prosecution, said in evidence that Knight's vengeful act of losing Pricey his job showed 'a level of ruthlessness that one does not usually anticipate'. Dr Milton continued: 'And I think it is the kind of thing that gives me concern, that retribution could take place in such a way without the normal limits at all . . . I think also there is a sense of entitlement, that Ms Knight feels entitled to certain things – a part of Mr Price's home . . . if it is not there then the anger comes out.'

Dr Robert Delaforce testified that the Howick Mines incident showed that Katherine Knight was a 'very pathological example of a paybacker . . . For a partner to do something like that which is, to me, gross; to do something to that extent is extreme, very extreme,' he told Justice O'Keefe. In his judgment O'Keefe agreed. 'This was said by her to have been done as an act of revenge,' he said.

Forty-four-year-old Bob Wells – blessed with Central Casting good looks and a blue-line integrity – was the detective heading the murder investigation into John Price's death. He interviewed Knight four days after Pricey's murder but before she had been charged. Knight told Wells that Pricey's son Johnathon 'hated my guts'.

'And can you tell me why, why that is?' said Detective Wells.

'Because I was with his father.'

'And he just didn't like you?'

'Mmm.'

'Is there any particular reason?'

'Because he lost his job in the mines.'

'Can you further explain . . . ?'

'Because his father used to hit me and I videotaped it, and took it to his company one day – he assaulted me again the second time, and he was sacked.'

Doctors Delaforce and Lambeth would both tell the New South Wales Supreme Court that Katherine Knight had a psychiatric disorder known as borderline personality disorder (BPD), which is characterised by inappropriate anger, a fear of abandonment and the need, in some cases, for revenge when the object of their affection disappoints them or is perceived to have disappointed them.

In his highly regarded book, *Homicide: A Psychiatric Perspective*, American forensic psychiatrist Carl P. Malmquist issued a chilling warning of the unstoppable need for revenge by some people with BPD:

> It is not unusual for BPD individuals to have engaged in a pattern of secret and devious behaviour over an extended period of time that is suddenly exposed. Many times, the history will reveal that person having behaved in unpredictable and unstable ways for some time. In a statistical sense, because dangerous behaviour represents only a small number of the deviant behaviours engaged in, there is always the difficult problem of predicting these rare events.
>
> Apart from the obvious – that instability in any setting increases the likelihood of a violent act – the question is whether there is any specificity connected to instability in BPD individuals. On one hand, their excessive adoration and groping for someone to idealise is doomed to disappointment given the nature of humans; however, in these individuals, such disappointment does not remain as a disappointment but goes on to a state of felt betrayal or a need for revenge in the context of unremitting hatred.

Malmquist could have been talking directly about Katherine Knight. In her bitter quest for revenge, she was consumed by an unremitting anger at John Price, and in it, she lost any foresight she might otherwise have had. It's a wonder she didn't stop for a moment to think about the consequences, but then revenge was all she cared about. Surely she must have known that by acting in such a calculated manner, Pricey would lose his job and would want nothing more to do with her? Maybe she did, but it didn't matter. As it turned out, Pricey disposed of her. What was done was done, and Kathy had done it.

Their separation may have been bitter but it didn't last long. Pricey was lonely, and he was now unemployed. As the weeks rolled by, Laurie Lewis was struck that his mate had started to recast Katherine's perfidy as his own fault.

'He started blaming himself for the way he treated her . . . I couldn't get it through his head. I said, "Jesus, mate, anyone that's set you up like that, how could you have any time for them again?",' Laurie remembered. 'He said, "Oh, I brought it on meself", and I said, "But look at what it's cost you", and he said, "Ah, I'll get another job, don't worry about that".'

Soon after, Kathy and Pricey were together – again – but she didn't move back into his house. Pricey's daughter Rosemary had a go at Kathy one day when she turned up at St Andrews Street and his son, Johnathon, opposed her moving back and thought his dad was a fool. Laurie and a few of his other mates agreed with Johnathon, and tried to counsel him against it.

'He said, "Oh, I love her", and I thought, "Oh, for god's sake. After what she's done to you?",' Laurie said.

Pricey's decision was derided by his no-nonsense mates. They lost respect for him. Most of them shunned Kathy, wanting nothing to do with her. Her actions had marginalised her and, to a lesser degree, Pricey.

Laurie Lewis told Pricey that he wanted nothing more to do with Katherine Knight and warned him off bringing 'that woman' to their table at the RSL club. He didn't want the poisonous speckled hen anywhere near him or his wife Fran. He was having none of her, and he made no bones about it. Laurie even fronted Kathy and told her to her face that he was finished with her.

'From then on Pricey didn't drink at the club anymore, he went up to the pub, because people would associate with her . . . at the club they wouldn't because they knew what happened,' Laurie said. 'And he was a lonely man just sitting there with her . . . he liked to have his mates.'

Frank Heap was another mate who couldn't believe it when Pricey reunited with Kathy. In his late teens Frank had moved from Murrurundi to Aberdeen in 1961 for a two-week stint as a motor mechanic. He never went back. Frank is a big bloke with broad hands and a long rectangular face emanating kindness. He tilts his chin down when he talks, making him raise both eyebrows at once when he looks you in the eyes. For a good part of the fourteen years they'd known each other, Frank and Pricey were drinking mates, sitting in the front corner straight ahead through the door at the top pub drinking Tooheys New. 'The best beer,' Frank declared. Every now and then if they were leaving the pub at the same time, they'd walk home together, with Frank peeling off Graeme Street to the left as Pricey turned right.

'That was the end of it, you know,' Frank said, referring to Pricey's sacking, which everyone in Aberdeen referred to as the 'Howick Incident'. 'I think that's where he lost a bit of respect . . . when he went back to her . . . But blokes did say it to him, "You're a fool", but like I said, one of his weaknesses was women.'

Laurie Lewis's younger brother, Trevor Lewis, also tried to talk some sense into Pricey, figuring the more pressure on him the better. Trevor, who invited Pricey and Kathy to his wedding a few years earlier, lived a few doors up the road and was part of the fishing crew that took week-long trips away to Ballina, Bonshaw and Deepwater. They were good mates. Trevor, four years older than Pricey, was the straightest with him. But even his tough talk couldn't persuade Pricey.

On one occasion Trevor and Pricey were working in Pricey's back yard and the on again, off again couple got into each other. Pricey told Kathy to 'fuck off'.

'You'll never get me out of this house. I'll do you in first,' Kathy yelled back as Trevor looked on. Pricey also confided to Trevor that he thought Katherine would kill him, according to Justice O'Keefe.

Whether Price was motivated by loneliness or whether he was still in love with Katherine Knight after what she'd done to him, no one could really say. If it was love, then he was as mad as a bloody cut snake. For all anyone knew, Pricey might have been in love with the idea of being in love with someone, anyone, and Kathy Knight, the speckled hen, was just there, available.

Pricey and Katherine had reconciled – he believed he was partly to blame for her vindictiveness – but it was never going to work. It had been a bitter separation, the scars of which could never fully heal. Pricey could forgive but, even though he tried, he could not forget. Their fights resumed, with increasing intensity. Later she would tell Detective Bob Wells that most of their subsequent fights were over Pricey losing his job at the mine.

Not long after Pricey and Kathy got back together, she was driving her daughter Natasha to Newcastle. Mother and daughter were talking about Pricey and the stress she said he caused her. Her mother said something like, ' "I told him that if he took me back this time, it was to the death",' Natasha told police a few hours after Pricey's body was discovered. Her mother also said: "If I kill Pricey, I'll kill myself after it".'

11

And then she stabbed him

Three things happened next. First, Katherine Knight continued to plot against John Price. Then she stabbed him, and finally, she tried to hire someone to steal his car and throw battery acid in his face.

Pricey had forgiven her for getting him sacked and took her back, but it hadn't placated Kathy. She was consumed by her poisonous need for revenge and carelessly revealed it. Street smart but not clever, she didn't keep her secrets.

'I'm going to kill Pricey and I'm going to get away with it. I'll get away with it 'cause I'll make out I'm mad,' Kathy said in 1999 to her older brother Charlie Knight. Charlie's daughter Tracey was also present.

Tracey, who was then twenty-four and pregnant with her first child, is a tall, lithe redhead with a splash of freckles across her nose, beautiful blue eyes, a crooked toothy smile and a gentle manner. In August 2000 she visited the Muswellbrook police station at the request of Bob Wells, who was heading the subsequent murder investigation into John Price's death.

It wasn't the first time Kathy had spoken about killing Pricey, and it wouldn't be the last. In fact, the New South Wales Supreme Court would later hear that she had made the same threat before, and, about five weeks before the murder Knight said to Charlie: 'I'm going to kill Pricey and the two kids too.'

Kath said something similar in front of Pricey's mate, Trevor Lewis, Laurie's younger brother. Detective Bob Wells said Trevor and Pricey were working in the backyard at Pricey's, when Kathy came out.

'I can't remember the exact words but Pricey said, "Get us a couple of beers, you red hen", because that's what he called her, or the speckled hen. Kathy said, "Get 'em yourself",' Bob Wells said. 'Pricey said, "You can fuck off then", she said, "You'll never get me out of this house, I'll do you in first". He called her a red-headed cunt, she called him – it just made me shudder. But that's the relationship they had. He just could not motivate himself to get rid of her and she was just showing that she was steadfast, not going to go unless she said.'

~

Jackie Price was a toddler when her mum left Pricey, eventually taking her to live in Tamworth, but the distance between her and her dad was measured in kilometres alone. Jackie has always been close to her dad and her older brother and sister, Johnathon and Rosemary, mostly because her mum and dad were sticklers about making sure they had as much time together as possible. Pricey was a caring, doting father and loved having all his kids together.

Johnathon had stayed with his dad when Colleen left, and despite the usual teenage friction, they were best mates and he wanted for nothing. Neither did Rosemary or Jackie. When Rosemary was a little girl, she asked for a horse. Her mum thought it was an extravagance, but Pricey bought her one just the same. Every year he sent Jackie his income tax return cheque.

Jackie is a strikingly pretty teenager who was born with her father's almond-shaped dark brown eyes. She got to know Kathy Knight whenever she spent the weekends or school holidays at St Andrews Street. Jackie, who wasn't yet ten when her father hooked up with Kathy, liked her and thought she was nice, but as she grew into her teenage years, she baulked at Kathy's attempts to 'mother' her or tell her what to do.

'I hate her now [but] she was nice, but weird . . . I liked her but I didn't because she was weird,' Jackie said, sounding like a typical teenager unable to quite define Kathy's nature but recognising it just the same. 'But it was never a weirdness to pick up on the extent of what happened. It was never, ever that. I was never scared of her, I'd back-chat her and everything.'

Even though Kathy was still living at the MacQueen Street house after the Howick mine incident, she had a free run at Pricey's. The kids kept their pyjamas under the pillows in the bedrooms and she had all her sewing equipment in the house and was always knitting. She would even bring her friends over for afternoon teas, talking over the television as Jackie tried to watch. Jackie remembered she frequently wore black jeans and was odd. One weekend they were camping and Kath and her two kids stayed in their tent and Jackie and her friend had another tent on the other side of a little creek. It was dark and all of a sudden, Jackie and her mate heard footsteps and whispering and panicked. 'So me and my girlfriend picked up rocks and we're pegging these rocks, it's pitch black. And we asked them the next morning what they were doing and they were coming over to start war with us . . . and I'm like, "Whaaat? . . . Haven't you grown out of that yet?" I would've been about 14 . . . as if you'd do things like that – being a teenager, that age, it's sort of like, you don't do stupid things, don't play stupid games.

'She was weird, too . . . I asked her to make onion gravy like Mum did – she put it out on the back porch in a frying pan and she said it was to let all the flavours go through it . . . I'm thinking, "You're a wacko".'

It was, as Jackie said, unusual behaviour. 'One night we were going to the club for dinner and she was all dressed up and we were waiting for someone, I think it was Dad we were waiting on, and she went out the back and started chopping firewood, I can understand getting firewood, but she was chopping it and she was all dressed up, we were going out for tea, it was just weird.'

Jackie said Kathy was strict with her two children, Sarah and Eric, just like most mums. She would make them sit at the table until they finished their greens and pick up after themselves, and occasionally she would try to use the same tactics on her and Johnathon.

'She tried to mother you but she didn't. And that's where Johnathon and Kath blued . . . she was trying to be this big mother, she tried to walk in Mum's shoes and Johnathon wouldn't allow it,' Jackie said. ' "You're not my mother, you're not telling me what to do".'

As Jackie got older, she started noticing Kathy's vengeful personality and became increasingly aware of her arguments with her dad. They were never physical and it was usually Kathy who would start them over nothing, 'going on about crap'. But what shocked Jackie most were the targets Kathy chose, including herself.

One time Jackie, then thirteen or fourteen, was minding her own business watching television in the lounge-room with a girl-friend when Kathy came in.

'She said, "Jackie, I've got to tell you something" and I said, "What?", and she said, "Well, your father is really not your father". And I'm a wreck . . . and I'm thinking, well, who owns me and I'm freaking out, my dad's not my dad, who is my dad?

'It's totally spinning me out. And so I rang here [home] that night. I'm bawling on the phone, and said, "Mum, I've got to talk to you", I said, "Dad's not my dad" . . . she was seriously telling me that my father wasn't my father.'

Colleen Price told Jackie to put Kathy on the phone, and when she answered, Col ripped into her.

'I had a word to her on the phone when I found out what she said about the kids and I said to her, "That's bullshit, Kath, if you say something say it to my face, you don't know what you're talking about". And then I thought, what am I doing here, trying to talk to her? I know who my kids' father is. You only have to look at them. She was always looking for some dirt, she always had to make herself look good, that was the thing with Kath.'

It was a nasty, spiteful thing to do to a vulnerable teenager whose parents were separated, but Colleen's admonishment was like water off a duck's back.

Katherine Knight's complicated character kept everyone guessing what she would do next. When she was good, she was very,

very good, and when she was bad she was downright devious. She would lend Jackie money if she needed it, and pick her up from the station whenever she made the trip to visit her father, but in the very next breath, she would try to bully her into doing the dishes or start ranting and raving, or torment her about her paternity.

Pricey's elder daughter Rosemary, who was married, also trusted her with her two young children. The kids called her 'Nanny Kath'. 'She wasn't lazy, and was often quite warm, especially with the kids,' Rosemary told *Who Weekly*'s Michelle Coffey. But, she could turn on you as fast as a scorpion.

'One day we were sitting on Dad's porch and she was sweeping the verandah,' Rosemary said. 'Dad picked up the broom and touched her on the bum and she went absolutely mental, screaming abuse at him. Then five seconds later, it was as though nothing happened.'

If she wasn't screaming and yelling abuse, swearing her head off, Kathy was conniving, doing little things to chip away at Pricey and irritate him. Revenge warfare. Pricey had his habits, one of which was always leaving the television and video remote controls on the arm of the lounge chair, within easy reach. One day Kathy hid them. Pricey's grandchildren had spent the day at his house and Kath led him to believe they had misplaced them. Pricey went crook at Rosemary blaming 'your friggin' kids' for losing the remotes. Rosemary protested, but Pricey was annoyed. Eventually, Kathy put them back and Pricey rang Rosemary to apologise.

Jackie was spooked when she witnessed Kathy rage at her own father, Ken Knight, gesticulating at him with a knife in her hand and ordering him out of her MacQueen Street home. Kathy and her dad had had a turbulent relationship.

'They were blueing about something . . . she was chopping food in the kitchen, and me and a girlfriend were sitting in the lounge-room and she's come out, talking to her father with a knife in her hand. "You wanna get out of my house",' Jackie said, waving an imaginary knife in her hand. 'At least you'd put the knife in your other hand and you'd be pointing the finger, or put the knife down.

'But she was talking to him using the knife as a finger and me and my girlfriend were like, "Yep, we've got our money, we're out of here". We just took off. It was freaky. Like, she's got these knives, it was pretty intense, you know? We scooted out.'

Colleen Price felt safe entrusting Kathy with the care of her younger daughter, and on occasion had dropped in to have a cuppa with Pricey and Kathy or go down to the club with them for a Coke – Colleen doesn't drink. But the year before Kathy executed her treacherous videotape plot, Col started to worry for Pricey's safety. She came to collect her daughter after she'd had a weekend with her dad, and Kathy raced out to the car ahead of Jackie and Pricey.

'She said to me, "I want to ask you something". It come out of the blue, and I said, "Oh yeah, what's that?" She said, "Did Pricey ever hit you?" I said, "What?", and I sort of laughed . . . because I was taken aback.' Pricey had never laid a hand on Colleen and she was lucky if she could remember three arguments with him during their fifteen-year marriage.

'And I said, "Who told you that shit?" She said, "Oh, a bloke that you gave a ride home from the club one night". And I said, "What bloke was that, Kath?" She said, "Oh, when you used to go into the raffles . . . you give a bloke a ride home one night". I said, "For a start, Kath, I've never given any bloke a ride home from the club". I said, "Who told you that? You go get him now, and I'll go with you, and I'll tell him in front of you that's a load of bullshit" . . . and she said, "Oh no, I might have got it wrong then."

'So she was trying to build things up for herself. She was building it up. And I knew. Pricey come out to the car and said, "Hi, darling", and she went back inside. I grabbed him by the arm and said, "Listen", and I made him look me in the face and I said, "She is going to do something to you, listen to what I am telling you . . . she is going to do something to you, mate . . . I don't know how bad it's going to be but she is going to hurt you, Pricey".'

Pricey told Colleen not to be silly, Kathy wouldn't do anything like that, but she insisted. Colleen's clairvoyant skills had shown her something.

'"I'm telling you now, she's going to do something to you,

Pricey, I can see it". I actually seen it. She put her hand on me and said, "Can I ask you something?" and she tapped me on the hand, and no sooner had she done it, I seen it. I didn't know to what extent [but] I knew she would hurt him . . . and that's why I told him.'

Pricey tried to play down any panic, ignoring the warning signs even if they were starting to get to him. It helped that he was distracted by his new job at Bowditch and Partners Earthmoving Pty Ltd which he landed a few months after getting the sack from Howick Mines. Geoffrey Bowditch, the owner of the company, hired Pricey after seeing him operate a loader truck as a casual worker for a rival company during an all-night shift on a rail construction site in the Upper Hunter Valley.

Pricey had recently applied for a job at the company that Geoff started in 1989 when he was just twenty-eight. Bowditch, who usually pulls 12–14 hour days, was driving a six-wheeler road truck tipper and was keeping an eye on Pricey to see how he operated. He liked what he saw and immediately offered Pricey a job.

Bowditch, then thirty-eight and a newly single father of two young girls, is a self-made man. His company contracts its services to the New South Wales rail authorities and various open cut coal mines in the Valley. It is tough, demanding and dangerous work, and he knows the value of quality workers when he sees them. Bowditch started Pricey as an operator but quickly discovered he was multiskilled and promoted him to supervisor. Pricey could operate any kind of machinery – a grader, dozer, scraper and loader, and even at a pinch an excavator – which was unusual. Geoff said he'd probably had three blokes in ten years who could run them all.

'It wasn't until sometime later that I found out why he was unemployed. People of his talent normally have a job for life. It's probably just our good fortune that she did get him sacked from where he was,' Bowditch said.

By the end of 1999, Pricey was running the Bowditch scraper crew – about a dozen men – at the Bayswater open cut colliery and operating a $1.6 million Caterpillar scraper. Ambition had never played a big role in Pricey's life – until now. He was even learning how to use a computer – an incredible feat for a man who could barely read and write – and had started drinking Lite beer at his boss's behest. Geoff Bowditch refused to stock his work fridge with anything heavier – for safety reasons – and when Pricey was at work, he converted. No problem.

'I think he actually had a responsibility now and he used to take it to heart if one of his scrapers didn't start or if someone was late . . . his production was up and he did a good job,' Geoff said.

Pricey's best mate Laurie Lewis also noticed a change in him. 'He was interested in his job and he knew his job, he was a good operator. He knew what he was doing and he knew what had to be done. He was teaching young fellas out there where they were going wrong, it interested him a lot. He was off the grog, he'd get on the grog once in a while but nothing like he used to. He lost a lot of weight and he looked a lot fitter, he looked really good and he was happy, except for her. Well, Keego told me, he said he was definitely worried about her, she was threatening more and more, you know, stabs and God knows what.'

~

Pricey was in his kitchen, having just hung up from Colleen in Tamworth. They had been talking about their youngest daughter Jackie. Col told Pricey that she didn't think Kathy had any right interfering in Jackie's relationship with her dad. Apparently, Jackie had been upset and Kathy told her that even though her parents were divorced, her dad still loved her. Pricey told Kathy what Col had said, and they got into an argument. It was spiteful. Kathy was at the sink doing the dishes as the argument got more heated. Pricey told Kathy she was being nasty and causing trouble.

The arguing sank to new depths, her against him and vice versa, and Kathy lunged at Pricey and stabbed him with a knife in the upper left chest right under the shoulder.

'It could have been a fork, a spoon or anything in my hand, it was a knife that you cut your meal with and I aimed it at him and it got him. He was leaning closer than I thought. And my eyesight was bad at that time, I've only had new glasses since then,' she told Detective Bob Wells later during the police interview which was played in court during her sentencing hearing.

Kathy claimed the stabbing was an accident and went to her solicitor in Muswellbrook and then to the police in Scone to report it, an act that would prompt forensic psychiatrist Rod Milton to make the following statement in court a little more than two years later after he interviewed Knight at the request of the Director of Public Prosecutions: 'She has got a kind of consciousness of the advantages to herself, like going and reporting the stabbing, I think of Mr Price, as an accident . . . She shows a certain astuteness, and I think there is some satisfaction from committing quite cruel acts.' Pricey did not report the matter. Nor did he get the wound treated – he just put a Band-Aid on it, his boss said later.

But Pricey told a few mates that Kathy had taken a knife to him, and when he showed Laurie and Fran Lewis the wound, Laurie said, 'Well, we've been telling you that for ages, we said "It will be worse than that"'.

'He was here one day with Fran and she got up him about bloody going back with her. She said, "She took your job off you and everything else and you're back with her?" He said, "I've got nothing else to lose". And Fran said, "Yes you have, Pricey, you've got your bloody life to lose".

'And that's when I said to him, "Yeah, she's already had one crack at you, don't forget". He said, "It wasn't nothing". And it wasn't much either, but the intention was there, enough to frighten.'

When Kathy was interviewed by Bob Wells four days after Pricey's body was found less than six months later, he asked her if there was any time during their relationship that she assaulted him.

'No,' she said.

'I've been told there was an incident . . . later on last year, in or around August 1999, that you caused a minor stab wound to Pricey's chest?'

'Yeah, that's right.'

Almost two years later in the New South Wales Supreme Court, Justice O'Keefe drew attention to the scar made by Katherine Knight's attack on Pricey that day in the kitchen when handing down his sentence after she pleaded guilty to murder. 'On another occasion she sliced Mr Price's left chest with a knife,' said the judge. 'The scar from this was still visible on his body following his death and skinning. It is perhaps no coincidence that the only part of Mr Price that was not skinned by the prisoner was that part of him which bore the scar which she inflicted.'

Colleen Price knew to be wary of Kathy, and remembered being told about yet another incident around the same time: 'She knew what she was doing. She walked into the pub there one night, she scratched herself on the neck with a fork and went to the pub so they would see the scratches down her neck . . . because Pricey was in there having a beer, so everyone could see, and make out that Pricey did it,' said Col. 'She was building everything up to make him look like a bad person.

'I think Kath liked to be in control and have the power and make you fear her.'

Katherine Knight was about to raise the stakes in her wicked plan, and she would double them soon after. But she needed the help of her nephew, Jason Roughan. Jason's dad Barry is Katherine Knight's half-brother, four years older than her but still the youngest of the four Roughan boys.

Whenever Jason visited his dad in Aberdeen, Jason would drop in on Katherine, either at her house or Pricey's. He was fairly close to her and his cousins, especially Natasha, who was only a couple of years younger than him.

Towards the end of 1999, Kathy, who is known as Aunty Kath by her nieces and nephews, asked Jason if he would steal and burn Pricey's private car as an act of vengeance. Jason asked why she wanted it done.

Aunty Kath replied that she didn't like the way Pricey treated her when they were at the pub together.

'He calls me a "slut", "moll", in front of the people at the pub. He offers to buy other females at the pub drinks . . . I'm sick of it,' Kathy told her nephew.

The car in question was Pricey's white Ford Mondeo which, brand new, was worth around $20 000. It was uninsured, which made Katherine's revenge even more satisfying. She told Jason she wanted to hurt Pricey in the hip pocket. All she cared about was inflicting as much damage as she could.

'I want to hurt him financially so he can feel it in his pocket,' the New South Wales Supreme Court would later hear she said.

When forensic psychiatrist Dr Robert Delaforce was in the witness box in October 2001, Justice O'Keefe asked about the significance of Knight's desire to hurt Pricey financially.

'It indicates to me the extent of the payback, absolutely,' he said.

In Katherine's cold, calculating world, she had turned her revenge into a conspiracy to commit a felony as well as a dirty business transaction. She knew that if Jason went ahead and did what she asked, she'd have to pay.

She offered him $500 and told him she needed a month or so to save the money. Later, Aunty Kath came up with a more violent strategy and asked Jason if he would throw some battery acid on Pricey's face. He said he wouldn't do it.

Katherine Knight seemed to have no conscience about corrupting her nephew by conspiring with him to steal Pricey's car and commit acts of violence with the intent to cause physical harm. If convicted of the felony charge of auto theft or conspiracy to commit auto theft or malicious assault with intent to injure, Jason could have been sentenced to jail.

'She wanted him [Jason] to smash him [Pricey] about, burn his car, get rid of his car for her . . . And Jason come up – and never done it, of course,' Barry Roughan said.

Jason visited Kathy and stayed at her MacQueen Street house for a couple of weeks, his dad said. But Aunty Kath's plan had completely unravelled and Kathy kicked Jason out of her house. He never stole the Mondeo and the closest he got to any acid was when Aunty Kath asked him to throw it at Pricey but he said he wouldn't do it. Pricey's car was sitting in his driveway alongside his Bowditch van the morning his body was found.

Twenty months later, Justice Barry O'Keefe noted Knight's plan of vengeance when he sentenced her for murder.

'Another matter of which Dr Delaforce became aware in the course of his interviews was the prisoner arranging for her nephew, in return for a payment of $500, to steal Mr Price's uninsured Mondeo motor vehicle and destroy it, so as to inflict financial harm on Mr Price,' Justice O'Keefe said. 'The same person had been asked by the prisoner to throw acid in Mr Price's face . . . Dr Delaforce was of the opinion that all these matters were indicative of her proneness to want to "pay back" persons who crossed her, even though she may have been in a relationship with them . . . I have no doubt that he is correct.'

~

Kathy's previous boyfriend John Chillingworth had turned his life around in Queensland and had started seeing a wonderful new woman named Janet*. She was a good few years younger than him, but that didn't matter. They were perfectly suited to each other. They met when she was working in a bank and Chillo came in to do some banking for the Salvation Army and started flirting with the women behind the counter. Janet caught his eye and she liked his charm.

After a few visits, he plucked up enough courage to ask her out for coffee, and pretty soon they were rock solid. In August 1999, after being together for three and a half years, John asked Janet to marry him, and she said yes. They planned on a November wedding, complete with all the trimmings and with his son Eric as a page boy. Eric was living in Aberdeen with his mother. Chillo rang Kathy and asked for her permission for the boy to travel to Queensland for the wedding and she said yes.

But Chillo's new happiness just gave Kathy another opportunity to exercise her spitefulness and exact another form of revenge against him. After saying her son could be his dad's page boy, she changed her mind just ten days before the wedding.

'It was just her mind games. We asked her in August when we decided that we were getting married and she said, "Yep, no problems",' said Janet, 'and then she waited until John had rung up the week before to say that we'd paid for everything and I had gotten the bow ties and cummerbunds made . . . and that's when she said to John, "The school said he can't get the time off". And he was in Grade 3 . . . She put us through a day of hell.

'It would have hurt Eric more, I think, because he was looking forward to it, carrying the rings,' she said.

'And we wanted him to be there too,' her husband said.

'That's what John said, "In the end, you are hurting Eric",' said Janet.

'That's probably why she reneged in the end,' said John. 'I said, "You are hurting me but you are hurting that boy more . . . he has been looking forward to coming up here for this wedding". I said, "It's not costing you nothing, we are picking him up, bringing him home, the whole bit".'

In the end, Kathy relented and Janet went down to collect Eric and brought him back with her on the bus. Kathy had sent a wedding gift with her son: a set of Chef knives.

12

Merry Christmas and unhappy New Year

Bowditch Earthmoving had two Christmas parties in 1999 – a small staff dinner for about ten people and a larger party at Geoff Bowditch's Muswellbrook house. Pricey, who had recently been promoted to supervisor, was invited to the dinner and he brought Kathy, who kept her vengeful nature hidden even though she was knee-deep in her plan. In previous years, Pricey would have tied one on, but his new professional responsibilities had influenced him socially and Geoff said he cut his drinking right back, especially at work functions.

It was Kathy who stood out, Geoff said. 'She was very different there, she talked about all these stupid things, it was completely different to the general [discussion]. I guess, you know what it's like to sit at a table with intelligent people and there's just one that doesn't fit in, she was sort of that one. Pricey, even though he couldn't read and write, could mix it with intelligent people. She was the odd one out, really was.'

At the party for families and children a few days later, Kathy embarrassed guests when she went topless bathing. Pricey had gout and his feet were playing up, and he couldn't dance with her.

'She got the shits and went swimming . . . She went bloody swimming topless . . . she took her top off and she went swimming in the pool,' Geoff said. Not wanting to add to the embarrassing scene, Geoff turned the lights off and shepherded the guests to the other side of his house, leaving Kathy in the pool on her own. It was pure Kathy. She didn't care what she did or who she upset, as long as she was happy and pleasing herself.

Christmas 1999 was John Price's crucible. He was on edge and nervous. He was determined to break up with Katherine, whatever it took. His problem was that he just didn't know how. He was a country bloke who didn't discuss the nuances of romance with his mates. He didn't watch Oprah and wouldn't have even heard of *Men Are from Mars, Women Are from Venus*. John Price simply did not have the skills to engineer a peaceable and final separation.

But he was worried about his safety and, more importantly, that of his children. Each time Katherine Knight did something violent or blew her stack, he'd ring a mate on the north coast and tell him to write it down, just in case something happened to him. He wanted Kathy's deviousness on record. His concerns were well founded even if he didn't know about her aborted plot with Katherine's nephew, and they would be proved right later.

It wasn't quite the spirit to go into Christmas with but, against the odds, Pricey pushed on. The house in St Andrews Street was in a festive spirit. Pricey's daughter Jackie was down from Tamworth and had some friends over. Rosemary and her husband Brad were there with their two littlies. Katherine was there with her two children.

Pricey's neighbour, Trish Gray, ran a party hire company that her father Bernie had started years earlier after getting out of the military. Pricey asked if they would inflate a jumping castle on the spare block between their houses and, in a neighbourly barter system, paid with a carton of Crown Lager. Everyone was happy. It was Christmas.

'There were kids everywhere. It was like a show, a little show in the paddock outside Dad's,' Jackie remembered. 'We moved everything from inside Dad's house out to this party. And she [Katherine] is sitting inside drinking this Bailey's, on her own, and I walked in and you could see she had the shits about something.'

It was on again. No one knew why Kathy had a bee in her bonnet.

One neighbour heard the fighting start later in the afternoon on the front verandah where Katherine was standing, drawing on a fag. 'They were saying effing this and effing c—,' she said. 'She said to him, "I know you fucked the woman up the road", and I said to my partner, it wasn't me,' she said as she cringed and pulled a face at the thought of being a target of Kathy's wrath. 'Then she said something to the daughter, "Oh, how would you know your father? You wouldn't know your father, your mother was a slut" . . . And all of these little kids were running around.'

She was shocked at the forceful language and the volume of the argument at the front of the house.

Rosemary, who Kathy was attacking, was ropable. 'Rosemary said, "If you don't get away from me, I'm going to kick you off the porch",' her younger sister Jackie remembered. 'Then she [Kathy] went inside and went to bed and Rosemary called the cops, and she said, "Dad, I want her out of the house".' Jackie said the police came, but Kathy had passed out on Pricey's bed. So much for a merry Christmas and happy New Year.

Rosemary knew Katherine and her father argued, but she never saw any physical violence between them. 'At times Kath was fine and she would make clothes for the kids, which was nice of her. But there was always something a little strange about her,' Rosemary told reporter Donna Page in an interview with *The Newcastle Herald*.

Sharon Turner said Kathy knew she had done some 'terrible things' and once told her she didn't want to 'snap' again. 'It was only when she was in a relationship . . . that she'd snap . . . And the only times she did ruthless things . . . was when she was having troubles with her relationships . . . She was generally a normal person until she had problems in her relationships and that brought the worst out of her . . . that brought the bad things out in her personality. It rocked her. You know, I don't think she could handle rejection and . . . that's why she did it to Johnny Price. Pricey, this time, had enough of her,' she said.

It was 2000 and nothing had changed. Pricey and Katherine were still together, and still fighting and making up. They talked about breaking up over the next two months, but they never got around to it.

Pricey had a job to do in Kempsey, and he took Kath along. She liked to watch him work. It was a good patch in a bad time. Towards the end of February, Pricey's first grandson was turning five and his mother, Rosemary, threw him a birthday party. 'Nanny Kath' came along. Katherine wore a locket around her neck with a picture of Pricey and herself on either side. The five year old clambered up on her lap and went to open the locket, but Katherine told him not to bother, the photos weren't there anymore. 'It was something he loved doing, but this night he couldn't open the locket,' Rosemary later told Michelle Coffey at *Who Weekly*. 'There's nothing in there,' Kathy told the little boy.

It was odd but Rosemary thought nothing more about it until later, when the full significance of the missing photographs would become evident.

Katherine still had sewing on Wednesday nights and played bingo twice a week at the Muswellbrook District Workers' Club with a few regulars including her sister Joy and an old friend from Aberdeen, Catherine Kennedy. Catherine didn't drive and couldn't get around much. She was about the same age as Kathy and had recently had her second hip replacement surgery. Kathy thought the bingo sessions each Tuesday and Thursday would be good for Catherine and generously offered to pick her up at 10.30 am and drop her off home twice a week. In between the morning and afternoon sessions, they headed into Bridge Street for lunch or went shopping.

'I've never had any problems with her. She seemed to be friendly to me. She'd do anything for you. She took me up to the hospital once when I asked her,' Catherine said. 'She would do anything for you. Sometimes she would come and ask me if I wanted to go to the pictures down in Maitland, take the kids down. We'd go together, have a day out.'

Catherine liked Kathy but was aware of her mercurial side. Nobody in Aberdeen wasn't. Her husband John Kennedy had warned his wife about Kathy Knight after his mate David Saunders had come to their house one morning years before with a stab wound to the stomach when she got him with a pair of scissors. The Kennedys' daughter was also good friends with Jackie, and Catherine often heard stories of arguments between Pricey and Kathy from the teenager.

Still, Catherine Kennedy had one rule: take people as you find them, and Kathy had always been more than kind to her, and they got on well, enjoying bingo and having a few laughs as they collected their prizes – they often won. Katherine and Catherine were tinny that way.

On the last Thursday of February, the 24th, Kathy was driving back to Aberdeen after bingo. Catherine Kennedy was in the passenger seat of the red Lite Ace.

'I can remember one thing she said on the way home in the car, she was saying something like, "I'm gonna kill Pricey one night" . . . but I just didn't believe it . . . she just said it,' Catherine said.

'Don't know what made her say that, I just didn't believe her. I just didn't think she'd do anything like that. But my husband didn't like her very much. He liked Pricey but he never went up near their place because of her. Oh, he thought she was a bit silly, you know, strange even.

'I don't think I said a thing. I just didn't think I'd believe her . . . She was just like normal till we started coming home in the car. I just couldn't believe her saying something like that. She did sound cranky sort of thing, you know. I just didn't think it would be real. Very strange.'

Remembering the conversation two years later, Catherine seemed to think Kathy 'said something about jealousy . . . Just jealous of other women, I don't know what it was.' She wasn't sure – after all, who would believe something like that?

Months later, after Katherine Knight had been charged with murdering John Price and was waiting to stand trial, her daughter Natasha visited her grandmother and told her that Katherine had made a voodoo doll of Pricey. Whenever she got mad with him, she stuck pins in it. Jean Dodson had no idea what the voodoo doll was, but from what her granddaughter had told her, Katherine had turned a rag doll into a replica of Pricey and had even attached some of his hair to it. It also had a penis, and some of Pricey's semen on it, according to the story that Natasha told her grandmother.

Towards the end of 1999 and the beginning of 2000, Katherine was becoming increasingly angry with Pricey. She had previously complained about his drinking to her girlfriends, and she was also upset at the way he spoke to her at the pub, telling her he didn't love her, saying he was still in love with Colleen. But Pricey had bought Katherine a ring, and when she wasn't complaining about him, she was showing anyone who would look at it and telling them they were engaged.

'He bought her a ring. Yes he did. I remember the day she showed me that. It wasn't long before she done him in,' said Sharon Turner, who had lived in Aberdeen for years and knew Kathy when they worked at the abattoir. 'She showed me, she said, "Look, we're engaged", and she showed me this ring. It had a blue stone in it, I think, and I said, "Well, Kathy, an engagement ring usually has got a diamond in it" . . . But she was that proud of it, and then they were fighting, and I know instead of being up at the [St Andrews Street] house she was back down the street a lot.'

On Saturday 26 February, Pricey and Katherine went to a party in Scone. Kathy's ex-de facto David Saunders was there. Saunders had lived with Knight for three years, more off than on, from 1987, and they had a daughter together. He was also mates with Pricey. 'He called me Saunders,' David Saunders said. They originally met when Saunders, a miner, was living in the Willow Grove Caravan Park. Two degrees of separation. That night, Pricey told Saunders that the time had come for him to end the relationship, once and for all.

'We're blueing again, I'm better off without her, I want to get rid of her,' Pricey said.

Pricey was up dancing with one of his daughters and David said that even though Pricey and Kathy were fighting, his mate did not appear nervous. 'He wouldn't be like that to me, because that was Pricey. You couldn't ask for a better bloke,' Dave said.

From his own experience, Saunders knew exactly what his mate was talking about. Saunders and Knight had started their relationship intoxicated by the exquisite pheromones that fuel new love, but within two months it had deteriorated and frequently descended into violence – her against him. He did a quick mental inventory of the violence: dead dingo pup with a cut throat, stab wound to the stomach, hit over the head with an iron, cut up all his clothes, damaged his car.

If Dave could sum up the relationship in one word it would be violent.

The day after the Scone party, the relentless summer beat down on Aberdeen. There had been no rain for days and the temperature settled early in the low 30s. On any given Sunday in Aberdeen, apart from the third of every month when the local market is held, there is little to do. The top and bottom pubs, the Aberdeen and the Commercial, are open for business, and if the occasion is right, like St Patrick's Day, a band might be playing, drawing a crowd. For those athletically inclined, there is a nine-hole public golf course with a $7 green fee, prepaid at the bar or dropped in the Honesty Box if no one is around to collect your money. Clay and grass tennis courts provide another sporting distraction. Lake Glenbawn is 10 kilometres up the road, but that's about it.

Forgetting the tensions of the previous night, or perhaps deliberately ignoring them for fear of having her fourth significant relationship disintegrate around her, Kathy Knight spent the day at Pricey's with her son. Sarah was at her dad's. Her second eldest daughter Natasha had moved out of MacQueen Street and into her own home in Muswellbrook a few weeks earlier with her daughter.

Before lunchtime, Pricey's neighbour and old mate, Ron Murray, a 66-year-old pensioner with nearly twenty years of Aberdeen in his blood, drove down from his place further up St Andrews Street. They sat in the kitchen for a while and cracked open a Tooheys New, like they did every Sunday. Ron popped his head through the lounge-room door to say g'day to Kathy, who was lying on the floral three-seater couch with a mask over her eyes, complaining of a sty or a head cold. Ron didn't pay much attention, just had a quick chat then went back with his mate.

Ron had known Kathy since she and Pricey got together, and thought she was a good-hearted woman, if unpredictable. She picked him up most Fridays at 4 pm for the unofficial pub run, before bringing Pricey up when he finished work. Sometimes she'd pop in and sit with them and have a Coke.

'He was a good little fella. Top little bloke, that's right. He liked a good time,' Ron said. 'She was alright but then she was a bit erratic at times. She would go a bit silly and go off her handle and they would have a blue and then kiss and make up again, like most de factos. It was pretty normal, it was over any little thing, any little thing at all. It would just flare up.'

Ron said Pricey sometimes jokingly called Kathy a 'mad cunt' and she'd fire back a comment straightaway, taking his comments on the chin, not getting upset, and giving as good as she got.

This Sunday the blokes went outside and sat on the front verandah and had a few more beers. Kath came out once to ask how they were going, and went back inside. It was too windy and glary for her with her crook eye, Ron remembered, and he left two hours later after four tins of Tooheys. Kathy took Pricey up to the top pub. When he came back, his workmate, Jon Collison, came over. Pricey asked Kathy to go up to the pub to buy another carton of Tooheys New, and complained when she came back because it cost $30 and not the usual $27.

Jon Collison lived around the corner from Pricey and worked in Pricey's crew at the Bayswater mine. They started at Bowditch about the same time, both as plant operators.

Later that afternoon John Price lit the barbecue and chopped the tomato and onion for dinner. Katherine Knight's niece, who lived on the other side of St Andrews Street a few doors up the hill from Pricey's with her parents John and Joy Hinder, had come down to visit her cousins. Pricey had a beer.

To outside eyes, it might have seemed like an average Sunday for an extended family but the image of a country idyll was a mirage. Around 5.30, the afternoon stillness was shattered by a torrent of verbal abuse. Pricey attacked Kathy about her children having four different fathers. Never one to lie down in the heat of confrontation, Knight had a go back at him.

'He was rubbishing me having different fathers for my children again, and I just said to him, "Hang on", I said, "You said last night at a party that your parents were married" . . . and they weren't,' Katherine told Bob Wells in her only police interview, which was played in court. 'And he just went off his brain and said, "Don't say anything about my mother". And then he attacked me.'

The kids, hearing the screaming, had retreated to one of the bedrooms and shut the door.

Knight knew how to push Pricey's buttons, and vice versa. Her words scalded him, lighting the emotions he'd been containing for months. Pricey launched himself at Katherine, grabbing at her throat and breast. In the scuffle, he ripped off her necklace.

'He stood up . . . in between the two lounges, the big lounge and the little lounge, and came over the lounge at me and I put me knees up and that's when he grabbed me by the throat,' she said.

Kath went to the kitchen and smashed his cigarettes up. Pricey was furious.

'Get out of my house,' he would have yelled.

Katherine told him to get out.

Pricey thought Katherine went for a knife and a flash of terror hit him – she'd stabbed him before. He panicked and fled through the front door and ran across the road to the safety of his neighbours, Anthony and Jillian Keegan.

'She's gone for the butcher's knife, so I got out of there,' Pricey told Anthony Keegan, blood dripping from above his left eye where Kathy had scratched him.

Keegan and Pricey had been mates for a couple of years and even though more than a decade separated them in age, they had become close. Keegan, who ran his own trucking business, knew how rocky Price and Kathy could be and tried to calm him.

Pricey did not know what else to do, so he rang the police, who arrived soon after. Pricey told them what he'd already told Keego, but when police walked over the road to see Kathy, she denied threatening Pricey with a knife and she showed the policewoman her bruises.

The police went back to Pricey. His frustration was rising. He said he wanted Knight out of his house. They told him he would have to seek a court order to do that. But it's my house, he protested, Knight doesn't live here, she's got her own place around the corner down by the milk bar, he told them. There was nothing the officers could do. No doubt about it, Pricey was in an invidious position. He was in his home, *his home*, and Knight was there too. He told the police he was worried about his safety but the law was impotent. Until she did something, they could do nothing.

Pricey told his work mates the next day, 'What if I wake up with a knife in my back?' He was trapped in his own home, caught between a dangerous and immovable rock in Katherine Knight and a hard place.

As soon as the police left, Knight, imperious as ever, cooked dinner for the kids and then sat down in the lounge-room and watched a videotape as if nothing had happened. Hadn't she just said this was her house too? John Price was defeated.

It was a crucial moment, and the real beginning of Kathy's cold and calculating plan to murder Pricey. As Justice O'Keefe said 18 months later: 'I am left in no doubt that the prisoner had determined at least by Sunday, 27 February, 2000, that she was going to kill Mr Price and planned the method of the execution between then and the time she returned to his home on the night of 29 February, 2000'.

In six years Price's and Knight's relationship had traced the arc of human emotions and as they had so many times before, that night they negotiated a fragile peace and Pricey retired to bed. Katherine slept on the lounge. He was fond of her, but his fondness could not quell his fears and anxiety. She had repeatedly threatened to kill him or cut his penis and balls off. She was volcanic and unpredictable, and it scared him. His chest bore a scar where she'd stabbed him in 1999. The wound wasn't serious and he let it slide. He regretted it now.

Making a racket in the back of his mind was his fear for his children's safety. Having ensured that Knight was legally entitled to none of his property, Price worried that if he left her, she would go after them. Vengeance is mine, sayeth Katherine Knight. It was hardly a lullaby. A low, persistent level of terror descended on Pricey as he drifted off to sleep.

At 2.30 am on Monday 28 February, an atomic fear gripped Price's subconscious and he woke with a start. In the darkened room he could make out Knight's silhouette as she stood at the

ohn Price, the proud father, walking his eldest daughter Rosemary down the aisle at
er wedding in October 1995. (Courtesy Laurie Lewis)

Pricey, all suited up for Trevor Lewis's wedding. Katherine and Pricey were dancing and Trevor's father said: 'If she keeps going she's going to shake herself completely to pieces.'

(Courtesy Laurie Lewis)

op: Four of the regular fishing boys on a very successful trip to Coventry in ∂97 – left to right: Dennis Costello, Trevor Lewis, John Price and his best mate, aurie Lewis.

(Courtesy Laurie Lewis)

ottom: Pricey with the catch of the day on a later fishing trip.

(Courtesy Laurie Lewis)

Top: This is one of the last photographs taken of Pricey and Katherine together. They were at a family barbecue at Lake Glenbawn with Pricey's eldest daughter Rosemary and her husband and their young children. Katherine's two youngest children Sarah and Eric were also there.

(Courtesy Rosemary Biddle)

Right: Katherine Knight, sitting in the floral armchair in Pricey's lounge room not long before she murdered him, could be as loving as she was violent. Even though Pricey had repeatedly asked her to leave his house and wanted to end their six-year relationship, she wouldn't budge.

(Courtesy Rosemary Biddle)

Top: John Price's body was found on the lounge room floor of his three bedroom house on 1 March 2000 after his boss, Geoffrey Bowditch, rang police concerned that Pricey hadn't turned up for work. Pricey had taken out an Apprehended Violence Order against Katherine Knight to get her out of the house just hours before she killed him. Police found blood stains on the outside of the front door, showing how close he came to escaping Knight's murderous fury. (Courtesy Sandra Lee)

Left: The house of a killer. Katherine Knight's modest timber house on MacQueen Street, Aberdeen, was boarded up soon after she murdered John Price when vandals drove by and threw rocks through the front windows. She decorated with a stuffed peacock and baby deer, and mounted animal skins, furs, motorbike leathers, steer horns and antlers on the walls. 'It is to me a place of death, of destruction. She is not in the garden and growing things. I am not aware there is a pet budgie there or something like that,' a forensic psychiatrist told the New South Wales Supreme Court during Knight's sentencing hearing in October 2001. (Courtesy Sandra Lee)

Top: The now disused Aberdeen meatworks where a sixteen-year-old Katherine Knight first went to work as a slicer and packer in 1971. For the next fourteen years, she worked in abattoirs in New South Wales and Queensland and loved her work. She had her husband David Kellett specially mount her slicer's knives on a board and hang them over her bed. (Courtesy Sandra Lee)

Bottom: It was in this normal kitchen where Katherine Knight had cooked so many meals before that she completed her most grotesque and evil act – cooking her de facto John Price's body parts and serving them up with baked vegetables for two of his children. She left his head cooking in a pot with vegetables on the stove. It was still warm when police arrived. (Courtesy Newspix/Bob Barker)

Left: Detective Senior Constable Peter Muscio from the Maitland Crime Scene ection told Supreme Court Justice Barry O'Keefe that Katherine Knight used three nives to murder, skin, and decapitate John Price and then cook parts of his body. The smaller knife . . . may have been used in the preparation of the vegetables,' he aid. 'The other two were quite capable of doing the major damage to the deceased.'

(Courtesy Newspix/Gary Graham)

Right: Detective Sergeant Bob Wells led the investigation into John Price's murder. It vas the most shocking thing he has seen in his career. 'After doing this job for 23 odd ears, you always expect to see something different, and it was really like a numbing ort of sensation to see what was there, and what had been done to this guy.'

(Courtesy Adam Hollingworth)

Top: John Price's relatives outside East Maitland Supreme Court after Katherine Knight pleaded guilty to murder. Pricey's eldest daughter Rosemary (back to camera) is hugging her younger sister Jackie, as their mother, Pricey's ex-wife Colleen, looks on. Pricey's brother is in the background.

(Courtesy Newspix/Guy Wilmot)

Left: Forensic psychiatrist Dr Robert Delaforce spent 8 hours and 46 minutes interviewing Katherine Knight in Mulawa Women's Correctional Centre in June 2000. He later told the NSW Supreme Court that 'control and power is usually present in crimes of this nature. It is a fundamental feature of it.'

(Courtesy Newspix/Robert McKel)

foot of the bed, not moving, just staring at him. Her arms were behind her back. Time froze. Horror shot through him like a wayward current. In that one split second of recognition his mind screamed: does she have a knife behind her back? Is she going to launch into one of her rages? Price wasn't waiting to find out. He threw the covers off and leapt out of bed.

And just as it started, it was over. Nothing happened. There was no knife.

Monday morning brought the safety and relief of work. By 5.30 am Price was heading east on the New England Highway to the tin shed office of Bowditch Earthmoving in Muswellbrook. His boss, Geoffrey Bowditch, is a man's man, his workforce is dominated by men just like him, no-nonsense blokes who do not scare easily. When Pricey walked up the unpainted wooden staircase to the office, Bowditch took one look at him and decided he'd never seen him looking more distressed. Price recounted the past twelve hours: the fight, the knife, the police, the unsuccessful attempt to have Kathy Knight removed from the house. He finished by telling Bowditch how he was woken from a deep sleep at 2.30 am to find Knight standing a few feet away from him.

'I thought I was a goner,' Pricey told Bowditch. The fear he felt was palpable. Geoff's second in command, Peter Cairnes, said it was only when Pricey saw the back of Katherine in the mirror on the dresser behind her that he realised she didn't have a knife in her hands. Bowditch offered him refuge in his house. Price thanked his boss but said he couldn't leave his home, he was too worried about what Knight might do to his kids if he wasn't around.

'You know, I told him to come and stay with me. He said he would rather she kill him than kill his kids,' Geoff Bowditch said. Later that day, Geoff dropped in on Pricey at the work site to make sure he was OK. Geoff was that worried. 'I remember Peter and I spoke at length after he left and that's why I went down and saw him at the site and I saw him again that afternoon. I was [fearful for him]. That's why I said, come and stay with me,' Geoff said.

Katherine Knight took her usual morning constitutional with her twin sister Joy Hinder. They walked the streets of Aberdeen, past the colliery and the recently closed abattoir where Knight and Joy had both worked on the slicing and boning floor years before. Most weekday mornings, the twins would walk with Joy's husband John Hinder, and the threesome cut a swathe up and down the steep hills on the eastern side of the railways tracks that run down the heart of Aberdeen. Some days they'd walk around the outside of the golf course. At the highest point on Graeme Street, which intersects with St Andrews to form a T, they could look down over Aberdeen and survey all it had to offer. It wasn't much and ended with the Aberdeen cemetery before folding into rolling fields leading to the horizon. They took their daily exercise for an hour, or maybe ninety minutes depending on their chosen route. Sometimes they were joined by others, at other times they took their dogs. They always talked.

Joy already knew about the previous night's brawl Kathy had with Pricey and the police intervention from her daughter, who was at the house when it unravelled like an American drama about a dysfunctional family. It would have been reasonable to think that the arrival of the police would have shaken Kathy a little, but it did not seem to play much on her mind and she didn't seem overly upset. Joy asked about Pricey bashing her and Kathy showed her the bruises on her breast and neck. Blood is blood. Joy told Kathy to leave, she later testified in court. Kathy said she would, but in her own time, and she also told her sister that she was going to the doctors to have the bruises checked. And that was it. That was the sum total of their discussion about the fight.

Then their walk was over. Joy went home, showered and spent the rest of the day awaiting the impending birth, keeping Val company in hospital and running errands. Kathy busied herself with her daily chores and plotting.

Meanwhile, John Price was sinking further into a depression. He was scared. He had a singular problem in Katherine Knight but he didn't have a single answer. Sometime after 6 pm he walked into the top pub and had a few drinks with Anthony Keegan. Pricey was in low spirits when he went home, but the day was about to get worse.

Pricey and Kathy sat down and conducted themselves like adults. For once, they managed to talk and not argue, Pricey told his bosses Geoff and Peter the next morning. The couple charted the course of their six years together and agreed it was not how a relationship should be. But Kathy did not want to move out of the house. Stalemate. He went to bed.

Later that night Kathy answered a knock on the door and found two policemen standing there, asking for John Price. She got him out of bed and he was served an Apprehended Violence Order taken out on Knight's behalf following the Sunday night incident. It was a standard order, in effect for two years – and, like all such AVOs, would have instructed Pricey not to intimidate, threaten or stalk the 'protected person'. As Detective Bob Wells told Justice O'Keefe, the AVOs were taken out by police on behalf of both parties.

It only served to highlight how their tortured relationship spun on its own axis in a parallel universe. Kathy Knight was there when police explained the AVO to Pricey, sitting in the kitchen, but she said they didn't read it out to her, and she didn't really understand what was in it. She later told Detective Wells that the AVO stated she had come into the lounge-room with a knife on the Sunday night, which she said was a 'lie'.

In the hospital interview with Detective Bob Wells four days after she was arrested, she said she asked the police: 'Where's my copy, and they said I don't get one.'

'Do you recall what happened that evening, did you stay at Pricey's?' Detective Wells asked.

'Yeah.'

'Did the children stay at Pricey's?'

'Yeah . . . Everything was fine between me and Pricey, even before they brought the order in . . . There was no problems between me and Pricey.'

She seemed to have overlooked the fact that in the hours before the police arrived, she and Pricey had just discussed how their relationship had the taste of sour milk.

The AVO set Pricey on his own trajectory. He knew she didn't want to call it quits but to him their situation was futile. The fabric of their relationship was a torn patchwork of constant warring, violence and threats, and, frankly, he was fed up.

And yet once again, Kathy and Pricey made their peace and took a few more faltering steps in their clunky dance. He didn't ask her to leave. They went to bed. It was the easier option.

13

The last supper

The year 2000 was a leap year and the last day of the month – the 29th – was a Tuesday. It was the end of the hottest summer in more than a decade and the front pages of the major Sydney newspapers reported that Cyclone Steve was battering northern Australia with 180km/h winds. Fashion designer Akira Isogawa was in Paris with his second ever show in the couture capital; new management at the Big Australian had come on board with a 'blueprint for recovery'; and the $690 million Olympic stadium reportedly was a dud in which flukey winds could swing from head to tail in the ten seconds it takes to run a 100 metre sprint. Sprinter Matt Shirvington was on record as saying, 'I have never seen that before.'

None of it meant a thing to Katherine Knight. She woke up and got John Price organised for work like any other day. The forecast was for a high of 31.3 degrees Celsius but Aberdeen, about 150 kilometres inland, felt hotter. Without a breeze, a shimmering haze played on the horizon as the sun moved over the earth, baking the countryside as it went.

At 3.30 am a baby boy was welcomed to the family at the Scone hospital and it was lost on no one that it would be four more years before the child really had another birthday. His grandmother Val Roughan was there, as was Joy Hinder, Katherine's twin. Around 5.30 am, Joy finally made it home after spending an entire night at the hospital.

Geoffrey Bowditch and his second in command, Peter Cairnes, were talking in the office at Bowditch Earthmoving when John Price came in. Geoff was more worried than he had been the day before and turned the conversation to the crux of the matter. What's going on? he wanted to know. Price told him that the night before he and Katherine agreed they couldn't go on the way they were. Bowditch thought that was stating the bleeding obvious.

Pricey also showed his boss the scar on his shoulder where Katherine had stabbed him previously. 'That was a bit different . . . I was a bit amazed. Probably a bit shellshocked at the time,' Geoff said. Even though he had had the scar for months, Pricey kept it a secret from his boss. Perhaps he was embarrassed that he had done nothing about it at the time.

'He showed us the scar, we'd seen the scar. So she, at some stage, had had a whack at him . . . He hadn't done anything about it, he just stuck a Band-Aid on it,' Peter Cairnes said. 'He mentioned that and said it had made him nervous, and that's why that night [Monday at about 2.30 am] that she was standing there he would've wondered if she had a knife.

'That's the sort of thing that, I guess, made him think that they shouldn't be together too much. He had a scar but he'd been living with her after that [occurred]. And you have got to remember that they mightn't have the same standards as you and I might have. They can get over something like that and be together, and that's just one of those things which might be the equivalent of having a shouting match for ten minutes. You don't know.

'He's a rough diamond and that sort of thing affects different people differently,' Peter said, speaking in the present as if his colleague was still alive. 'Certainly not to you, you'd be long gone, wouldn't you? And me the same, probably. But somehow he got over it and they'd been camped together after that. But it must stay in your mind. There was something on his mind.'

To Geoff Bowditch, the scar spoke of potential dangers ahead. He suggested that maybe Pricey should head north to Queensland to get away for a while, to let things simmer down. Price demurred. He had commitments. 'Mate,' he said, 'I just can't do it. What about me kids?'

Pricey asked Geoff for time off to visit the chamber magistrate at the Scone courthouse. He was obliged to adhere to the rules of the AVO and he wanted to know where he stood, legally. More importantly, he wanted to take out his own Apprehended Violence Order against Knight. The court was his last chance to claw back his life. Geoff told him to take whatever time he needed. Pricey left to get his crew started at Bayswater.

It was just after 6 am when Katherine strolled from Pricey's up the road to Joy's for their morning walk. Joy was in bed and her husband John played gatekeeper and begged off, saying Joy was too tired to walk. Up all night at the hospital, he told Katherine at the front door. Joy could hear her sister's voice but didn't drag her tired bones out of bed. Unperturbed, Katherine returned home and got her children, Eric and Sarah, ready for school.

Katherine drove Sarah to school in Aberdeen, then drove to Muswellbrook where Eric went to school. The day would get busier as her plot was woven with forensic precision.

Mid-morning. Katherine Knight visited her solicitor in Scone, then unexpectedly dropped in on an old friend, showing her the bruises from Sunday night. She also pulled her top to the side and showed another friend the bruises. That friend told Sharon Turner that Kathy had said, '"That bastard's not gonna get away with this, I'm gonna bloody get him". But we all say that when we're cranky,' Sharon said.

Twelve noon. Pricey walked into the Muswellbrook courthouse where Scone chamber magistrate and clerk of court Glenn Dunning had set up shop for the day, as he did twice a month. Country courts are a moveable feast and officers of the Crown routinely travel to service members of the local community who have wittingly or unwittingly gotten themselves into trouble, or simply need the guiding force of the law behind them. Dunning is a seasoned officer of the court who knows how to dispense

advice without drowning it in pompous jargon designed to alien-
ate and mystify those unschooled in the law's arcaneness.
Dunning is of average height and has a pleasant unthreatening
face topped off with a non-judgmental Mona Lisa smile and a
kindly manner. He comes across like a country doctor who makes
house calls. To someone with his first-hand knowledge of the
possibilities of human behaviour, Pricey's concerns might have
sounded routine. Here he was, forty-four and previously
divorced, another damaged party seeking justice and sanctuary in
what the court can offer.

For Pricey, every syllable carried the full weight of his fear. In
plain-spoken language Price said that he wanted to end the relationship with Katherine Mary Knight. He pulled no punches.
This was not a time to conceal or obscure details due to a false
sense of machismo or embarrassment. He'd been living with her,
on and off, for six years and it wasn't always easy. But now, he
said, he wanted to stop her from entering his home. Dunning
listened and explained the process of applying for an AVO.
Price recounted how Katherine had stabbed him a few months
ago, and to prove it, he undid a couple of buttons on his work-
shirt and showed Dunning the scar on his chest. And, Price
added, man to man, Katherine had threatened to cut off his
penis. An interim AVO against Knight was issued on Price's
behalf.

Later, Katherine Knight visited the Muswellbrook police
station where she recounted the Sunday night fracas to a policewoman manning the front desk, mentioning the bruises she had
on her neck and breast. You should visit your doctor, the officer
told Knight. Just what she wanted to hear.

En route to Natasha's in Muswellbrook, Kathy popped in to
Woolworths and ran into her friend Amanda Pemberton, who
had her baby with her in a stroller. Kathy nursed the infant and
exchanged baby talk about Natasha's little girl Angela*. Amanda,
who had recently returned to Muswellbrook after 18 months in
Alice Springs, thought Kathy seemed normal. 'She seemed happy,'
Amanda said.

She drove back to her nineteen-year-old daughter's house
and made an appointment to see her longtime doctor in Scone

at 5 pm. For the next couple of hours, Katherine was with her daughter and granddaughter – a matriarch presiding over the next two generations of females.

At 2 pm Katherine Knight drove back to the Hinders' home in Aberdeen. Joy was not at home, but Kathy was like a sister to John Hinder and she went in. It was the second time they'd seen each other that day. Kath wanted to borrow some videotapes but John told her she should pop back when Joy was home. Katherine left to collect her children from school, the youngest of whom got off the bus from Muswellbrook at 4 pm. Kathy returned to the Hinders, and this time Joy was home and the sisters did a quick trade in videotapes. They frequently watched graphic horror movies together, and between them and their brothers Barry and Shane, they made and shared their own copies of films, some with titles like *Resurrection* and *Jason Goes To Hell*. Joy later testified in court that Kathy and she liked 'murder movies'.

Kathy and Joy chatted about Kathy's plan to take her and Joy's children camping in the national park at Nundle the coming weekend. Kathy also asked her sister for her video camera, which she had left at Joy's because Pricey didn't want her having it in his house. He was firm on it, especially after Katherine used it to get him sacked in 1998.

With grandmotherly pride, Katherine told Joy how Angela had been showering her with kisses all day and she wanted to capture her on tape when she returned to Natasha's that afternoon before taking the kids out to dinner. 'The little one, she was giving me heaps of kisses and cuddles and I wanted to get it on tape,' Katherine told police later. Kathy left for her 5 pm doctor's appointment in Scone.

She did not present with any ailments, but wanted her doctor to record the bruises Price had given her two nights earlier. A preemptive strike. Katherine Knight was building her defence. In his judgment twenty months later, Justice O'Keefe noted that her doctor wrote in his medical report: 'The consultation was fairly brief, she seemed mainly concerned that the injuries were recorded.'

'From a review of the prisoner's history, I am satisfied beyond a reasonable doubt that the prisoner was throughout her various relationships a person who was prone to violence and vindictiveness, malice and possessiveness and to cruelty, and that she was also a person who was anxious to present herself as an innocent victim whereas in fact she was not infrequently a serious aggressor,' Justice O'Keefe said.

Around 6 pm, Katherine Knight returned to MacQueen Street. She grabbed some money to pay for the 'special dinner' she planned with her children that night, collected a few things and then repeated the drive she had taken earlier that day to Natasha's home.

Pricey was inside the top pub having a drink when Katherine drove by in the red Toyota Lite Ace. If she had a sixth sense, she might have felt her ears burning. Pricey was not a happy man. The visit to the court furnished him with the same legal clout that Katherine Knight had, but it gave him no sense of security. How could it? Kathy ignored the AVO the night before when she stayed the night at his house. What would his do? It was just a piece of paper.

Publican Sharon Simmins was in the bar, her husband James was behind it pulling beers for the regulars. James and Pricey were good mates and the previous October had taken a road trip through the western part of New South Wales and ended up in Wee Waa where Pricey showed James where he had grown up. Publicans are one part friend, two parts counsellor and three parts listener. Each day they hear a different heartbreak in a different voice, but the themes are always the same: shattered dreams and fading optimism. Sharon turned a kind ear to Pricey, it was the least she could do for one of her favourites. He drank at the bar a lot, and had never given them any trouble. Any publican would be lucky to have such a patron. With a beer in front of him, a maudlin Pricey talked about his life.

He talked about his ex-wife Colleen and the possibility of getting back together with her, things he'd told his mates before. They were the words of a desperate man who was living in a half-world of terror.

Frank Heap was sitting in the bar and joined Pricey and Sharon. He noticed Pricey was out of sorts and had a scratch on his face from the blue on Sunday.

'I said, "Oh, the red hen's been at ya?",' Frank remembered.

'You're the first one to comment,' Pricey replied.

'I just said, "Mate, you want to be careful, she's going to get you", and he said, "Ah nah, she won't get me". You could see it.

'He was agitated, sort of thing. I don't know, but I think, deep down, he knew himself. Well, he did, he ended up saying to Keego, "If you see me vehicle there in the morning don't bother coming across – ring the police".

'He must have known . . . I think he had a feeling, knew that something was going to happen . . . because that's what he said to Keego.

'He had changed, he was a bit frightened, you know. But she was just that way, you know, and like I said, he had his weakness for women. What happened, it's a mystery.

'She'd encouraged him like she did . . . that's the sick, frightening part of it all, what she done. He should have just told her to buzz off and get away but she had her ways to get him around like I said, he had his weakness and that was it.'

To Frank, Pricey was a 'loveable rogue. Everyone loved him, like I said, he would hurt nobody, only himself, and he did a pretty good job at that.'

~

Katherine Knight pulled up out the front of her daughter Natasha's not long after 6 pm. She had the video camera and made a big fuss about filming loving and affectionate scenes of herself with her three kids and granddaughter. The video showed Natasha's first child Angela bouncing on Grandma Kathy's knee as she sat in the lounge chair, while her two youngest children played together. A voice in the background, maybe Natasha's, can be heard complaining about housework and other things most women complain about – and then there are tears, probably Natasha's, but no one can be sure. The person is off camera.

Kath hugged her youngest daughter Sarah, and in a knowing mother-to-daughter confidence, told her to make sure she gets the pram that her own mother Barbara gave her when she was about eleven, the same age as Sarah was then. It was as if Kath was passing down a family heirloom through three generations of women. 'I love you very, very much, my darling girl,' she says.

A bit later, when no one else was in the room, Kath looked at the camera and said: 'I love all my children and I hope to see them again.' What was she thinking? What was she planning?

Natasha thought her mother seemed unstable in herself. Her mum's strange behaviour got Natasha thinking about a chat she had had with her about sixteen months earlier during one of the offs in her on again, off again relationship with Pricey. 'I told him if he took me back this time, it was to the death,' Natasha remembered her mum telling her at the time. 'If I kill Pricey, I'll kill myself too.'

It was like a warning.

That night Kath treated the kids to dinner at the Muswellbrook Chinese restaurant. Natasha thought it was a 'special night'. Kath rarely took her children out for dinner as a family. She was on an invalid pension and a night out was an expense she could little afford.

Five days later Kath would tell Detective Bob Wells she thought Natasha needed some cheering up because she'd been having man trouble with Angela's father. Kath Knight knew all about man trouble.

Inside the restaurant, Kath and the kids sat at a big table. Kath ordered standard dishes from the stock Chinese menu which offered sweet and sour, sweet corn soup, dim sims, spring rolls and the specialty of the house, steak in plum sauce. Angela was as cute as a button, playing and exploring like any toddler.

But something was wrong.

'At first they loved each other so much it was great, but then things started to change,' Natasha told *The Newcastle Herald*'s Donna Page. 'Pricey was always a good fella but he started to change towards Mum in the end.' Natasha said she never saw Pricey hit her mum – it was more a 'mental abuse'.

'I think Mum was asking me for help,' Natasha said, 'and I

didn't click on. The way she was expressing it was by saying, "I'm going to do this and I'm going to do that".'

Mothers and daughters often share a bond that lets them know instinctively when something is wrong, no words need to be spoken, although, as any mother and daughter will attest, they usually are. In spades. Natasha was well aware of her mum's careening relationship with Pricey that shifted as if resting on tectonic plates. All day Natasha sensed her mother was 'unstable in herself'. It was hard to describe, but it was there.

The red van pulled up at Natasha's after nine-thirty, and the five of them piled out.

'I was watching a video and it was too late to take the kids home to bed, so they spent the night at Natasha's and I just went home to Pricey's,' Kath told police. To keep herself awake, she slipped the video of the kids that she had made earlier in the machine and sat down to watch. Natasha was upset and went 'walkabout', Kathy said.

It was around 10 pm and, out of the blue, Kath asked Natasha if she would mind baby-sitting her younger brother and sister for the night. Natasha said she would. Her mum never did that. She never left the kids without new clothes and their schoolbags on a school night. Natasha walked to the door with her mother and brother.

'You're not going to kill Pricey and yourself, are you?' Natasha blurted out as her mum got to the door.

In his sentence Justice O'Keefe said it was significant that Katherine had left her children at Natasha's: 'The true explanation in the light of subsequent events is that she did not want to go to her own house with her childen, and that she did not want the children at Mr Price's house on that night.'

~

John Price was holding two stubbies of Tooheys draught when he knocked on Anthony Keegan's door across the road from his St Andrews Street home at 8 pm. Keego asked Pricey how he had gotten on with Kathy after Sunday night. Geoff Bowditch dropped in on the way through from Scone to see how Pricey was. Geoff thought Pricey was out of character. 'I think probably enough to arouse suspicion that something wasn't right, but you couldn't have pinpointed it. There was no way in the world you would have thought that was going to happen.' Geoff also noticed Pricey wasn't wearing any shoes because his gout was giving him the 'irrits'.

Pricey told his mates he went to the court to get his own AVO and that he didn't know where Kathy was.

It was 9.30 pm and Pricey went home.

'Love youse forever,' Pricey said as he walked out the door.

~

Aberdeen is 15 kilometres from Muswellbrook down the New England Highway. Around 10 o'clock most nights, there is little traffic on the road except for the 18-wheeler semi-trailers that barrel down the highway en route to their next delivery or pick-up. It's almost a straight run from Natasha's place to Kath's on MacQueen Street, just two right turns and a left and two sets of lights in Muswellbrook – the first on Sydney Road, the next on Bridge Street. Then it's all open road. Rattling along in her red Toyota Lite Ace, Kath Knight was home in fifteen minutes.

It was dark when she returned to Aberdeen. The moon was a half-crescent hanging in the eastern sky, painting it a deep indigo blue. A smattering of clouds cast dark grey shadows which shifted and changed shapes as they blew along. The night had cooled to a pleasant 22 degrees.

Katherine Knight had one last visit to make. She popped in on her half-brother Barry Roughan and his wife Val, who had become a grandmother that day. The women gathered in the lounge-room and quickly watched a videotape of the hours-old baby before going into the family room to chat. Kath cooed over the pictures and apologised to Val for not having seen the newborn yet, but she'd had a busy day. Barry, who sat at the table watching television, thought Kath was her usual self. Nothing out of the ordinary.

He walked her out just on ten-thirty as the new police drama from America, 'The Third Watch', was winding up on Channel 9. Before she left Kathy darkened the mood when she complained about Pricey to Barry, who had heard it all before.

'I've had a gutful of him,' she said, and was gone.

14

Sex before murder

The past forty-eight hours had been sheer hell for John Price. As he climbed into bed sometime after 10 pm on Tuesday night, he figured he had one thing going for him. Katherine Knight wasn't there. It must have been an utter relief. He'd also been thinking about a new future, one that involved going back to the past and resurrecting his marriage. Earlier that night he gave some serious thought to ringing the ex-wife Colleen and talking about the chance of them getting back together, even though they had been separated for twelve years.

Pricey felt as safe as he could; he was alone in bed in his own home, but the dramas of the past two days – and the past few months, for that matter – were playing on his mind. With the sedative effects of a few beers in his belly, John Price fell asleep.

Around 11 pm, the supposedly magical forces of the Apprehended Violence Orders failed. The documents that should have kept them apart were worthless. Despite the heavy legal implications they carried and for all the anxiety they caused, they were as effective as an electronic shark repellent in the Great Australian Bight.

Katherine Knight drove into Pricey's driveway. The house was in darkness. She walked up the front steps, lit a cigarette and sucked deeply. A 25-a-day smoker, it was a habit she couldn't quit. Like her baby brother Shane, Kath liked to roll her own, but tonight she was puffing away on Winfield Blue. She finished the ciggie and let herself into Pricey's house through the front door with her key.

She knew he was home. His white work truck with the word 'Bowditch' painted on the rear window was in the drive, as was his white Ford Mondeo sedan, the same one she wanted to have destroyed as part of her payback. Kath walked through the entrance hall and in to the kitchen and spotted Pricey's wallet and car keys on the bench-top near an empty stubby of Tooheys New. A man of habit, he could be counted on to leave them in exactly the same spot every night, knowing they would be right where he left them in the morning. Kath went to the fridge and helped herself to a soft drink. There were two overturned bowls on the dish-rack, and an upended glass beer mug in the sink. A green electric kettle and toaster were in the corner near the microwave, where they always were. His work bag was open on the kitchen table.

Thinking Pricey might have been asleep, she didn't bother calling out to him.

Kath felt at home – in fact, she believed Pricey's home was hers as well. She'd often spoken about it as her own and told people that if Pricey wanted her out, he'd have to give her $10 000. She went into the lounge-room, turned the television to Channel 9 and settled back to watch 'Star Trek: Deep Space Nine', which had started at 11.05 pm. She only watched a tiny bit before hitting the off button on the remote and going to the bathroom for a shower. After drying herself, Katherine padded down the carpeted hallway and into the bedroom where she had spent many nights during the past six years. Pricey did not respond to the familiar footsteps of his lover and Kath still assumed he was asleep. The humming of the air conditioner filled the silence. His blue thongs were on the floor between the bed and the window, his cigarettes on the dresser.

She quickly put on a short black nylon nightie with buttons that did up the front. It was lying over the end of the bed where she'd left it. She hadn't worn it yet, and only recently picked it up from St Vinnie's in Muswellbrook for $4. All the nighties are $4 and dressing gowns are $5. Kath got into bed.

One can only wonder what was going through her mind.

An easy intimacy takes time to build in any relationship, but after several years, couples develop a coded language for initiating sexual congress. Sometimes it is a word, other times a gesture or a look. For couples as riven as Pricey and Katherine, sex comes as a welcomed equaliser, an act so primal as to mollify a swelling rage. Knight rarely rejected Price and never withheld her sexual favours as a silent punishment when they were at war. On the contrary, they sought physical respite in each other's arms, even in recent nights when the tension was at its height.

Pricey woke up and was sweet and kind in the way he frequently was.

'Where's the kids?' he asked.

She told him they were at Natasha's, and later she told a forensic psychiatrist that she left the kids there because it was late and it was her sewing night the next night, and because Pricey wouldn't let them sleep there. Kathy had said, 'If they went home that night and made a noise, Pricey would get pissed off,' the psychiatrist told the New South Wales Supreme Court at Katherine's sentencing hearing.

He rubbed his hand across her soft tummy, rounded by middle age and loose after four pregnancies. She read the gentle caress as a signal for intimacy and didn't ignore it.

'He had sex with me and I had sex with him. He went off for a pee. I remember him coming back,' she said later. She watched him walk back into the bedroom and climb into bed.

John Price was as unguarded as most men are in their immediate post-coital exhaustion. Or perhaps, because of all that had gone on before, the release of testosterone in that final moment of sex masked his more consuming terrors and fears. As Pricey lay on his back next to his lover and closed his eyes in a sexual coma, he could have been forgiven for thinking that the previous forty-eight hours had been nothing more than a nightmare.

'He was over at Keego's . . . and said he was scared to go home,' Pricey's best mate Laurie Lewis said. 'I suppose I can see her like a black widow spider. She's conned him in and said, "Oh,

darling, let's make up", and all this. And Pricey, being the bloke
he was, "We'll make up, be friends again, that's it, it's all over",
like they've done before. Once she got him relaxed, that was it.
[Pricey would have said] "I'd rather make up and forget about
it". I imagine that's what went on, and she got him completely
relaxed and the next thing – whack. When he's least expecting it.'

The master bedroom, like the rest of the house, was in darkness. Outside the night was still and mild. A few clouds were scattered in the sky, and the cicadas were making the last racket of
the evening signalling the end of summer. The neighbours to the
west, who they hardly ever heard, were silent as usual, having
long gone to sleep. An empty block of land was next door to the
east and the couple who lived in the house next to that, were
away on holidays. Their place was being minded by a guest, who
was out like a light.

Sometime before crawling into bed, or maybe while Pricey was
in the toilet, Kath hid a knife within easy reach of her. Wrapping
her fingers around the handle, she felt its familiar weight in the
curved hollow of her hand. Knight had been an expert meat
worker, the knife becoming an extension of her hand. She wielded
it as effortlessly as a magician does a wand, and she wasn't afraid
of using it.

Without warning, Katherine Mary Knight struck. Finding a
ferocity she'd kept in check until now, she leaned over her lover
and plunged the steel into his exposed body. Once, twice, maybe
three or four times she brought the knife down, smashing it into
his naked chest. Stab. Stab. Stab. Stab. Droplets of crimson flew
off the knife and beaded against the wardrobe on the wall opposite the bed, more blood spurted on the wall above the bed-head,
drops ran down, pulled by gravity. The pillow was spattered with
droplets. Kathy was doing what she had threatened to do so
many times. She was killing John Price.

The shock hit him first. Victims of stabbings often don't feel
the attack. A sharp, expertly delivered knife can slice elegantly
into the soft tissue of the human anatomy, making its intrusion
easy to miss. A merciful biological imperative protects the body
from recognising pain, but in a slow instant, a searing reality
takes hold.

It was like being hit by a train, it happened so fast. As blood gushed from his chest, terror seized John Price and a deep-seated instinct for survival kicked in. He staggered out of the sheets, staining the left side of the bed with blood. Adrenalin pumped through his assaulted body and he ran for his life. But the chest wounds had immediately started to constrict his breathing.

Price found the doorway to the hall and staggered, searching for the light-switch, the fingers of his right hand smearing it with blood. As his heart raced, it pumped sprays of blood out of his wounds, hitting the wall near the light, a telltale mark of the fear he felt. Holding on for balance with his left hand, he smeared blood onto the door which was flat against the wall. He turned left and fled down the carpet towards the nearest exit – the front door. Knight, strong and fit, followed, punching the knife through the air and stabbing him in the back, between the shoulders, and down his torso to his buttocks. Stab. Stab. Stab. Six. Seven. Maybe eight times.

Price banged against the hallway, smudging blood on the white paint. Arterial blood, pumping faster and faster as his panic rose, sprayed the walls around shoulder height. At rest, the heart runs at 60 beats per minute and pushes blood through the body at a rate of 100 millilitres per second, or 5–8 litres per minute. Excited or exerted, its load doubles, working at 120 beats per minute. Panicked, the pace is more furious, maybe three times as fast, 150 to 180 beats per minute – blood would have been spurting out of his wounds, hitting anything around him, and filling his body.

In extreme panic the body shakes and sweats, the heart beats irregularly, the pupils dilate and nausea takes hold, but John Price kept running, closing in on the door 10 metres away, each step more agonised than the one before as his body's pain receptors sent one sharp message after another to his brain.

Knight was relentless in pursuit. The slashing thrilled her, propelled her on. Her adrenalin was surging. She'd been preparing for this carnage for days and now she was the mistress of it. She knew how to do this. Katherine Knight had spent fourteen years slicing her knives through thick chunks of flesh and scraping congealed blood out of cattle carcasses. Guts and gore didn't worry her. She loved all of that, she was good at it and she knew what she was doing.

Her knife sliced through Price's skin and connected with a lung. Gasping for air, Price would have heard a slurping noise echoing in his ear as his damaged organ spewed air into his chest cavity where it shouldn't have been. An excruciating pain assailed him as each exhalation pushed air into his body, putting pressure on his heart and his other lung. He banged against the wall. More blood stained the white paint. His body was sucking in air through the stab wounds, causing pneumothorax, a condition which creates a blistering pain as air pushes down on the organs, constricting them, collapsing them.

Price kept running. A ghastly artwork of tadpole-shaped splotches appeared on surfaces he passed, flung from the tip of the blade as Knight charged, swinging the knife at Price's escaping form. Blood hit the wall forming near perfect arcs as if they were part of a grotesque mural.

Kathy kept after Price. She kept raining wounds on her lover, slashing at him like lightning and hammering deep punctures into him, hitting almost every internal organ except, oddly, his heart. Most major organs, except the skin, do not have pain receptors but the muscles around them do, so each time the long blade plunged into him, John Price would have felt the torture. He was losing blood fast, he could hardly breathe, and worse, without any air in his lungs, he couldn't scream for help. His voice was impotent. He couldn't alert anyone to his torture. He had to escape. He didn't fight back, he just tried to flee. He rounded the corner into the entrance hall. His exit was only a metre away.

Knight plunged her weapon into his neck. Arterial blood spurted, hitting the wall, leaving a telltale sign that a vital artery had been cut, possibly the carotid.

Stubbornly clinging to life, Pricey slumped against the wall and grasped for the light-switch, flicking it on. Blood was pouring out of him. The lower half of one kidney was sliced off. How long had it been now? Just one savage minute, maybe two? What body could survive this?

The knife pierced his chest again and slashed through the lining of his second lung. The blow would have felt like a hot needle hitting a raw nerve. Agonising. Price was barely breathing. He was desperate. He wouldn't have been able to draw any air into his lungs, which were drowning in his own blood. Punctured, both collapsed.

Kath launched a savage blow at Pricey from the front and her hand connected hard. The blood-covered blade sliced a clean hole in his aorta. With his aorta cut, he had no hope. Death was guaranteed.

But Pricey was not going to go down like this. He kept moving, staggering. His bloodstained hands turned the handle to the front door, trying to drag his body outside, holding on to the brown, wooden doorframe. Knight kept stabbing. Thirty-one, thirty-two, thirty-three. Her black nightie was spattered with blood but as long as Price was moving, her murderous obsession drove her on.

Medical practitioners don't know how long it takes for a body to bleed itself out. Five litres of blood from a healthy male aged in his forties could drain into and out of a punctured human within two to five minutes, maybe ten at the outside, at once drowning and robbing it of life. It is impossible to know how long John Price survived the attack but it is possible to know he suffered terribly.

He held on. Pricey was almost outside. He left a bloody hand mark on the doorframe, a testimony that he was propelled by sheer willpower and a survival instinct, but he hadn't escaped. Kathy dragged him back into the hallway, and he collapsed. It was too late. His lower colon had been damaged. Stab. Thirty-five. His pancreas. Stab. Thirty-six. John Price slumped against the wall in the entrance foyer and slid down, blood tracing his path. He was dead. His ordinary brick veneer home had been turned into a slaughterhouse. Blood poured from his body and pooled around him creating a gruesome pond that spread over the cork-tiled floor.

In the silence of the night his lover stood over him, breathing heavily from the exertion and the chase, looking at what she had done. Blood was everywhere. Her new black nightie had tiny bits of John Price's flesh stuck to it. The knife felt sticky in her hand, covered with hot blood that had already started to clot. Part of the blade had broken. She didn't care. This is what she wanted. This was what she had threatened to do so many times during the past six years, and now she had done it.

But Kath Knight wasn't finished. It took at least another hour for her to complete the final strokes of her ghastly masterpiece, leaving the wreckage of her evil on display in an act of the most spiteful revenge.

Pricey didn't have a single defensive wound on him.

15

Missing in action

Gerri Edwards is tall and slim, one of the lucky women in life who have been blessed with the legs and body of a super-model. Naturally attractive, Gerri dyes her hair blonde from its natural brown and wears it pulled back and twisted up in a hard-working kind of way. Gerri never goes by her given name of Geraldine, it wouldn't suit her if she did, and she moves in a hurried, purposeful way typical of a woman with a thousand things to do and a small business to run. When she speaks, it's with a thick, raspy, smoke-filled voice tinged with inherent kind-ness. Gerri owns and runs the Aberdeen General Store in Mac-Queen Street, directly next door to Kath Knight's.

Gerri was up and about at 5.45 am as she is most mornings, getting ready to open her shop for the early starters who pop in on the way to work for the odd pack of ciggies or a can of Coke for a quick sugar fix to sort out last night's hangover. Gerri hadn't been outside all morning but at about 9.30 am on Wednesday 1 March a friend banged open the fly-wire door and rushed in, asking her what was going on. There are a couple of Ds outside, she said, using slang for detectives. Gerri went outside and heard male voices up the side of the house in the space that divided her house from Kath's. Urgent footsteps crunched on the driveway.

She saw a couple of men dressed in blue overalls with POLICE spelled out in orange block letters on their backs, their guns unholstered. They were stalking around the timber house next door. White marked police cars lined the streets, their sirens silent, their blue lights flashing.

'Who are you? What are you doing here?' Gerri remembered she asked, worried. 'You just don't go and do stuff like that,' she said later, recalling how she felt seeing police with guns drawn. Gerri is a pacifist.

'Who are you?' an officer commanded in reply, ignoring her question.

'I live here,' she said.

'Do you know where the children who live in this house are?' he barked, gun at his side.

'I have no idea,' Gerri said. She didn't. The kids, Sarah and Eric, were always with their mum and Gerri assumed they would be wherever she was. She was Kath's neighbour, but you could hardly call them close friends, and she didn't keep tabs on her.

'Have you seen the woman who lives in this house?'

'I heard her last night. I heard her put the bin out,' Gerri said she told the policeman, pointing to the bin further up the driveway. Each Tuesday night in Aberdeen, residents haul their wheelie bins out to the kerb. Wednesday morning is rubbish day.

As she turned, Gerri spotted Kath's red van parked right up the back of the yard, near the rear fence. Gerri realised that Katherine hadn't put the bin out as she had thought while showering the previous night when she heard Kathy pull up around 10.30 pm. She had moved it so she could drive her van in. That was unusual, Gerri noted silently, something Kath never did. Kath was territorial about her property and preferred to park the van on the street in front of her house in what she believed was her rightful spot. If anyone else parked there, she'd have a go at them.

'Kath hadn't driven it on the property for two years,' she remembered.

The police wouldn't tell Gerri anything. But Aberdeen is a two-policeman town and that morning there were at least four of them at Kathy's. She didn't know there were at least that many again at Pricey's house a few blocks away and that blue and white chequered police tape had been stretched across the front yard from fence post to fence post, but she knew something was not right. Police were asking pointed questions about the children.

Gerri was worried.

~

The sun was up and it was just after 6 am when Peter Cairnes arrived at the Sir Thomas Mitchell Drive office of Bowditch Earthmoving in Muswellbrook. The summer had been long and hot, and this Wednesday the mercury was expected to climb into the mid 30s. Peter Cairnes put the electric kettle on and waited for Pricey to arrive.

Usually they were the first two in. Their open-plan office was at the top of a flight of stairs in the two-storey corrugated iron shed which has a cavernous space for storage and is surrounded by a massive yard out the back for machinery and equipment. Peter would unlock the front gates and open the office. Pricey would head directly from his home to the pit at the Bayswater mine to make sure the conditions were safe for his crew to work. Then he'd get on the two-way radio and call in to Peter. If everything was A-OK, he'd go into the office to start the paperwork.

'He would normally be up and about before daylight, and I would normally open up here about five or six,' Peter said, munching on a dry Vita-Weat biscuit, his preferred way of eating them. 'He would normally drop in and say g'day. Quite often the first thing I heard from him was when he'd been around the pit to check that everything was right and that we could work. And he'd say, "Everything's right, I'll come in".'

For a couple of hours they might be the only two in the office. They'd shoot the breeze, have a cuppa, tea for Peter, whatever was going for Pricey, and get down to work. They couldn't have been more different. Pricey was lucky if he was an inch over five and a half feet. 'There wasn't much of him,' said Peter who, on the other hand, is tall and lean and as neat as a pin. He wears his shirt tucked in and his pants have deliberate creases, not military issue sharp, but just enough to show appearance is important. His thick-soled work boots are clean. He looks younger than a man of fifty-five should, and is ruggedly handsome and quietly amiable in a way that telegraphs that Peter Cairnes is a man you could rely on in an emergency. Decent. Strong handshake. Direct eye contact. Softly spoken.

Peter is a self-made man. He runs his own business and contracts his services to Geoff Bowditch. Pricey reported to both men, and by 6 am most mornings, the three of them would have spoken to each other several times. They all had company four-wheel drives – Pricey's was 009 – with two-way radios that were able to get through in remote country areas where mobile telephone signals had trouble finding a satellite to bounce off.

Geoff Bowditch had had a restless night, waking up about three times worried about Pricey. He woke around 1.30 am and the timing makes him shudder now. On each of the previous two days Pricey had confided in him, telling him what Kath Knight had been up to, and to Geoff, she sounded like a dangerous woman. Geoff was so concerned that he dropped in on Pricey at the mine to see how he was going, and joked about living the bachelor life once Pricey got his AVO sorted out. There was little true humour in the joke, but it somehow made the situation easier to deal with. He started to ring Pricey at 5 am from home but got no reply.

As soon as he was in his truck he started calling Pricey on the two-way. He got the 'not home' response. Geoff used the two-way to ring the office from his truck and he and Peter discussed Pricey's absence. All night and into the early morning Geoff had a raggedy, gnawing feeling in his gut. He knew something was wrong.

'I remember that night I woke up at least three times and wanted to give him a ring and I held off till five in the morning to ring him. It was me who actually sent the police up . . . I think he left that much of an impression that [Tuesday] afternoon, that's why I didn't sleep that night and that's why I was looking for him so early the next morning,' Geoff remembered.

'He knew it was coming. I guess at the time – how would you put it politely? – you knew it was a problem, but you didn't think it was to that extent, you knew he was serious, but to what extent, you weren't sure. I think blokes tend to deal with their own problems and probably not exaggerate it too much, to play it down rather than up.'

Peter took a considered, methodical approach. There had to be a reason Pricey was late. He tried to raise him on the two-way. There was no answer. He didn't panic, but tardiness was unlike Pricey.

With Geoff on his way to the mine, Peter kept trying to raise Pricey. He punched in Price's telephone number at St Andrews Street. No answer. Pricey was a creature of habit who dropped in to the top pub for a beer most nights without fail. So Peter rang the pub. It was after 6.30 am – he had no qualms it was too early. This is the bush. Everyone is up at sparrow's fart. The publican answered. Peter asked if Pricey had slept the night at the pub. No, he hadn't, came the reply.

'My first call was to his home, and probably the next one to the pub, thinking if he is not here, either he has slept in, unusual for Kathy to do, and if he hasn't done that, perhaps there was a party on and he fell asleep at the pub,' Peter said. 'It hadn't happened before, but it's one of those things. It's happened to other blokes.'

Peter was ticking off the possibilities in his head. Had Pricey run off the road on the way to work? Unlikely, but still he called police to see if a car accident had been reported in the previous hour. Thankfully, no.

Geoff Bowditch arrived at the office at 6.50 am. Pricey still hadn't shown up. His concern was mounting because Pricey had always been so reliable. He kept trying to reach Pricey on the office two-way radio and again there was no response.

There were a few things about Pricey that you could rely on: he was always about an hour early for work, he was never, ever late, and he was never too hungover to work. 'He was just there, like clockwork. I can't think of a day when he didn't turn up,' Peter said later. 'If there was one, he would have given you plenty of notice, whatever reason. So when he wasn't here, I knew it was a matter of there was going to be a reason.

'It'd be very easy in hindsight to say we suspected all sorts of nasty things, but I don't believe that was the case. Maybe a little bit later,' he said. A little bit later was a matter of minutes.

Geoff was getting worried. Real worried. 'Ring Pricey at home,' he said to Peter, who called St Andrews Street again.

'No answer,' he said to Geoff.

~

In Aberdeen everyone is somehow connected, even if it is only through social networks at the top and bottom pubs or the club, or through routine neighbourly alliances. Anthony Keegan, who lives opposite Pricey, had gone to school with Pricey's son Johnathon. And it was to Keego's that Pricey had fled two nights earlier when he claimed Kath had gone at him with a knife.

Keego has his own transport business and his custom is to start the day early, but not as early as Pricey. At 6 am when he was getting ready to go to work, he spotted Pricey's four-wheel drive up the side of his house.

Keego went outside, headed across the road and strode up the six front steps of Pricey's house. The front screen security door was closed. The curtains were drawn. The motor from the air conditioner was humming and clunking. But apart from that, nothing. Silence. Pricey's work boots were lined up at the front door, beside the mat.

~

Jon Collison was at the yard just before 7 am. His boss Geoff Bowditch and Peter Cairnes were worried because Pricey still hadn't shown up. Jon, remembering that Pricey told him he was leaving work early the day before to see the doctor, thought his absence might have something to do with his health. Peter and Geoff were ringing around looking for Pricey, and Jon called Kath's house in MacQueen Street. No answer there either, he told them.

Peter and Geoff asked Jon to drop in on Pricey to see if he could suss anything out. No worries, Jon said, and he hit the road heading straight for Pricey's. 'We sent one of our fellas up, to go up and find out what the hell was happening because he just hadn't turned up,' Peter Cairnes said later.

No one had heard from Pricey. Many of the men on his crew lived nearby. Peter and Geoff knew at least three in the streets around St Andrews. Two degrees of separation. Geoff asked Peter for Anthony Keegan's number and punched it into the keypad as Peter read it out. Geoff and Peter didn't know that Keego was already searching for his mate, worried by the presence of his work truck in the driveway. Jillian Keegan answered.

'Have you seen Pricey? Is the work truck there?' Geoff asked, trying to keep his voice calm, and explaining that he hadn't shown up to work yet.

'No,' Jillian replied, 'the work truck is there and Anthony's just going for a walk to see if he's there.' Peter thought Pricey might be in the shower, and he reasoned that if his work truck was in the driveway, then he 'hasn't run up a tree somewhere'.

'Is Kath's little van there?' Geoff remembered asking her.

Jillian is a petite woman with a direct gaze, beautiful brown eyes and an open, honest, friendly face. She has the manner of someone who goes out of her way to help you, and she does. The Keegans' house is directly opposite Pricey's. All Jillian had to do was look out her lounge-room window and she had a clear view of the brick veneer home.

'No,' she said.

While they were talking, Keego returned and Geoff overheard him telling Jillian that Pricey's work boots were still on the verandah. Jillian told her husband it was Geoff Bowditch on the phone, worried because Pricey hadn't shown up for work. Geoff told Jillian that he was going to ring the police, which he did from his office before leaving to take care of business. Pricey's crew were at the Bayswater mine waiting for work directions, so Geoff jumped in the truck and drove over, keeping in touch with Peter on the two-way.

'I guess by then we were starting to worry,' Peter Cairnes said.

Senior Constable Scott Matthews was on duty at Muswell-brook police station with Senior Constable Robert Maude, both of whom were based at the Scone station but rostered at Muswell-brook for the day. Forty-five minutes into their shift, the phone rang. Matthews picked it up and Geoff Bowditch introduced himself, quickly outlining his concerns. He asked if the police could go up to Price's house to see if he was there. He was worried that he might not be alive. The call was logged at 7.45 am.

Sergeant Graham Furlonger was the relieving duty officer for the Hunter Valley Local Area Command, stationed at Muswellbrook, making him the senior officer on the watch that day. When Matthews hung up, he told Furlonger it was a 'concern for welfare' call and repeated what Geoff Bowditch had told him. Furlonger dispatched Matthews and Maude to St Andrews Street and using the call sign 'Muswellbrook 15', they took the police paddy wagon. Sergeant Furlonger followed immediately in a marked police van using the call sign 'Hunter Valley 10', denoting his seniority.

The three officers hit the highway. They didn't have much information. All they knew was that John Price had not arrived at work and his bosses were worried about him. They also knew that his girlfriend Katherine Knight had recently threatened him with a knife, so it was alleged, and that she sometimes slept at his house. She had two children aged eleven and eight who lived with her. If she slept at the subject's house, then they did too.

'I took the call at Muswellbrook. In myself I knew that probably something was wrong. Just experience, and the fact that his employer seemed so concerned that he hadn't turned up, and it was so out of character, and the fact that he had mentioned he had trouble and he'd been feeling the way he had been,' Senior Constable Matthews said. 'But I thought the other way, that he had done something to himself. That's the way I was thinking.'

Matthews, then thirty-six, has been a police officer for eleven years, and moved to Scone in 1997.

'You just get a gut feeling, you just get that uneasiness when you are driving to the job . . . We often get jobs regarding concern for welfare where people have rung up and haven't seen someone for a while and unusual things happen. All these things go through your mind when you are driving there – something might have happened and you have to deal with that.

'It's probably the worst job you can go to because it's the unknown. Every other job you know what's happened, whether it's a domestic or a break and enter or something – you know what you are going to find when you get there or what people have told you.

'But where you go into a house where you are unsure of what is inside, it's always the worst job. It's the fear of the unknown. And nine times out of ten your gut instincts are right, but like I say, I didn't imagine that. I thought he may have done some harm to himself.'

Every police officer starting his or her career is drilled on what to expect at a crime scene, and they are told to expect the unexpected. Don't always assume the worst, but be prepared for it, just in case. Years of experience arms police with a built-in radar system for sensing a scene before they go in, like a wolf sniffing the wind. Some, like Scott Matthews, describe it as a gut instinct. Others just reckon they know what's coming well before they've reached the threshold and before they've had to kick down a door with their weapon raised at shoulder height. All coppers prefer it when their radar detects nothing, or at least, something manageable, but sometimes their gut tells them it's going to be bad. The most jaded and hard-bitten cops expect the worst. Always. They know, and have seen first-hand, the capacity for evil that some humans have.

St Andrews Street is divided in two by the CountryLink track that runs from Sydney to Brisbane. On the east side of the track where Pricey lived, it starts with a slow incline before the gradient climbs steeply. Anthony Keegan was walking up the hill towards Ron Murray's place on the next block up from Pricey on the same side of the street. He'd been up for a while when Keego knocked on his door. It was close to 7.30 am. In a few short sentences, Keego told Pricey's mate Ron about his worries, that he'd already been over and couldn't raise Pricey, and that his boss had been on the blower asking him to check things out.

Ron said he thought Pricey was home and saw his four-wheel drive ute in the driveway as he drove past to drop his son at work at 6.30 am.

The 66-year-old pensioner jumped in his ute and followed the the 27 year old down the hill to Pricey's. His truck hadn't moved from the driveway where Ron had seen it earlier. They walked up the steps, Keego for the second time that morning. This time, he opened the screen door and noticed what he thought was blood on the wooden frame. He pointed the blood out to Ron, who sang out to Pricey and tapped on the window.

'We did go down, me and Keegan, and have a look at the front door and seen the blood stains on one of the front door knobs, where apparently he's tried to get out and she's grabbed him and pulled him back,' Ron said. 'But we tried to get in and we tried to look through the windows and thank Christ we never did.'

Peter Cairnes was in the office when the phone rang. It was Jillian Keegan. They'd been over to the house, knocked on the door, and Peter remembered her saying that she sure hoped she was wrong, but there was blood on the door.

~

Sergeant Furlonger and Senior Constables Maude and Matthews arrived at the same time in their separate vehicles. They noted their arrival at St Andrews Street as 08.10 hrs. The first person they saw was Jon Collison, who told them what he'd seen. He showed them around the house, up the six tiled steps to the front verandah, and around the side to the rear entrance.

The doors were locked and an air conditioner servicing the main bedroom was operating. The police knocked but got no answer.

Adrenalin was coursing through their bodies. They banged harder. The silence that had greeted Anthony Keegan, Jon Collison and Ron Murray greeted them. They noticed smears of blood on the outside of the front door, which was locked.

Matthews said they went around the side of the house to the back yard. They spotted a lump of meat thrown into the yard, but there was no dog. They kept moving. They checked the back sliding door. Locked. They tried to force it open but it wouldn't budge.

There was a small gap at the edge of the curtain of the kitchen window, and Matthews could make out the archway between the lounge and kitchen area where he saw what he thought was bunched-up blanket. 'I thought it was an old blanket or something, just a sheet like you might hang up in an archway as a partition,' Matthews said. 'Who is to know, who is to think what it was? . . . I registered it was unusual, I said, "What the hell's that" . . . I probably wouldn't have went into the house if I had've known for sure what it was.'

Senior Constable Matthews wedged a crowbar in between the flimsy door and wooden frame and popped open the laundry door. Jon Collison was told to wait outside the door. Sergeant Furlonger went in first, his heart beating, his gun drawn and raised in front of him. Matthews and Maude stood at the door, waiting for orders. Furlonger shouted to them to draw their weapons and come in.

Between them these three police officers had more than forty years of service. But no amount of training could ever have prepared them for St Andrews Street.

Furlonger, taking steady, cautious steps and listening for noise, walked into the kitchen and dining area. Blood was on the floor and walls in front of him. A pool of blood fanned out before him on the floor of the entrance foyer. It was about one metre wide and two metres long and glistening wet in the middle, with the edges a bit darker as the blood had dried and hardened. Furlonger didn't want his junior officers to look, Matthews said.

A split second later, Matthews looked up and realised that what he had thought to be a bunched-up blanket was in fact the skin and hair of a human. The skin had collapsed in on itself, following its natural folds like a coat hung from a peg.

It was John Price. His entire body had been expertly skinned. His face, his hair, his genitals, his fingers and feet were part of a full human pelt that had been hung on a stainless steel hook in a grotesque display. It was like a sick Halloween costume. 'It was particularly horrific. Even at that point we didn't know what was hanging up against the wall . . . I brushed up against it . . . as we moved through, because you really couldn't get through the archway without touching it, and I remember looking down and seeing blood on the back of my hand – that's when I knew definitely what it was,' Matthews said. 'It doesn't look human. You have to look at the whole picture, you have to look at him, as soon as we saw him the Sergeant said, "Oh, she's skinned him".

I don't know how he knew it was male but he said it . . . he knew straight away.'

Furlonger and Matthews looked past the skin into the lounge-room. Lying diagonally on the floor just through the doorway was the body of what looked like a man. Matthews knew it was John Price but he couldn't tell for sure. The body had no head. It had been decapitated. The torso was raw and, oddly, bloodless. The body's legs were crossed at the ankle, left leg over right, but there were no genitals. One arm had been pulled out and left draped over an empty plastic soft drink bottle. They didn't need to check a pulse to know he was dead.

Police had a victim, but they had been told a woman might be there too. And kids. Where was the girlfriend? A greater panic grabbed them like they'd been kicked in the guts: where were the kids? Police hate nothing more than when children are victims of crime. It sickens them. It drives them. They must have been wondering if this was a multiple murder-suicide.

They had a body, they needed to search the house. They drew their Glock .40 calibre weapons and moved forward. They were fast, following the blood trail on the floor and walls. They all noticed the huge amount of blood. 'I thought, "Well, whoever had done this obviously hasn't done this to himself, whoever has done this is maybe still in the house". That's why we had our guns out, because whoever has done this is obviously not going to think twice about killing a police officer,' Matthews said.

The house was silent. Matthews described the moment, saying it was like he was moving in slow motion. 'You do get frightened or you are not human, but you just get adrenalin,' Matthews said. 'You become more aware, your hearing and your eyesight, every-thing is more acute. Everything goes in slow motion. It has to. If you start to panic and you have got two or three guns drawn in the house,' he said, then stopped. 'You don't want to start panicking or have any sort of reaction.'

No one was in the kitchen, but something had been cooking on the stove and two meals had been prepared and served on plates. Was John Price killed as he was about to sit down to dinner?

They checked the lounge-room to the right. No one there. Furlonger paced down the hall, the walls of which were covered in blood sprays and smears, and Matthews followed, covering him.

The bathroom was off the hallway to the left. It was empty, but grey fleshy matter was clumped over the drain in the shower recess. A black nightie was thrown carelessly over the side of the bath. It was covered with blood and what police learned later were specks of John Price's flesh.

The second bedroom was on the right of the hall opposite the bathroom. It took only an instant to note the two single beds were empty. No children. No Katherine. The door to the third bedroom was directly ahead at the end of the hall – another empty single bed, an empty sofa bed and a wardrobe.

Furlonger, with Matthews on his heels, found the main bed-room. As they approached, they could hear a person snoring. They said nothing, angled their weapons in front of them and looked in through the door. Blood was smeared on the light-switch.

A woman was lying face down, fully clothed, on the double bed. The source of the snoring. Parts of the green sheets on the bed were stained red. Blood was on the wall above the bed-head. Blood had congealed on the wardrobe and walls, dripping down. It was a blood bath but the woman, who Matthews and Furlonger presumed, rightly, was Katherine Knight, had barely a drop on her.

Furlonger stepped closer to her, his gun raised, just in case. He tried to wake her but she didn't budge. He checked and found a regular pulse. She wasn't dead. He shook her. She was coming around. With Matthews, he lifted her off the bed and tried to get her to stand. She's a big, strong woman and felt like a dead weight.

'What happened?' Furlonger asked, nearly shouting.

Nothing. No answer.

'Where are the children?'

No reply.

Where were the two children? The house was empty. The two children were nowhere to be found. They had vanished, if they were ever there to begin with.

Matthews snapped his handcuffs on Katherine Knight.

Immediately, the police assessed what they had: a victim of a brutal, stunning act of violence the likes of which none had ever seen before except in movies and on American news shows. They assumed it was John Price. They had a woman who they couldn't get a coherent sentence out of. They assumed she was Katherine Knight, possibly the killer. But they had no children.

Furlonger and Matthews walked a staggering Katherine Knight down the hallway and out through the laundry door past Jon Collison. It was about 8.14 am. The house had turned into a crime scene. They called for an ambulance and police back-up.

When Kath was brought outside, she looked sprightly, as if she'd just recently showered. Police asked Jon Collison to follow them to the front of the house, where they told him that Pricey was dead.

Ron Murray, Jillian Keegan and her father-in-law Larry were standing over the road watching as the police took Kath Knight to the paddy wagon and sat her on the ground. One of the officers was talking to Jon Collison and writing in his notebook. Jon looked over at Pricey's neighbours.

'We were standing on the opposite side of the road, and that's when they came out and [Collo] just put his thumbs down. And that was it – I knew he was done then,' Ron Murray said later.

~

Peter Cairnes was still at the tin shed office in Muswellbrook. Geoff Bowditch was at the Bayswater colliery having started Pricey's crew. Jon Collison rang in from his two-way. 'He was the first one who told us what they found. He got the effect across that he'd been killed,' Peter said. 'And I don't know if he said murdered or what. I guess the fact that it was in the house that would have been the inference. So whether he said he'd been killed or been murdered, or didn't know, obviously, it was one and the same.' Peter Cairnes was shocked. He hung up and immediately contacted Geoff.

'I got Geoff and I remember he asked over the two-way what I had found out and I think I said, "The absolute worst. You had better come through". So he picked me up and we went straight up. Not that that helped,' Peter said, looking down at his empty cup of tea.

~

Jeffrey Harrington had been an ambulance officer for twelve years and had spent the past five of those based at the Scone ambulance station. A carpenter by trade, he wanted a change and joined the service whose motto is 'for love and life'. He was at the Scone base early, just after 8 am, waiting to start his 9 am shift when a call was placed to Charlestown dispatch from the police radio.

'Query: Code 4. Deceased. Query: Suspicious death.' The call was logged at 08.21.57 hrs.

Harrington's partner of four years, Bob Kembrey, was at home when Newcastle Ambulance Operations Centre rang him at 8.25 am. Harrington and Kembrey were officially given the job at 08.25.39 hrs. Kembrey immediately swung by Scone base and picked up Harrington. They flicked the siren on and tore down the New England Highway at 100 km/h, covering the 15 kilometres, with the sun in their eyes. En route they were mistakenly informed: 'Male offender in custody of police at scene. Query drug affected. Requires ambulance.'

The sirens pierced the morning silence of Aberdeen. They raced up the street. Neighbours were standing on their front lawns, trying to work out why the cops were at Pricey's, and now an ambulance. Kembrey pulled up in St Andrews Street at 08.44.17 hrs. Twenty-two minutes and twenty seconds had passed since police radioed in the call.

Katherine Knight was sitting on the ground at the back of a police vehicle with three police standing by her. She had her head down and her eyes shut. Harrington checked her vital signs.

Police told him several nearly empty blister packs of medication were lying on the kitchen bench. Harrington sent Kembrey into the house looking for drugs. He needed to know what she'd taken before they could start treatment. Kembrey saw the carnage as he looked for drugs. A blood test taken later that morning detected promethazine and fluvoxamine in her blood and that it was well within the therapeutic dose that had been prescribed for her. What she had taken was not going to kill her, but police and the paramedics didn't know that then.

Kembrey and Harrington strapped Katherine Knight onto a gurney and wheeled her to the ambulance. Senior Constable Scott Matthews, who had taken Geoff Bowditch's phone call at 7.45 am, rode with her in the back as a guard while Harrington took care of her vitals. The sirens went on again, and Katherine Knight left St Andrews Street for the last time. It was 09.15.36 hrs.

~

Detective Bob Wells was the head detective for the Hunter Valley Local Area Command, which takes in a huge sweep of the rich wine-growing and horse-breeding area including Singleton, Branxton, Muswellbrook, Scone and Aberdeen, all the way up to Murrurundi. He was based at the Singleton police station. As the senior detective for the past three years, the case automatically landed in his lap. John Alderson, a plain-clothes officer from Muswellbrook, took the call over the police radio system from Furlonger at the scene. At 8.15 am, Alderson rang Bob Wells and told him the situation. Wells told Alderson to go to the scene. With plain-clothes officer Michael Prentice, Wells jumped in the car and drove to St Andrews Street, arriving at 9.10 am.

It doesn't take a detective as seasoned as Bob Wells too long to get the lay of the land. With two decades of police work under his belt, including service at some of New South Wales tougher beats, like Bourke and Moree, he is prepared for most things. Furlonger had already taken steps to ensure the house was being treated with the caution a murder scene requires, so that no evidence was contaminated. He was on the front lawn behind the blue and white chequered police barrier tape that stretched across the front of the house. Furlonger told him what they had, and together they went inside the house.

Wells checked the premises and did a quick inventory before leaving through the back door and making sure the scene was preserved for the crime scene unit which was en route. 'Our concern was at that stage, where were the kids, where were the two little kids, Eric and Sarah?' Wells said. 'I had a very quick look at the headless body, the skin hanging up, very quick look around the kitchen . . . It was a bad, bad brief.'

Wells sent officers Mick Prentice, John Alderson and Robert Maude to Katherine Knight's MacQueen Street home to look for the children. Dead or alive, they had to be found.

'We didn't know. Just didn't know,' Wells said, but his police instincts, honed after twenty-one years in the service, told him they would be alive. 'I thought really, I suppose if she was going to do that typical domestic situation, all the bodies would be in the house. Especially if she was going to do it and remain at the scene herself and attempt suicide, she'd want to be close to the children anyway. Gut feeling said I thought they'd be alive, if they weren't at the house I thought they would be alive. Just off gut and quick thinking, because our minds were racing a fair bit.'

The children were not at MacQueen Street. Police interviewed the nearest neighbours, including the next-door neighbour and shopkeeper, Gerri Edwards, and she said she had no idea where they might be. 'We eventually located them at her daughter Natasha's,' Wells said. 'It took a little while.'

~

John Price's only son Johnathon was sitting on the front lawn of his dad's house when Peter Cairnes and Geoff Bowditch arrived. Police confirmed Pricey was dead. Peter Cairnes shook Johnathon's hand. 'That's the first time I met him,' he said later. It was the worst moment of his young life. Johnathon was twenty-six. He wasn't allowed into the house where he had grown up to see his dad and he didn't know what Kath Knight had done to him. What do you say to a man whose father has just been killed?

Jon Collison was on the road, staring in disbelief. Jillian Keegan, who couldn't raise Pricey earlier that morning, was standing in her driveway across the road with her father-in-law Larry. Geoffrey Bowditch could smell perfume, Katherine's. When Peter Cairnes found out later that day how Kath Knight had spent the early hours of that morning, he was glad the police got to St Andrews Street before him or any of the boys. He was relieved they weren't the ones to discover the carnage, because he wasn't sure what they would have done next had they found Kath Knight lying on Pricey's bed.

The hard men from the bush stood in silence together as the ambulance left, too stunned to say a word. 'They hauled her out on a stretcher,' a shocked Peter Cairnes said. 'She was out to it, apparently . . . It didn't matter much anyway.'

16

Deadly news travels fast

Even before a barely coherent Katherine Mary Knight had been wheeled away on a stretcher, placed in the back of an ambulance and admitted to Muswellbrook hospital with a suspected yet failed drug overdose at 9.24 am, Aberdeen had woken to news of a murder. There is nothing like the bush telegraph in a small town to spread a story, especially one as grisly as this. A lot of people said they just *knew* that Kath Knight was capable of violence. Some even said they always believed she had it in her to kill. It was only a matter of time. She'd been walking around with a storm warning attached to her for as long as anyone could remember. There were a lot of 'I told you so's' and more than a few 'I knew it's'. Gossip had a new currency that day. Stories about Katherine Knight's past exploits were repeated in a communal game of Chinese whispers, changing slightly with each retelling.

One of the most retold was how she had left her baby Melissa on the train tracks after a row with her husband David Kellett in 1976. No one witnessed her putting the child there, and some retellings had it that the baby was tied down. Old Ted Abrahams was said to have rescued the baby girl, but he was long dead, his body found at the back of the Aberdeen Hotel where he lived.

Lorna Driscoll, the storekeeper, swears it's true and says she saw Melissa in Ted's arms that very day. Another story retold was how Katherine had once pegged one of her children to the washing line by way of punishment.

Almost everyone had an opinion, even if they said they didn't. Word of the murder was like rolling thunder, picking up energy as it was passed from one person to the next. Up one hill on the east side of the New England Highway and all the way down another to Segenhoe Street on the west, phones were ringing, tongues wagging, two-ways pulsing. People were dumbstruck. Shocked. Horrified by what they were hearing.

Each day the Bowditch Earthmoving two-way radio network is chock-a-block with blokes organising jobs, cracking jokes and taking pot-shots at each other. It is the surest way to communicate. The morning that Pricey didn't turn up for work as usual, the network was deathly silent. The men had heard what happened.

'If you listen to our two-way system during the day, it's just games all day. It was the quietest I've ever heard it on the two-way,' Geoffrey Bowditch said.

Peter Cairnes said a pervasive sadness descended on the workplace. 'He was one of nature's gentlemen . . . It's just a huge shock and suddenly there is that total emptiness where the bloke was and he is no longer there, and there is no reason why. You just think "Why?"' he said.

By day's end, it would be a rare person who didn't know that Kath Knight had killed John Price, and by the first ad break in the 6 pm news, they all knew how she had done it, to some degree.

Crime is a barometer of social standards in the bush. In the big cities, man's abhorrent behaviour towards his fellow man is expected – even murder, which is now so commonplace that it only makes the front pages of the newspapers when the murder has been most foul and the victim so innocent and unsuspecting. While politicians massage crime statistics for their own purposes – down if they hold office, up if they don't – there is no denying that crime in the city is a constant. It is the price one pays for living in an urban metropolis where neighbours prefer to remain anonymous despite living side by side for years.

It's not like that in the bush. In the Australian mythology of country life, you *can* leave your doors unlocked and your car keys in the ignition. You don't have to worry about keeping an eye on the kids playing in the street. Predators don't cross country council lines. Crime is not welcome in those tiny towns that form a chain of dots along Australian highways and are never destinations but merely a row of family-owned shops and a petrol station blurring as you drive past. Crime dirties a place, muddies its name and permanently stains its reputation. And it had been a long while since a devastating murder had touched the small town of Aberdeen.

It was 1973, the day after the nation stood still to watch 41-year-old jockey Frank Reys ride underdog Gala Supreme to victory in the Melbourne Cup. Frank Reys' gutsy performance was on everyone's lips the next morning and his and Gala Supreme's photographs were on the front pages of every news-paper in the nation, especially around Aberdeen, which announces itself as the 'gateway to the horse capital of the nation'. The same day, a young farmer's wife by the name of Virginia Morse was abducted from her family property at Collarenebri, about 40 kilo-metres as the crow flies across parched country from Lightning Ridge in northern New South Wales. Collarenebri is a long way from Aberdeen, but when it came to Mrs Morse, the distance was purely geographical. Mrs Morse was a former Aberdeen girl. She was raised on a farm in the district and another one further east in Gloucester. Once of Aberdeen, always of Aberdeen.

Kevin Garry Crump was from Cessnock, further south but still in the Hunter Valley, and his partner in crime, Allan Baker, was an outsider. He hailed from south of Sydney but had worked on the Morse family property for three weeks the previous year. Crump and Baker were ex-cons who had done time together in Long Bay jail. They were no-hopers looking for an easy living, thieves who had graduated to murder the day before they knocked on Mrs Morse's door on 7 November.

Virginia Morse was the mother of three primary school children who had already been packed off to classes that morning. Her husband had left to take care of business in another town. As she opened the front door, Virginia Morse recognised Baker instantly. Had she known that he had callously murdered a man named Ian Lamb the day before in the course of a $20 robbery, and had similar intentions for her, she wouldn't have been so welcoming. Crump and Baker forced her into a stolen car, at gunpoint, and drove to Queensland. They raped her and kept her staked to the ground, spreadeagled, torturing her for hour on excruciating hour.

Terrified, humiliated, injured and crying, Mrs Morse pleaded with Baker and Crump to spare her life for the sake of her three children. They ignored her. They tied her to a tree and then they shot her as if she were facing a firing squad. The bullet entered her head just below her eye. Aged twenty-six and twenty-four, Baker and Crump, two heinous and depraved cowards, were playing judge, jury and executioner. Mrs Morse was dead.

After shooting her, they defiled her body, an act of gross depravity the details of which the judge presiding over their later trial refused to let into evidence. In the final hours of her life, Mrs Morse was allowed no dignity, and in death there was even less. Her ravaged body was stripped and dumped in a river before Baker and Crump drove back into New South Wales, robbing homes and committing crimes along the way.

Two days later, they were arrested in East Maitland after a shoot-out with police. It was another year before a Supreme Court judge handed them the toughest sentence possible – life in prison, stamped never to be released – for conspiracy to murder Mrs Morse. If they are freed from jail in New South Wales, they will be driven across the border to Queensland, where Mrs Morse died, to face trial for murder.

Virginia Morse's murder had left an indelible mark on Aberdeen because she was of it. Yet as bone-chilling as her death was, it hadn't happened there. This time, though, murder was on their doorsteps and the killer, as well as the victim, was one of them.

~

Sharon Turner was getting ready to leave for her regular Wednesday business in Muswellbrook. She had a strict routine and liked to stick to it. She tried to be out of the house and on the road by 9 am to be at her destination, parked and ready to work by 9.30 am. Sharon was about to leave when the postman rode up her driveway on his motor-scooter. He didn't have any mail, he hadn't even started his rounds yet, but he had news.

The postie told Sharon and her partner that police cars were all over St Andrews Street outside Johnny Price's place. There was an ambulance too. Neighbours were on the street, looking, not believing what they were seeing. Blue and white chequered plastic police tape ran across the front of the house from the fence to the tap to the letterbox and all the way to the other fence. It sealed off Pricey's house as a crime scene. The postie didn't know what had happened, he was only telling what he saw. Swear to God.

'I said to my partner, I said, "There you go, I bet you any bloody money you like she's done him in",' Sharon said later. 'He said, "Oh, don't be stupid". I said the same thing to the postman . . . Yep. And that's what happened. I said, "There's tape up, someone's been bloody murdered". I said to Mum, "She's done him in, Mum, I bet ya, she's done him in".'

When the postie told Sharon Turner about the police cars and blue and white tape, she was not shocked. 'It didn't surprise me. It. Did. Not,' Sharon said later, stopping between each word for effect. 'I thought she probably would have shot him or stabbed him, mainly stabbed, because she liked the knife, you know, with Molly Perry, 'n that. But it did not surprise me one little bit. But I didn't think she would desecrate his body like that. That was awful. I knew she was capable of killing him. I knew she was capable of that. Any woman that can cut a dog's throat, a *woman* especially,' Sharon said, placing heavy emphasis on the word 'woman', 'get a dog and cut its throat, is capable of anything as far as I'm concerned.'

~

Bill James* was born and bred in Aberdeen. A compact man of impeccable manners and fastidious presentation, he had worked at the abattoir with Katherine Knight for years. His parents knew her parents, and probably the generation before on his side knew the generation before on hers. Bill worked alongside Kath's brothers on the slaughter-floor and he knew Joy Hinder, her sister, too.

'I was told she murdered John Price,' Bill James said later. 'A shopkeeper told me. My first assumption was, and I didn't know there was an AVO out against her, I just assumed there had been a physical fight and she grabbed a knife and hit him in a critical spot,' Bill said. 'And the more we learned . . . for me, I have worked in an unpleasant environment all my life, it was hard for me to believe that somebody would do it.'

~

Ken Knight, Kath's father, wasn't well. His ticker had been doing poorly in recent years and even though he carries just the right amount of weight on his tall frame, his arteries needed to be propped open by a couple of stents to keep the blood flowing through them. Touch wood, he hadn't needed a bypass. Ken, who had just turned seventy, had a scheduled appointment with his heart specialist in Newcastle that morning. Knowing how hard it is to get appointments with cardiac specialists, Joy Hinder and Val Roughan, her sister-in-law, volunteered to take Ken to Newcastle to make sure he got there on time. They picked him up early for the 70-minute drive down the New England Highway. On the way, they swung by Muswellbrook to collect Ken's family friend of several years, Elaine Smith, who went with them.

Ken was with the doctor when a message reached the surgery from Aberdeen. Barry Roughan, Ken's stepson and Kath's half-brother, had rung in and left a message. Someone had to ring home in Aberdeen. It was urgent. Barry spoke to Val, his wife. He told her that Kathy had killed Pricey, but said she shouldn't tell Ken the details because of his bad heart and warned them against having the radio on in the car on the way home. Ken was told that there had been a death in the family, nothing more.

A baby had been born the day before, and Ken and Elaine put it down to the baby. Val's daughter had given birth to a son at 3.30 am in Scone hospital.

Ken, like most of Aberdeen, found out the details of what his daughter had done that night on the 6 pm news after he returned from Newcastle. He was so upset, it would be at least another six months before he visited Katherine in jail.

'The TV,' confirmed Ken. He sat on a high stool in his kitchen, on the other side of the laminated breakfast bar which jutted out from the sink to form a U-shape opposite the green-painted walls and cabinet. A toaster and electric kettle sat on the bench, and a few clean dishes were turned upside down to drain on the sink. Ken was hunched over the breakfast bar, looking straight ahead, folding and refolding my business card. It was two years on, and still Ken doesn't like remembering.

Barry Roughan had been on his way to Muswellbrook at about 9 am when police cars with their sirens wailing flew past him en route to Aberdeen. Barry had seen Katherine around ten-thirty the night before when she dropped in unexpectedly, complaining about 'all the shit with Pricey and how she was leaving and all this . . . that Pricey hurt her that night and she's been to the police and how he's been to the police,' Barry remembered. 'And I just told her to piss off, I didn't want to hear it . . . I did not want to hear a thing about Pricey because I got her out of the house once before . . . I went up and got all her stuff out.' That was after Pricey kicked Kathy out of his house when she had him sacked from the Howick mine. Barry also said that he had never seen Pricey hurt Kathy physically, 'but he played her mentally'.

'Katherine had a heart of gold, it was just the stupid things she done, you know. The way she'd carry on with Pricey. It was just stupid some of the things she done, as I said, she would go and do all this to hurt him and five minutes, she's back with him. That was her life, she hung around with the wrong people.

'It was just the usual thing, they fought today, made up and kissed tomorrow and then fought again the next day, that was their relationship. It was a bad relationship and everyone in the town knew that, you know . . .' Barry said.

'Now, driving down to Muswellbrook, the sirens were going past me in a detective's car. I thought, that bastard Pricey's finally killed her. It was only the night before that she was at our house saying one way or the other, you know. It was a feeling we had that they were threatening to kill each other and I thought, oh, just back of my mind, oh shit, that bloody Pricey's killed her.'

Barry was home thirty minutes later and, within the hour, police arrived at his front door and told him that Pricey had been killed, but nothing more. They informed him the children were missing and asked if he would go with them while they broke into

Kath's house in search of the kids. Barry was worried. Kathy didn't have them with her the night before and he thought they might have been at Pricey's, the scene of the crime. Barry went with the police to MacQueen Street and by the time they'd broken in and determined the kids weren't there, they had been located at Natasha's. And so the job of informing the family fell to Barry.

After ringing a message through to his stepfather at the heart specialist in Newcastle, Barry got on the phone to Shane Knight, his youngest half-brother who was at home at the Rouchel Road property where he'd lived with his dad since Ken moved the family there in 1979. The last of the Knight children, Shane is six years younger than Katherine and Joy.

'I was devastated. I couldn't believe it,' Shane said, in the same slow, considered tone that his father uses. He is sitting on a plastic outdoor chair, elbows on his knees, and holding an anorexic roll-your-own cigarette between the thumb and forefinger of both hands, looking down at the concrete beneath his feet.

'I found out off Barry, he rung me up and about ten minutes later the coppers rung up wanting to know where her kids were,' he said.

'I just thought she stabbed him to start with and the coppers never come and told us anything. Took eight or nine months before we even seen a copper. They never even come to inform us what happened. He wouldn't have even told me anything if I wouldn't't've asked him. He was only a desk sergeant from Scone, or somethin'.

'And I asked him if it was true what happened, and he said, "Yeah". But at that stage I only thought she stabbed him. It wasn't until the news, the six o'clock news that night, we found out what really happened. My old man got home just as it was coming on and he'd just come back from seeing his heart doctor in Newcastle. There was no sleep in this house for a few nights after that. I think it was about two weeks before I got any sleep.'

A few doors down from Kath Knight's house live the Ryans, Kevin and Pat, an elderly couple who had moved to Aberdeen six years earlier. They live in a quaint and pretty white weatherboard house with a covered verandah that runs across the front and part way down one side. Kevin Ryan is a polite, humble man, friendly and kind. He prefers to find the goodness in people, not the bad, and if pressed would probably say there isn't much bad about. Kevin and Kath Knight were good neighbours and often spoke over their front fences. Occasionally he'd hear her getting stuck into one of the kids, giving them an earful about their behaviour. Other than that they didn't have much to do with each other. In fact, Kevin Ryan thought Kath Knight was a decent woman.

'There were a lot of heads together at that time. You would see people standing around and all they would be doing was talking, mostly in the streets, in the paper shop,' Kevin Ryan said, staring out across his front lawn. 'There was talk about it everywhere. I wouldn't repeat it. Some people were sorry for her and some weren't. She has had a problem for a long, long time. I think she had a breakdown earlier in her life and a lot of people knew about it.'

'I was bloody shocked because I was only talking to her at the gate two days beforehand,' Kevin Ryan said, gesturing with his chin towards the front gate that stands under a pretty white archway with flowers trailing down from it. 'She seemed normal to me and everything looked alright to me.'

They talked. Neighbourly talk. 'Everything in general, nothing specific, just the weather. She priced me a pot plant and she said, "I will bring it to you", and the pot plant never got here. It was a white geranium.'

Detectives spent several hours interviewing shopkeeper Gerri Edwards, asking her about her neighbour. She told police that Kath had once told her that she 'threatened to cut his dick and balls off'. Her day had turned into a nightmare from the moment she first saw the police.

'We just had cops here all day. It just got worse and worse and worse and we all freaked out and I couldn't sleep. I wouldn't have thought that any human being could have done that to another human being. If Katherine had've done that, it was an argument on the spur of the moment, but not that methodical,' Gerri said.

~

Detective Senior Constable Vic Ford joined the police service in 1985 when he was nineteen years old and had worked in

Scone and Muswellbrook for all but one year of his law enforcement career. He knew of the Price family, and knew Johnathon. Ford took his statement the morning his father's body was found. Johnathon told Vic about the arguments between his dad and Kathy, and the police being called to the house during their relationship. The policeman also remembered that he'd been called to one of the domestics years before when Kathy whacked one of her exes with a fry-pan. At that point that Wednesday morning Vic and Johnathon knew it was horrific but neither fully knew what had happened to Pricey. It wasn't until later that day that Vic Ford knew the full story.

'The hardest thing out of all that for me was that night I told him [Johnathon] the full story of what happened. It was the hardest thing I have ever done in this job. Because at that stage he knew he had been stabbed but didn't know the ferocity of it all,' Vic Ford said. 'I argued . . . that someone has got to tell him the whole story because it's going to come out in the media.

'So that was sort of later that night, I took him out the back here at the Muswellbrook police station, and I had to go through the whole thing, what happened, the cooking, the skinning. I just said I will explain exactly what's happened because you are going to hear things and I want you to know exactly what we know.

'It had started to filter through a bit. My missus works at a pub up at Scone and she rang me during the day and said, "Listen, are there heads cut off and cooking?" It had all started, being a small town, it had started people talking and that was why I thought it's important he's got to know. I didn't want him going home that night and then hearing all this later.

'And he was just, like, stunned and obviously upset and still all shocked from the whole day – and once he heard all of that, you can imagine.'

Lyn and Danny Buckman were like second parents to Johnathon Price. After Colleen and John Price separated in January 1988 after fifteen years of marriage, Johnathon's mum Colleen moved out of St Andrews Street leaving his dad with the house. The young teenager spent a lot of time at the Buckmans' house on the other side of MacQueen Street and Danny took to calling Johnathon 'young Pricey' to distinguish him from his father, John, who he called 'old Pricey'.

When Danny married Lyn, she already had three children from a previous marriage, and he became an instant father with a ready-made family. It suited him perfectly. Lyn's eldest son was one of Johnathon Price's best mates. They played rugby league together in the Aberdeen Under 18s and were coached by Danny, who was still playing a mean game of footy himself.

Danny Buckman is a miner who has lived in Aberdeen all his life and worked on the kill floor in the Aberdeen meatworks for a few years when he first left school, the same time Kath Knight was in the boning room. But he never had anything to do with her, work-wise or socially. Their paths just didn't cross, except if she was up at the top pub having a beer with Pricey.

'They were at the pub a bit together,' Danny said. 'Didn't take a lot of notice. She was just as loud as he was after a couple of drinks, not swearing, just, like, voice-wise. You always sort of knew that they were there in the pub.'

Even though Johnathon Price didn't like Kath Knight and was not backwards in coming forwards about it, he never said anything to Danny Buckman about the relationship, nor did he ever come 'straight out and [say], "Well, I think Dad's in danger", or anything like that. Because Pricey was a fairly tough man, he could drink hard and work hard, and you sorta got to be a little bit tough, I suppose.'

Danny Buckman was at work at the mine when his wife called him on the mobile around ten o'clock. Lyn told him what she knew, and he asked her if she wanted him to come home, but he added he wasn't sure he could do anything, and he was right. It had all been done. All he and Lyn could do was be there to comfort Johnathon Price and his family. Lyn came home from work, and Danny got home at the end of his shift at 3.30 pm.

'[I] found out what was going on and all I was told was they found old Pricey dead that morning. When he never showed up for work people went looking for him. So that would have been half past seven, eight o'clock, and I don't think anyone went into the house until police got there because there was blood on the front door. Then I was told that he was murdered and I asked where young Pricey was . . . and they said, "Oh, they're all down the top pub".

'By that time old Pricey's brothers and uncles and relatives were sort of there too. I went and seen how Pricey was and he just looked at me as if to say, "What can ya do, I can't do nothing". And as you know, there's not a lot you can do because he wasn't allowed in the house, he wasn't allowed to look at anything. He just sort of stayed down there for a while . . . he wanted to stay with his uncles and things like that. And his sister was there, she'd come down [from Tamworth].

'It was awful for everyone in the town. Just couldn't believe what happened and why it had happened. I think they are only speculating as to what did happen – whether he walked straight into it or he was asleep. You can't stop anything when you are asleep.'

The horror had only just started to set in. That night in Aberdeen, some people locked their doors for the very first time, and then double-checked them.

17

The charge

If anyone in Aberdeen missed the six o'clock bulletin the night before or was not plugged in to the bush telegraph when the news of what Katherine Knight did to John Price crashed through town like a tidal wave, they were left in little doubt when they opened *The Newcastle Herald* the next morning. 'Slaying of a battler' the page one story trumpeted on Thursday 2 March. It was less than twenty-four hours since Price's body had been found. The content of reporter Dan Proudman's tightly written 448 words was shocking.

THE decapitated body of a father of three was discovered yesterday at his Aberdeen house after concerns were raised when he failed to report to work.

Police made the grisly discovery of John Price's body after the 44-year-old's boss at Muswellbrook-based firm G. & T.A. Bowditch Earthmoving became worried about his reliable and hard-working supervisor.

The bush battler, who moved to Aberdeen 20 years ago from western New South Wales, is believed to have been stabbed several times in the attack. Police sources said the mutilation was so severe that dental records would be needed to formally identify Mr Price's body.

The words were enough to stop everyone cold. What had Katherine Knight done to Pricey to warrant the use of dental records? Dan Proudman's story continued. Aberdeen's residents were reeling from the discovery. He painted a picture of John Price as an avuncular bushie, a regular fellow who had a beer and a yarn at the pub the night he was killed. But it offered scant details about what torture he suffered at his lover's hands. As for Katherine Knight, the *Herald* was equally circumspect, stating only that she was in hospital and 'she was expected to help police with their inquiries'.

On Tuesday 7 March, the *Herald* ran a 193-word report on page three announcing that the day before Katherine Knight had been charged with the murder of John Price in a special bedside sitting in Maitland hospital's psychiatric wing. Knight's doctor was also present in case her medical condition deteriorated. She coped just fine. Three days earlier, Maitland hospital's head psychiatrist Dr A. Johansson said she was well enough to be interviewed by police. It was the first and would be the only time she spoke to police about what she'd done.

Detective Sergeant Robert Wells had one chance to have a crack at Katherine Mary Knight, the prime suspect in the murder of John Price, and he got it at 10.29 am on 4 March, ninety-eight hours after she was arrested. He'd been living on adrenalin and mainlining coffee for the past four days, interviewing friends and family on both sides of the tragedy, and building a brief for a murder case.

Wells had also been inside the St Andrews Street house and seen first-hand what John Price went through. It was mind-numbing, unlike anything he'd ever seen in more than twenty years in the police service, and it stunned him, but he couldn't let it affect him, at least not then.

'At that stage we knew that this was going to be a helluva shit fight in court. It had to be done right. The thing was, I wanted to make sure that she was capable of being interviewed, she wasn't under the influence of any drugs,' Wells said, both hands wrapped around a mug of instant coffee. 'We weren't prepared to go at her until Johansson said that she was right. There is no use interviewing her if the interview is going to be tossed out because she was not in any mental state to be capable of being inter-viewed, or under the influence of any medication . . .

'You learn through years and years and years of being smashed up in the witness box by good barristers about that. It doesn't matter how many courses, what they teach you in detectives course, the only place you learn is by jumping in the box and getting beaten up. And you always say to yourself . . . I will make sure I don't make that mistake again, because you don't like to be made a goose of in front of a jury. And that is what their job is, a barrister, to call you a goose in front of a jury.'

At forty-four, Wells is fast-talking, straight-shooting and has a signature walk that is naturally commanding – ramrod straight, shoulders held back square. He's on his second marriage, has five kids, swims to keep fit and doesn't suffer fools, liars, cheats or crooks. Forget gladly – he just doesn't suffer them, period.

Bob Wells knew he only had one shot. Katherine Knight's defence lawyers had put him on notice to tread carefully during the interview or else it would be stopped. Witnesses had already spoken of Katherine's violent, wicked ways, and her daughter had said she asked her mother that night if she was going home to kill Pricey. He didn't want to blow the case before it had even started. He didn't want to miss something crucial in the interview. The pressure was giving him the bends.

'What it was all about was putting a brief together that would block any defence that this woman could've thrown, and the first one could've been insanity, the second one, which becomes obvious by her interview, was that this poor woman has been battered, the battered wife syndrome. So then it was all about getting the nose to the grindstone to negate anything she raised, you know,' Wells said.

'The video at the end of it gives a lot of indication of what she was going to do. It's just the way it was done, even Price having sex with her that night – that's just the way he was. If she come in with the skimpy black gear on and he's half full . . . got his usual amount of alcohol in him, he'll have one more for the road.'

10.25 am, Saturday 4 March 2000.

Katherine Knight walked into a stark room in the hospital wearing a navy blue and white print dress that buttoned up the front with a scoop neck. Her hair was down and her glasses were on, and a hospital tag was on her right arm. She was accompanied by her solicitor, and took a seat to the right of Detective Wells. Her Queen's Counsel Peter Thraves paced outside in the hall. Also present were a male nurse and four other policemen, including Vic Ford, the officer who, three nights earlier, had broken the news to Johnathon Price.

The official interview with Katherine Mary Knight started at 10.29 am and finished at 11.50 am. Wells said he knew straight-away that she was never going to confess. Experience. Cops know when a suspect is not going to change their story.

After the introductions and preliminaries were out of the way, Bob Wells opened the questioning: 'As I've told you, Kathy, I'm investigating the death of John Price . . . I have reason to believe that you may be the person responsible. Is there anything you can tell me about that matter?' Wells asked.

'I don't know anything on it,' Katherine Knight replied.

'Can you recall the last thing that you do remember?'

'The last thing I remember was going out for tea with me daughter and the kids coming home.'

'Can you tell me anything about that?'

'No, then I don't know anything about the next day then.'

'Right. Can you tell me what time [was] the last thing you remember about the previous day, the Tuesday, when you went to dinner with your children?'

'Yeah, I had to go to Muswellbrook for the test, to show the doctor the bruises on me breast, and I asked me daughter would she like to go to tea, 'cause she was upset . . . So we went out for tea and we, I was watching a video and it was too late to take the kids home to bed so they spent the night at Tasha's, and I just went home to Pricey's.'

'Do you know how you got to Pricey's?'

'Yeah. I drove my car.'

'Do you recall going into Pricey's at all?'

'I really don't know nothing.'

As the questions continued, Katherine described herself as Pricey's fiancée and said he was nasty to her and her children and had been physically violent. She remembered the fight they had on Sunday night and Pricey being served with an AVO on Monday.

Throughout the interview, which was played on the fifth day of Katherine Knight's sentencing hearing in East Maitland Court in October 2001 after she pleaded guilty to murder, Wells kept returning to Tuesday the 29th. Katherine recalled making the family videotape at Natasha's, going out to dinner, then coming home and watching the video.

'Can you just take me to the last thing that you actually recall on that evening, which is the Tuesday, the 29th of February?' Bob Wells said.

'The last time I recall was, I don't know about your dates, but I went inside and watched a bit of TV.'

'Right. Was Pricey there?'

'Mmm.'

'Do you, can you tell me where he was?'

'Not particularly.'

'Okay. So you remember going to bed?'

'Mmm.'

'Okay. Was Pricey in bed with you when you went to bed?'

'Mmm . . . He had to have been.'

'Do you recall that he was there or not?'

'I don't even remember meself, so, I just remember watching a bit of "Star Trek".'

Wells kept at it. 'So, you recall going to bed and going to sleep?'

'I don't remember anything, so, I would have had to have gone to sleep.'

'Can you tell me the next thing that you remember after that?'

'Them telling me that I'm in the Mater Hospital.'

Detective Ford asked some questions. Katherine Knight said Johnathon Price hated her guts because his father was sacked from the mine, and said she admitted she stabbed Pricey and hit David Saunders over the head with a frying pan and cut his dog's throat.

Wells returned to the 29th. Again. It was well into the morning.

'To go back to the Tuesday, just past, when you tell me that the last thing you remember is going to bed after the "Star Trek" on television. That's still the case?'

'Yeah. I only watched a little bit and I went to bed.'

Instincts are important for a cop, and Bob Wells relied on his going into the interview and they were right. Katherine Knight had not confessed nor was she going to deviate from her story.

'And that's when the investigation started, really . . . We knew she had this violent nature, knew that she had a lot of boyfriends, we knew that her and Price had a lot of stinks between themselves, we knew that the relationship wasn't that flash, we knew that he wanted to end the relationship but obviously the power of too many years with the pussy kept him there, she kept flashing it at him and he kept using it,' Wells said.

'She kept hanging around and I think he was unable to motivate himself to make the break and I think that's what a lot of it was . . .

'They spoke to each other like they were . . . I would be embarrassed in their company to hear them talk like that . . . I think sadly, he wanted to end it but he wasn't motivated to pursue it, to say, "Kath, that's it, finished, done, I don't care what you say, it is no more". And she was a person who just hung around. And the thing was she just refused to accept it, that came out in the evidence . . .'

Immediately after the interview Katherine Knight was taken back to her ward in the hospital, and Bob Wells was on the F3 driving to show the videotape to Phil Lloyd, the senior police prosecutor for the Hunter Valley region, who would handle the early stages of the case. The burden of the past four days had been slowly constricting him when he suddenly realised he had missed something. The realisation hit him as if he'd pulled the pin on a hand grenade.

'I realised that I missed part of what her daughter, Natasha, said; "If I kill Pricey, I'll kill myself after it". That was what she said to her daughter once. And I realised that I left out putting that to her,' Bob Wells said.

Bob Wells was passing a place called Ryhope and pulled off the freeway onto Awaba Road, which runs from the F3 to Toronto. Sitting in the driver's seat, he could hear nothing but a white noise. His heart was pounding and his head was spinning. He felt as if everything around him had stopped. He called it a crash. For the next ten minutes the seasoned cop took stock and gathered himself. In the investigation leading up to the interview, he'd been in the zone – totally focused – afterwards, he crashed.

'It was a build-up of things, it's not like hyperventilation or things like that, my head was just in a spin, you know, and especially after interviewing her it was a fairly climactic thing to get that done and out the way because we had been waiting to have a chop at this woman for days and when it finally came, and I think time just caught up and the magnitude of what had happened, the magnitude of what the brief was going to be. It was just that build-up of things, that, because of the brief that it was and what it was going to be and what we were faced with, ahead of us. Trying to get to the first base with this woman as far as her not being mad but bad. The brief could easily have been written off if she played the insanity role and the pressure that was brought and all the work that was going to be done and had to be done would amount to nothing . . . and in the end you think to yourself, I don't want it all to come to an anticlimax.'

Bob Wells showed Phil Lloyd the videotape. He had missed it, but it wasn't a lost cause. Lloyd said that on Monday when Katherine Knight would be officially charged in front of a magistrate with her barrister, they would address the issue.

'We would type up a short screed: Your daughter, Natasha Kellett, made a statement to police. Amongst other things, Natasha said on one occasion after you and Pricey got back together again, after a split up, that you said something like, "If I kill Pricey, I will kill myself after it",' Bob Wells said. 'Would you care to comment about that? You are not obliged to comment unless you wish to do so, any comment made by you may be submitted as part of the brief against you, do you understand that? Her answer was "I don't know". She signed it K.M. Knight, 6/3/2000.'

Out in the back yard at the Lloyds, Phil put his hand on Bob's shoulder. He could tell his mate was carrying an enormous load. At home that night, sitting on the bed next to his wife, Bob Wells broke down sobbing. 'Wondering what this woman had done to this man.'

On the morning of 6 March 2000, Maitland Local Court magistrate Richard Wakely convened his court in a nondescript, windowless conference room known as the Tribunal Room in

Maitland hospital's psychiatric wing. He is familiar with it. Each Friday he holds mental health hearings there for patients wanting to know if they qualify as well enough to be discharged, but that Monday was the first time in his seven years on the bench as a magistrate that Wakely used it for a criminal matter. The walls were bare. There was no clock. A folded-up wheelchair leaned against a corner, as it always does in case a patient needs assistance being removed. Wakely sat at a large table with an empty whiteboard behind him, left for when the room was being used for medical conferences.

Katherine Knight came in with her barrister Peter Thraves and his assisting solicitor. Detective Bob Wells took a seat on a row of chairs in front of the table next to police prosecutor Phil Lloyd. A clerk of court sat nearby, recording the proceedings. A doctor was in attendance, just in case Miss Knight felt unwell. All up, there were eight people around the makeshift courtroom. It was crowded and stifling, but not uncomfortable.

Without much ceremony, Magistrate Wakely announced that he had convened Maitland Local Court in the Tribunal Room and called to order what is known as a 'special bedside sitting' (even though it was not held at her bedside). After accepting appearances from Peter Thraves and Phil Lloyd on opposite sides of the legal system, Magistrate Wakely read out the two charges against Katherine Knight: That sometime between February 29, 2000 and the early hours of March 2nd, 2000, she did murder one John Charles Thomas Price of St Andrews Street, Aberdeen. That sometime between February 29, 2000 and the early hours of March 2nd, 2000, she had improperly interfered with his body.

Phil Lloyd then presented the magistrate with a short resume of the facts of the murder and indicated that the accused still needed treatment.

Katherine Knight did not enter a plea. She was not compelled to do so. And because it was a murder case, there was no presumption for bail, which was formally refused even though her barrister Peter Thraves had not asked for it. It was a matter of procedure. Magistrate Wakely then ordered that she be remanded in custody for full psychiatric evaluation at Mulawa Women's

Correctional Centre. It was over in twenty minutes, and Katherine sat in total silence throughout the hearing.

'She was controlled. It was chilling. She was controlled,' Phil Lloyd recalled. 'To my lay mind, well, it's just not normal to be capable of generating that kind of demeanour in the wake of such horrendous conduct. She is not like anyone else I have ever seen or anyone else I care to encounter again.'

There is something uniquely repellent about the phrase 'improperly interfering with a body', and the very fact that such a charge exists is even more repulsive, a shameful indictment of the depravity and the capacity for evil that some people have.

Evil is a slippery, elusive subject, a concept so innately ugly and confronting that many people prefer to dismiss as abnormal or sick the kinds of acts with which Katherine Knight had been charged. For many, defiling a corpse, decapitation, sexual sadism, torture and cannibalism are too disgusting to accept for what they are – the dark side of human behaviour. People capable of plumbing those depths, some might argue, have got to have something wrong with them. It's easier to deal with them if they and their perversions can be categorised as abnormal or sick. It offers a glimmer of hope that they can be made normal and well again.

But the reality is that evil people do exist, and they do unspeakable things for their own perverse gratification. They kill, maim, rape, brutalise and torture, and they do those things simply because they enjoy it and get a sexual charge out of it. They do it because they can. Philosophers have long debated whether a person is born evil – the bad seed – or whether evil is learned behaviour, driven by circumstance, geography and experience. Biology versus psychology. There is no consensus. Philosophers and psychiatrists may disagree, but police, prosecutors, and priests all believe that evil is not an intangible concept. They know because they have seen it. Some people are just plain evil and do evil things.

John Douglas, a former special agent in the FBI's groundbreaking Behavioural Sciences Unit at its Virginia headquarters, spent years questioning murderers and serial killers to work out what makes them tick. In his book *Journey Into Darkness*, he writes that he and his partner Jim Wright 'live every day with the certain knowledge of people's capacity for evil. Serial killers and sexual predators, the type of people I have spent most of my career hunting and studying . . . do it because it feels good, because they want to, because it gives them satisfaction.'

'It almost defies description what one person can do to another,' Jim Wright said. 'What a person can do to an infant; to a child less than a year old; the evisceration of women, the dehumanisation process they go through.'

American forensic psychiatrist Robert I. Simon in his book *Bad Men Do What Good Men Dream* argues 'the dark side exists in all of us'. The fundamental difference that divides the good from the bad is that good people do not act on their darker fantasies, bad people do. They 'translate dark impulses into dark actions'.

In his definitive book *Signature Killers*, Robert Keppel distinguishes between a murderer who kills in the commission of a crime, such as a bank robbery gone wrong, and the 'signature killer', for whom degradation, humiliation and murder are the desired outcomes. The homicide is deliberate and not the by-product of another crime. A signature killer keeps trophies of the murder and uses a unique 'signature' that is his, or her, trademark. According to Keppel, their calling card at the crime scene, their signature, is to be found in how they mutilated or manipulated their victim and the dead bodies, and what they did with the corpse, where they left it or dumped it.

Signature killers are after sexual gratification, and they get it from their crimes. For many, an integral part of the process is returning to the place where they committed the murder, out of guilt or because it thrills them remembering the murder. Some move the corpse, or sexually explore the dead body, and all feel they must have control over the victim, whether dead or alive. 'What separates the signature killer from the dysfunctional person who doesn't kill? Nothing more than a choice, nothing more than a decision about how selfish to be at any given moment,' Keppel writes.

For investigators like John Douglas, Jim Wright and Robert Keppel, evil exists, and as the number of victims rises with each new year, none of them are optimistic about the future. The criminals they deal with are determined and deliberate, their crimes beyond barbaric. The behaviour they see is learned and refined over the years. What they do, Robert Keppel said, is 'a learned response, a choice, you are learning about things that make you feel good, so you are constantly trying'.

John Douglas believes evil is hard-wired into a person's nature and refers, by way of explanation, to an analogy used by a fellow FBI agent that changes slightly in the country of telling:

You've baked this chocolate cake which smells great and looks terrific, but as soon as you bite into it you realise something is very wrong. Then you remember that you mixed in some axle grease with the milk, eggs, flour, butter and cocoa.

If I can just figure out a way to get the axle grease out of the cake, it will be perfectly fine to eat. The fact of the matter is that in the vast majority of cases, the urges, the desires, the character disorders that make them hurt and kill innocent men, women and children are so deeply ingrained in the recipe of their makeup that there is no way to get out the axle grease.

18

The skinning

Peter Muscio sees dead people. He joined the New South Wales Police Service crime scene unit as an investigator in May 1991. He's a stocky fellow with dark brown eyes and brownish-auburn hair. Before joining the police, Muscio was an industrial chemist employed by BHP in the steel chemistry laboratory, mainly working on water chemistry and electrical instrumentation.

While in the police service, he studied for a Diploma in Applied Sciences majoring in forensic studies. Science is empirical data and, unlike humans, it doesn't lie. As a crime scene investigator, it is Muscio's job to piece together the facts from the grisly evidence before him. To let dead men talk.

He has, by his own count, dealt with about seven hundred bodies, all victims of one crime or another.

Peter Muscio arrived at John Price's house in St Andrews Street at 10 am on the first day of March 2000. In his nine years with the crime scene unit, Detective Senior Constable Muscio had seen a lot of things, but nothing could compare with what he would see that day. Like the other officers who went in before him, the images would stay with him forever.

Peter Muscio was sound asleep in bed when his phone rang at 1 am on 1 March. The time meant nothing to him, but looking back on it, he wondered about the coincidence. He was told there had been a fire at Toyota in Maitland. He dragged himself out of bed and drove to the scene. Arson. The fire had been controlled, Muscio determined no one had been injured or killed and he decided to return at daylight to investigate. At 8 am he and his boss, Detective Sergeant Neil Raymond, were at the scene. Sometime in the next hour, his mobile phone rang.

Muscio quickly got a sense of what was ahead. A male victim had been decapitated. A murder. He was told to leave the arson crime and head straight to St Andrews Street, Aberdeen. Muscio was thirty-nine years old. His victim was just five years older than him. En route, he was told the body had been skinned, and then he called the crime scene video unit to meet him at the house.

Bob Wells met Muscio and Raymond on the front lawn at John Price's home. Sergeant Furlonger and Senior Constable Mick Prentice were with him. They huddled in a circle as Wells briefed Muscio and Raymond on what was inside the house. The information would spare them the shock suffered by officers Furlonger, Matthews and Maude. 'The pre-warning by Bob Wells was a big plus, I wouldn't have liked to be Graham Furlonger or Scottie Matthews, because they just walked in cold,' Muscio said.

The two crime scene police suited up, pulling on blue disposable overalls with Forensic Services spelled out on the back. They slipped the throwaway cover-alls over their work boots, not wanting to contaminate the crime scene. Muscio took a Polaroid camera.

Bob Wells led them around the side of the house. Muscio checked off what he saw: three vehicles, all white, two four-wheel drives and a sedan. Two galvanised iron garden sheds, one in each rear corner of the back yard. A brick barbecue up against the eastern boundary. He noticed small things. Habit. His senses are trained to observe things most humans miss. Investigators file inconsequential details at the back of the mind, to retrieve later when they need help to crack a case.

Then, something unusual. Prentice pointed out a piece of cooked meat on the lawn in front of the white car. Muscio remembered that he didn't know what it was and told Prentice he'd come back to it.

Bob Wells went through the back door first. Muscio and Raymond went next. The instant they walked through the laundry,

Peter Muscio detected a smell. A body had been in the house for several hours. Mutilated corpses left exposed for a long period of time develop a certain stench. But strangely, it wasn't the hard odour of death that Muscio noticed. Rather, it was the familiar smell of cooking, like a casserole. It was a perverse irony. Muscio was at a crime scene and what was there also bore all the hallmarks of one of the most violent crimes imaginable. And yet, the house smelled so, well, so *homey*.

Once inside the house Muscio saw what the other officers saw, the skin hanging to the floor and the debrided torso. He knew it was John Price. For Muscio, the scene spoke of vengeance.

The victim was lying on an angle with his legs, from the knees down, jutting out into the entry foyer under a bricked archway. The top of his headless body was at the foot of a functional grey armchair which had bloody hand-prints on the arms and back. An open packet of Winfield Blue cigarettes was on the seat cushion, next to a sharpening steel, the kind you see hanging from a butcher's apron. It was a macabre and spitefully deliberate sight.

John Price had been carefully posed, as if, in any other circumstance, he were lying on his back ready to watch the footy. His legs were crossed, his left ankle over his right. It was symbolic, an act of defilement and contempt. The wrist of his left arm was draped casually over an empty plastic bottle of soft drink, Shelley's Club Lemon Squash. The lid was screwed on. A cigarette butt had been dropped carelessly on the carpet on John Price's right. More than twelve hours later, parts of the debrided torso had started to yellow as the air affected it and the crimson of the exposed muscle seemed to darken.

A few inches away was a bloodstained knife, 31.5 centimetres long from its yellow plastic handle to its sharp steel tip. The blade was 17.5 centimetres long. A later examination would reveal that some of the blade edge had been broken off.

The furniture was arranged as it would be in any house lacking ostentation. There was a floral three-seater couch against one wall, three more armchairs, one in each corner of the room, a slow combustion heater for cold winter nights, and a coffee table. A large display cabinet on the other side of the doorway to the kitchen housed the television, positioned directly opposite the three-seater. A smaller cabinet was butted up next to it. Lying face up on top were two picture frames. They had been smashed.

'I remember walking down the hallway [and at] about shoulder height there were all these blood spatter marks on the walls. To me, it's indicative of each attack . . . He's absolutely fighting for his life,' said Muscio. 'The bloke's just had a bonk in the bed and then wakes up, then stab, stab, stab. He's getting up, there is arterial spurting on the robe and the bed, and on the doorway there's a bloodied handprint or swipe on the western side of the door near the dressing table, and blood around the light switch. It looks like he's tried to turn the light switch on. And then all down the hallway, they're everywhere. And he's almost made it, he's opened the front door, the screen door is shut, there is blood staining, trajectory again, flicking out across the front door, he's almost made it . . . but he wouldn't have survived.

'He had initial fears for her and that's why he didn't want to go home in the first place and all his worst fears have come to reality . . . He would be absolutely horrified, terrified – probably terrified more than horrified – trying to get out and all the time being stabbed.'

Muscio took Polaroid images of the crime scene, then he and Raymond walked out the same way they had come in.

Sometime in the previous twelve hours, as the blood drained from the wounds in John Price's ravaged body, pooling around him, Katherine Knight had gathered the implements of her destruction: a stainless steel meat-hook, two smaller knives in addition to the one she had used to kill him, a sharpening steel and a Norton sharpening block.

She grabbed hold of John Price's right arm and dragged him about a metre from the front foyer through the pool of blood, onto the carpet in the lounge-room. She laid his head on the carpet near the foot of the grey armchair. An outline of blood traced Pricey's head as it settled into the carpet.

Kathy lit a cigarette and inhaled, leaving the packet of Winfield Blue on the chair. She removed Pricey's watch from his wrist and smashed it down on a framed photograph of his son Johnathon on the bureau along the wall, breaking the glass. Another frame with a photograph of Pricey's younger daughter Jackie had been broken and was lying face up on top of a bloodstained, hand-written note with vindictive references to Johnathon, Jackie and Pricey, left by Katherine. The contents of the note would later be suppressed by the judge in court. When Muscio and Raymond collected evidence the next day, they noted the watch was covered with blood, and the note had small pieces of flesh on it.

No one knows what was going through Katherine Knight's mind as she gave life to her monstrosity. Knight would tell police and several psychiatrists that she could not remember what happened, or anything at all of what she did. The police didn't believe her, nor for the most part did the judge at her sentencing hearing.

Bob Wells was unequivocal. He thought Katherine Knight was faking her memory loss. He's interviewed enough crooks to know when they're lying, he said. It's in their eyes. It's a look they give. 'And that's when you catch her eye and I'd say "ah fuck, this sheila is just stringing you along". But we'll play your game, play their game, and at the end of the show, we will see what we can get out of the wreck.'

Katherine Knight was variably diagnosed with dissociative amnesia. The psychiatrists who treated and examined her in jail for her trial were divided, not equally, on whether they believed her and how much they believed of what she told them.

Dissociative amnesia is a recognised mental disorder included in the American Psychiatric Association's Diagnostic and Statistical Manual of Mental Disorders, Fourth Edition, Text Revision (otherwise known as DSM-IV-TR). The DSM-IV is a handbook used by psychiatrists to classify whether a patient is suffering from a mental disorder or disorders, as many often suffer more than one at the same time. In the medical, psychiatric and legal worlds, dissociative amnesia is a complex issue. Not all psychiatrists agree it is a legitimate mental disorder. Psychiatry is an organic subject, not a precise science. A handful of doctors examining the same patient, for example, may not arrive at consensus with a diagnosis.

Under the DSM-IV classification, a person suffering from dissociative amnesia experiences a 'marked but reversible impairment of recall of important personal information or experience, usually involving emotional trauma . . . The symptoms cause clinically significant distress or impairment in social, occupational, or other important areas of functioning'. Its essential feature is an inability to recall important personal information, usually of a traumatic or stressful nature, that is too extensive to be explained by normal forgetfulness.

Len Lambeth is a highly polished man who is a wing commander in the Royal Australian Air Force Reserve. He's been a doctor, a surgeon and is now a consultant psychiatrist to the Air Force and a forensic psychiatrist in private practice who has a passion for aviation and flying in F-111s and F-18s.

Dr Lambeth was brought on board by the defence lawyers to examine Katherine Knight's psychiatric condition. Lambeth, who spent three hours and fifty minutes interviewing Katherine in Mulawa Women's Correctional Centre in September 2001, diagnosed her as having borderline personality disorder, post traumatic stress disorder, and dissociative amnesia.

Dr Lambeth believed it possible that Katherine Knight had been amnesic about the events on the night of the murder, he told the New South Wales Supreme Court on 31 October 2001. 'As to when that amnesia began, I could not say,' he testified.

Knight's lawyer, Mr Thraves, QC, said: 'It's not abnormal in your experience for people to be amnesic after the traumatic event of committing a murder, is it?'

'No, it's not.'

'In your dealings with the prisoner . . . have you come across anything which would incline you to believe that she is in fact feigning amnesia?'

'Not in my dealings, no.'

Katherine Knight said she can't remember what happened on the night she murdered John Price. But, she can remember some things right up until moments before she plunged the knife into him. She remembered sitting down and watching television. She remembered having sex with him, although she didn't tell police this. That was 'pleasurable', she said. And she remembered Pricey getting out of bed to go for 'a pee'. But that's it.

Dr Robert Delaforce is a forensic psychiatrist who spent eight hours and forty-six minutes examining Katherine Knight over two days at Mulawa Women's Correctional Centre before she was scheduled to stand trial for murder. He was called in by the prosecution, with the consent of Knight's own lawyers.

Katherine Knight told Delaforce the same story: that she could not remember what happened.

In court later Dr Delaforce said: '. . . The indications are that she remembers more than she admits and I have a lot of suspicion about her claim of amnesia after the event . . . Amnesia after the murder is quite common, some reports have it up to 65 per cent of cases.'

Criminals can be canny.

But, as the psychiatrist pointed out, Katherine did tell him she and Pricey had 'pleasurable sex' and that she slipped into her new black nightie for the occasion which, he said, introduced the possibility of an element of sexual sadism and narcissism. 'Imagine that, you know, sex that night if she had planned to do that.'

~

It was after midnight on 29 February, and although John Price was dead, Katherine Knight hadn't finished with him just yet.

She pushed a knife into his corpse, just under the collarbone. It would have met with slight resistance from the skin, but with a sharp blade Katherine was able to slice horizontally across the top of his body, from shoulder to shoulder, right under the clavicles. It was a straight, clean cut, anatomically precise. She then turned and cut the knife down his chest and over his stomach to his pubic hair line. She had made a T with another straight line.

Tracing the knife tip around his pubic area and careful not to cut his penis or genitals, Katherine Knight cut down the front of John Price's thighs, over the knees and to his feet. It was horrible work, gruesome and bloody. But nothing that she hadn't seen done before to animals in the abattoir. In fact, it was as if Katherine Knight had taken herself back to the boning room at the meatworks she left fifteen years ago.

She moved up his body, held his arms up and cut down the back of each one. Skilful, precise. Katherine cut across the top of her dead lover's head. A small piece of skin with hair on it was tossed on the carpet, and would be found the next day by police. With the incisions complete, Katherine Knight then peeled John Price's skin off, including his head, his hair, his face and all the way down the length of his body to his feet. When the skin was removed some of the stab wounds were clearly visible, and part of John Price's intestines were exposed.

It was barbaric. But Katherine Knight was not content. She wasn't through with her evil just yet. Before the night was out, she retrieved a stainless steel meat-hook, about 10 centimetres long, and pushed one pointed scoop of the S-hook through his curls which were stiffening with blood and got ready to hang John Price's curtain of skin – what police and lawyers called the human pelt. She hoisted the skin up and attached the top of the hook to the architrave on the archway leading from the lounge-room to the kitchen and dining room.

If anyone had been looking through the drawn curtains on the window, they might have seen what they thought was a silhouette of a macabre dance illuminated by the overhead kitchen light. There, swinging from the hook like it was an animal carcass at the abattoir, was the human form of John Price. His entire skin was in one piece including his hair, face, ears, nose, mouth and genitals. His feet touched the floor. Blood dripped down his skin. Slashes and stab holes tore through the human pelt, a testimony to the wounds he suffered before dying.

Eighteen months later. October 2001. The barrister driving the murder trial against Katherine Knight was Mark Macadam, a Queen's Counsel with twenty-five years experience as a prosecutor for the Crown. He was eighteen months away from retirement. His offsider was Kylie Henry, an attractive and petite brunette who had joined the Director of Public Prosecutions in April 1998.

Forensic pathologist Timothy Lyons was the first witness to take the stand at Knight's sentencing hearing which had started on 18 October 2001. Dr Lyons was sworn in at 12.08 pm on 23 October. By then he had performed more than 5000 autopsies in his career, including the one on John Price. He was the chief pathologist at Port Arthur when gunman Martin Bryant murdered 35 innocent people in 1996.

Prosecutor Macadam wanted to know how difficult it was to skin a human being and how long such an endeavour might take: 'Doctor, in your experience of years of attending at crime scenes and the like, I imagine that even in your past experience you would never have come across a case such as this before?' Mr Macadam said.

'I have never seen such an unusual a case as this before,' Dr Lyons replied, his voice still carrying an English accent despite years of living in Australia.

'Doctor, so far as the skinning of the body was concerned, whilst I appreciate of course that this is not something that is often even considered or looked at as the ordinary course of experience, certainly I presume even in your vast experience, you have little to go on in terms of the skill or otherwise that would be required for that to be done,' the prosecutor said to the forensic pathologist. 'But are you able to just express any opinion as to whether or not it would require some degree of expertise in terms of at least dealing with skin and bodies to get it off?'

'Only in the most general terms from one's experience in the autopsy room,' Dr Lyons replied. 'I can say to you I think it would not have taken just a few minutes, but it is something that could have probably been completed within thirty minutes to an hour.' He came to this conclusion based on 'certain dissection techniques' he performed every day during autopsies.

He said John Price's skin had been removed in virtually one piece, and he estimated it weighed 20–25 per cent of his total weight. Timothy Lyons said what was left of John Price's body weighed 70 kilograms.

'The skin component was to all intents and purposes the entire body, including the head. So the sequence of events must have been the skinning and then decapitation,' Lyons said.

John Price was dead and his human pelt removed from his body. Katherine Knight picked up the knife. She went to his bloody corpse and looked at the grotesque vision of his skinned face. She would have had to hold on to part of what was left of John Price for leverage, then, taking the knife, she cut off his head, clean at the C3-C4 junction, right at the top of the shoulders.

She had used a very sharp knife. The cut was clean and precise. Lyons noted in his report on the autopsy, conducted on 2 March at the city morgue in Newcastle, that there were 'no obvious marks in the adjacent bony aspect of the vertebral bodies . . . (all) transected cleanly, leaving an incised type wound'.

Those who saw John Price's body on the carpet in his lounge-room and the crime scene video in court were struck by, among other things, the sight of his windpipe – so perfectly round and white.

Justice Barry O'Keefe, sitting behind his raised bench in East Maitland Court, had some questions for the forensic pathologist: 'It is one thing to chop a person's head off with an axe or meat cleaver or something like that with brute force, but this was a much more delicate operation, if delicate is the right word?' the judge said.

'Yes, it appeared to, if I could use the word, have been anatomically dissected,' Lyons replied.

'Doctor, the process of removing a head is not something that you would normally do in the course of your autopsies, is it?'

'No, it certainly is not.'

'Could you give any indication as to the sort of time that it would be likely to take to carry out a decapitation of the kind you observed here?'

'I would think with a sharp knife that it would not take very long at all.'

'What is "not very long at all" though?'

'I think if I said, you know, a few minutes, meaning, say, five to ten minutes at the most.'

When cross-examined by Katherine Knight's counsel, Peter Thraves, QC, about whether any luck was involved in the decapitation, Lyons conceded that yes, he could not rule out luck in anything. But, he said: 'The decapitation looked – the incisions were neat and clean and not ragged and untidy. They did look as though they had been undertaken in a way that one wondered whether someone had had some anatomical dissection experience of some sort.'

Sixty minutes to skin John Price's corpse. Ten more minutes to cut off his head. Katherine Knight was skilled. Fourteen years in the meatworks. She was strong.

'Dismembering a corpse is not an easy task even with the aid of a sharp knife. Cartilage and bone are tough materials, but the skilled dissector can disarticulate a corpse if he has enough time. Some often take pride in their work', wrote J.H.H. Gaute and Robin Odell in their book *Murder: What Dunit?*

Katherine Knight could have stopped after she stabbed John Price just once. She could have stopped after she stabbed him to death. She could have stopped before she skinned him and hung his human form from the architrave, and she could have stopped before she decapitated him. And she could have stopped after she cut his head off.

She didn't.

Peter Muscio was in the dining room at St Andrews Street. The smell of cooking was in the air. The kitchen was much like any you'd find in any house in suburban Australia. The image was that of manageable domestic disorder, with all the telltale signs of life in neat disarray.

Pricey had knocked back a stubby of Tooheys New the night before and left the empty on the laminated breakfast bar near his Winfield Reds and black leather wallet. A full bottle of Tooheys lay on its side on the carpet in front of the fridge, forgotten. It was, after all, a man's home.

There were three chairs around the table, and a fourth one under the breakfast bar. An electric toy gorilla sat on the wooden table-top, evidence that children sometimes stayed here. When it was turned on, the gorilla moved.

Clothes were piled on the table next to Pricey's work bag, which had been left open, a nectarine, the fruit of summer, and an apple visible inside. Also on the table next to a bowl of fruit were three packets of Pricey's prescription medication.

The curtains, an orangey brown colour printed with swaying palm trees, were drawn closed, yet the sun wasn't due to hit that side of the house until early afternoon.

As Peter Muscio moved around the kitchen, he noticed a black-handled knife and four more strips of three types of Kathy's prescription medication on the breakfast bar near a Norton's honing block used for sharpening knives.

Dishes and vegetable peelings were in the sink, two meals had been cooked and placed to the right of the stove-top. The microwave door was open, its light left on. A toaster and green electric kettle, its handle bloodied, were in the corner, where they are in most kitchens. The louvre doors to the pantry were shut.

John Price's skin was hanging from the archway. Blood drops tracked across the carpet and led across the corked kitchen floor to the stove-top. In the middle of the floor was a single bare footprint in blood. Just one. Peter Muscio couldn't work out how it got there. Usually a footprint is preceded by others. This was on its own, as if someone had hopped down on that one spot and then moved off, deliberately stamping their identity in blood. Blood smears were on the door handle and the side of the refrigerator, and a blood-stained blue shirt was hung over the back of one of the chairs.

A pot was sitting on the right rear electric element, still warm, with its lid on. The policemen who came in earlier didn't lift it to see what Katherine Knight had been cooking. A large baking tray was to the left of the pot. Cooking implements were on the sink – two forks were beside a bloodstained, yellow-handled vegetable knife on a chopping board with a brown cup of what looked like gravy. Leftover cooked cabbage was in a microwave dish.

Katherine Knight had gone to a lot of trouble to prepare the two meals sitting on the opposite bench near the stove-top. Sticking out from under the plates were two ripped sheets of paper towel with the names of Pricey's son and younger daughter. She had prepared the meals for Pricey's children, like she was playing at being a kindly stepmother making a Sunday roast. Each plate held two pieces of cooked meat, surrounded by baked pumpkin, baked potato, zucchini, yellow squash, cabbage and gravy. The pumpkin and potatoes, which were cut in quarters, would have taken about forty-five minutes to bake in the electric wall oven. Katherine Knight had been kept busy.

When Muscio gingerly lifted the lid on the aluminium pot on the stove-top, he and the crime scene camera operator were staring at the skinned head of John Price. Muscio was expecting to see it. It had been shoved in tight and was lying on its right-hand side, further damaged by the cooking process. She had tossed an array of sliced vegetables – including potatoes, zucchini, pumpkin, carrot and squash – into the pot on top of John Price's head.

Forensic testing on the meat on the plates, and the meat that had been thrown out into the back yard, later proved it had been sliced from John Price's right buttock. Katherine Knight had cooked her lover and prepared him as a meal for his unsuspecting children.

Katherine Knight went into the bathroom and draped her blood-spattered black nylon nightie over the side of the bath, inside out. Leaving faint bloody footprints on the bathmat and on the floor in front of the vanity unit, she ran the shower and hopped under. The next day Peter Muscio found blood on the bathroom wall and a piece of human flesh over the drainhole in the shower.

Katherine Knight dressed in the same denim shorts and sleeveless denim shirt she had been wearing all day. It was around 2 am. Katherine Knight walked out of the house, hopped into the red van, and drove the 15 kilometres down the New England Highway into Muswellbrook. It takes twelve minutes at that time of night. What was she thinking as she came over the last rise in the asphalt road out of Aberdeen, away from the scene of the crime? The Dartbrook colliery was on the left, its machinery lit up like an industrial Christmas tree. Then, as the amber glow from the last street-light fades from view, the countryside goes dark, lit only by the moon and the stars.

Whatever Katherine Knight was thinking as she drove along the highway away from Aberdeen, it wasn't about fleeing. She had no intention of driving as far and fast away from the scene of the crime as she possibly could. At the small bridge over Sandy Creek, an 80 km/h signpost welcomes travellers to Muswellbrook. She passed the Vietnam War Memorial on the left, a sombre grove of trees that runs for more than a kilometre with signs listing the regiment and the number of servicemen and women killed in action. Five hundred and three in total. Katherine Knight would have been oblivious to the body count. She passed the memorials erected to honour WWII veterans and the 'Nashos' and another for those who served in Korea, Malaya and Borneo. Then she was in Bridge Street, Muswellbrook. Her destination.

She pulled up outside the Upper Hunter Credit Union at 87 Bridge Street. John Price's credit union. The streets were deserted. She didn't have to worry about being seen. It was two-thirty on Wednesday morning. Not even the district dairy farmers who supply the Oak dairy plant around the corner are up at that hour.

Katherine Knight slid Pricey's ATM card into the slot, punched in his pin number and withdrew $500. The date and time on the receipt were precise: 01/03 02:34:29, transaction number 009949. Fifty-nine seconds later, Katherine Knight withdrew another $500. The time read: 02:35:28 transaction number 009950. Pricey was dead. Knight had just stolen $1000 from his bank account in two separate withdrawals. Pricey had a $1000 daily limit.

She drove back to her house on MacQueen Street, manoeuvred the red van up the narrow driveway between her house and that of Gerri Edwards, and parked it up the very back of the yard.

At 3.30 am, Lisa Logan was standing on her front verandah waiting for her Maltese terrier to do its business. Lisa and her husband and two little children had lived down the bottom of St Andrews Street for about a decade. Lisa worked in the office at the abattoir for ten years until she had her first child, but Katherine had left by the time she joined. They never worked or socialised together but they knew each other and were friendly, as one is in a small town. Lisa occasionally saw Katherine walking up the hill with Pricey or some other locals, coming home from the top pub or the club. Lisa also knew John Price. 'He seemed quite nice,' she said.

Each night Lisa followed the same routine, getting out of bed to take her house-trained pet outside. Most nights the streets are empty, but early this Wednesday, Lisa was surprised to see Katherine Knight.

'I saw her walking up the hill, I think it was three-thirty. I have a little house dog and I take her outside to go to the toilet, and that's when I saw her just walking up the street,' Lisa said, pointing to the other side of the street. 'She was under the light. I thought it was odd, a lady walking up the hill at that time. As soon as I saw someone coming, I grabbed my dog and jumped back. I don't want anyone to see me in my jarmies.'

Katherine Knight was on her way *back* to Pricey's, back to the scene of the crime.

She'd walked from her house at MacQueen Street. Her walk took her past the police station which, heading to Pricey's, was on the right-hand side of the highway. She'd already passed it as she drove back to her house from the credit union. She turned left and walked over the railway bridge, then right into Mount Street, and left into St Andrews. She was half a block away from Pricey's when Lisa Logan saw her.

Not five hours later, at 8.14 am, police officers Graham Furlonger and Scott Matthews woke a snoring Katherine Knight, snapped a pair of handcuffs on her and led her out of St Andrews Street for the very last time.

19

A top bloke

If there is one way to measure a man and the sort of life he has led, it is his funeral. John Price's was standing room only. On Friday 10 March 2000, several hundred people came to pay their last respects to the little fella who had touched their lives. The pews were packed and people stood lining the back and side walls of St Alban's Anglican Church in Muswellbrook. Those who couldn't fit inside spilled out onto the church's picket-fenced grounds.

The collective grief was like a heavy cloud, but when Pricey's best mate Laurie Lewis and his two bosses, Geoffrey Bowditch and Peter Cairnes, stood before the congregation to deliver their eulogies, the sorrow was briefly lifted. Laurie had planned to read a poignant poem he wrote about his mate and the loss he felt, but decided instead to honour the bloke that Pricey was, to remember his easy-going nature and sense of humour.

As Laurie recalled a fishing trip they took to Bonshaw when they got flooded in a couple of years earlier, he began to mimic Pricey's voice and smiles spread knowingly through the church.

'Hey, Pricey, we're locked in by flood,' Laurie said, standing a few feet away from Pricey's coffin.

' "Fiiiiiiiine," Pricey said.

' "Hey Pricey, old Ted's got a poisoned hand."
' "Fiiiiiiine," he said.
' "Pricey, Marty's car's got washed away."
' "Fiiiiiiine."
' "I said, it looks like we're here to stay."
' "Fiiiiiiiiiiiiiiiine."
' "Pricey, it looks like there's not enough grog to shout."
' "What?" he said. "Quick, let's get out." '

Everyone laughed. Laurie's simple anecdote had perfectly captured Pricey's spirit.

At the end of the service, the funeral cortege made its way along the New England Highway to the Aberdeen cemetery where John Price was laid to rest.

Katherine Knight was in Mulawa Women's Correctional Centre at Silverwater the day John Price was buried, having been officially charged with his murder and remanded to custody by Magistrate Wakely four days earlier.

Since being arrested on Wednesday 1 March she had been kept under guard at Newcastle's Mater Misericordiae Hospital and then Maitland hospital while being treated for a suspected overdose. In the hours after she killed Pricey, Katherine Knight had taken something. The next morning at nine-twenty, she told medical staff at the Mater she had taken two types of 'nerve tablets' and a strip of Pricey's blood pressure tablets. A blood test taken the day before showed she had taken an anti-depressant fluvoxamine and an antihistamine promethazine – two of the drugs found in Pricey's kitchen the morning his body was discovered. The trace levels of drugs in her bloodstream were within the recommended dosages. Nothing lethal. The two drugs had been previously prescribed for Kathy by her longtime doctor in Scone.

In handing down his sentence in November 2001, Justice Barry O'Keefe told the Supreme Court: 'I am satisfied beyond reasonable doubt that there was no genuine attempt on her part so to do [commit suicide] . . . These drugs had been previously prescribed for the prisoner and as a consequence, she was well aware of the therapeutic dose.'

Katherine Knight was recovering and had received a steady

stream of visitors at the hospital. She had spent nearly two hours that Saturday morning being interrogated by police about the murder, but said she could remember nothing about the night.

Among the visitors were Kathy's daughter Melissa, her twin sister Joy, her sister-in-law Val and four of her six brothers, Patrick, Neville and Barry Roughan and Shane Knight. Melissa, who came down from Queensland where she was living with her husband and their child, visited on Friday with Joy.

Shane Knight visited his sister the next day, Saturday, and said she seemed normal – not happy, but not like there was anything wrong with her either. His twenty-minute visit was supervised by a nurse. Shane had been instructed by doctors not to talk about what had happened, so they avoided the subject and chatted about old times. Kathy didn't mention a word about Pricey's death and neither did Shane.

'I think she thinks she was just in there for trying to kill herself,' Shane said, adding that it felt odd that they were talking as if nothing had happened. 'Yeah, that's what, um, that freaked me out . . . I knew what happened . . . I knew that night. I was devastated, couldn't believe it possible.' Shane never thought his sister would be capable of doing what she did. It was a theme echoed throughout Aberdeen.

'Not that,' he said. 'Everyone knew she was crazy. I don't think she should be in jail; in a mental hospital somewhere. I just don't think that anybody in their sane mind could do what she done. She'd have had to have snapped, it's just the way I feel about it.'

Shane knew the full details of what had happened, but it didn't turn him against his sister. 'No, I love me sister, even though she done a horrendous thing,' he said. Instead, he was overcome with guilt, thinking that had he stepped in when he believed there was violence between the couple, he could have stopped what happened. Like everyone else in Aberdeen, Shane knew that Kathy and Pricey had a love-hate relationship.

'I used to get on pretty well with Johnathon and the daughter, Rosemary, but I never liked the father and I wanted to flog him one day, but she wouldn't let me flog him,' said Shane. 'He belted her one night and I wanted to go up and get into him and she wouldn't let me. So that was it, I turned my back on them, which now I'm suffering for. I feel guilty. If I went and flogged him or something, it might never have happened. But she wouldn't let me do it. She loved him.'

On Monday 6 March Katherine Mary Knight was formally charged with the murder of John Price and turned over to the custody of police. Detective Sergeant Bob Wells and police prosecutor Senior Sergeant Phil Lloyd drove her the 30 kilometres from Maitland hospital to Newcastle police station where she was to be processed before meeting the prison truck which would take her the next 226 kilometres to Mulawa Women's Correction Centre at Silverwater.

Wells was driving, Lloyd was in the front passenger seat and Katherine Knight was handcuffed in the back seat. A couple of 'highway jockeys' in a marked police vehicle drove behind them. Katherine's suitcase of personal clothing was in the boot. The fifty-minute ride had a surreal feel about it. The two experienced policemen knew they couldn't breathe a word about the crime, and it would be ungentlemanly of them to ignore the lady in the back, so they chatted like you'd chat to anyone you were forced to travel with but you didn't really know well. Polite conversation.

'It was quite funny actually,' Detective Bob Wells remembered. 'Here we are with this horrendous murderer in the back seat, Phil and I are talking to her about fishing, how she likes fishing with the kids . . . they go fishing, camping. All this other rot. And she was just talking like, you know, we were all sitting in the pub together talking about our interests. She spoke quite openly, sounded like one of the boys.'

Phil Lloyd was stunned. He hadn't seen the crime scene video of what happened at St Andrews Street. Bob Wells had it when he visited Phil on Saturday, but Phil decided not to watch it. There was no doubt about the identity of the perpetrator, and Bob Wells' investigation – still less than a week old – had already dug up evidence of her past violent behaviour and a souring relationship with Pricey that provided a motive. Had Phil been a young policeman at the beginning of his career, curiosity might have got the better of him, but he was secretly glad he didn't need to watch the crime scene video. Knowing what was on it was enough and that was what was playing on his mind during the car trip with Katherine Knight chatting about how she liked to go fishing. Surreal.

'My experience of dealing with people who have been involved in those sorts of quite grisly homicides is somewhat limited but I have dealt with a few,' Lloyd said with classic understatement. He's been in the police service for thirty-seven years, thirty of those as a prosecutor, and once attended the scene of a double murder in the sandhills at Stockton beach in Newcastle with a co-accused in the murder. Two bodies had been burned to destroy evidence, and then buried.

'It was sufficiently unsuccessful for there to be positive DNA of extraordinarily barbecued remains,' Lloyd remembered, 'and I had been in the company of the accessory who had been directed . . . to continue to fuel the fires on his own in the night time and spend the whole night with these bodies.

'And he was suffering, this person, when he took us out there to the bodies to be found. And he was profoundly visibly affected by his involvement and you can contrast that completely with the demeanour of Katherine Knight who was composed and quite happy to engage in conversation and took the conversation in new directions.'

~

Two trees were planted in memory of John Price, one in the Lions park on MacQueen Street and another in the back yard of the top pub. But Aberdeen was changed. People were terrified to be on their own at nights, especially the women whose husbands worked different shifts in the mines around the Valley. They locked their doors for the first time ever, some couldn't go to work on their own and others didn't like leaving the house at all. The elderly feared opening their doors to the Meals on Wheels lady, not knowing if a stranger would be on the other side. An irrational fear gripped the towns-folk. They knew it didn't make any sense, yet they couldn't help but feel it.

The trauma had also left an indelible mark on those who knew Pricey and Kathy and their respective families. They felt their loyalties and affections were in conflict. It was difficult for people to reconcile that a woman they knew and liked and shared a history with had murdered a man about whom they felt the same way. Guilt had seeped in too. Could anyone have done anything to stop it? It was a rhetorical question; of course, the answer was 'no'. On top of that, the close-knit community felt their town had been damaged, as if an ugly burr had rolled into the middle of the fabric of Aberdeen.

The country rumour mill was spinning hollow tales about - reprisals and vigilantism, and rubber-necking tourists drove through town to perve at the St Andrews Street house where Pricey was murdered. Somebody had already gotten to Kathy's house, smashing a window, and the wooden home had been boarded up. It was impossible to escape Katherine Knight's savagery.

Senior Constable Troy Conway had been the lock-up keeper at the Aberdeen police station since 1996 and knew just about everyone in town. He was the type of country cop who was comfortable having a beer with the locals in either the top pub or down the hill at the Commercial. He carries his authority casually and in a way that invites people to confide in him rather than fearing him as the local law enforcer. Troy Conway knew Aberdeen was suffering like never before: 'I think it [the town] became really withdrawn. You picture a person being withdrawn and within themselves, it was like the whole town was like that. The town was just overtaken by it,' Conway said. 'It was shock – shock just lasted a long time . . . because it's such a small town everybody knows everyone no matter what, and everyone knew John. He was a super bloke, fantastic bloke.'

During his years as a copper, Conway got to know about the Homicide Victims' Support Group and thought that if the group could help a single family work through the shock and trauma of a murder and brief them on what to expect in the legal process, it could do the same thing for a small community like that of Aberdeen. After all, Conway rationalised, small towns are big families. A community debrief, as it is known, had never been done in Australia before, but the group's executive director, Martha Jabour, and Conway's boss, Superintendent Beverley Blanch, who was then the local area commander for the Hunter Valley, couldn't see why it shouldn't be done now. It was an extraordinary case. Extraordinary measures were called for.

At the time New South Wales was in the middle of the worst mouse plague in a decade. Mice, a pair of which can produce five hundred offspring in twenty-one weeks, were everywhere in the south and northwest of the state, including Aberdeen and the surrounding district. Crops and sheds of hay had been destroyed by the voracious rodents. They chewed through electrical wiring in farm machinery. Windows rattled after the mice ate the putty in the frames. They got into kitchen cupboards and closets and ate their way through edibles, wearables and collectables. Baits and poisons had been flown in from the United States and Egypt to cope with the plague, but still the numbers grew.

The locals were talking about the plague when Martha Jabour and her counsellors, accompanied by the New South Wales Police Assistant Commissioner John Laycock and Superintendent Beverley Blanch, walked into the Aberdeen RSL at 6.30 pm on 13 April for the community debrief. They were surprised at the turnout. About eighty people had come out on a rainy night. Martha Jabour knew it would be an emotional one too. As people shuffled into rows of chairs, she urged them to grab a cuppa or a soft drink. It was an informal night, but alcohol was banned just the same. Emotions and alcohol are not a good mix. A few weather-beaten blokes who didn't want to appear to be involved stood at the bar, silently sipping a beer, but they listened just as hard. The local cop Troy Conway was there, a familiar sight in blue.

Assistant Commissioner Laycock opened the evening and talked the crowd through the legal process. Of course, he said they could not discuss the ongoing investigation, and most were happy with that. They probably knew enough already. Counsellors ran through the services that could help them cope with their grief and trauma. They were told that post traumatic stress disorder could be causing sleeplessness, nightmares, flashbacks and other unexpected fears, and that this was perfectly normal and should, in time, pass. Then the floor was opened to the locals who were invited to ask their questions in writing if it made them feel more comfortable.

'It was done in a very civilised way and it gave people the opportunity to raise issues without being identified,' said Superintendent Blanch. 'So if they had a fear or concern they could do it almost anonymously. And there were a number of issues raised and even, for example – and I suppose it just shows you how fear works – even some men were having trouble leaving their wives to go to work on night shift because they were fearful, their wives were fearful. And because this is a very working-class town and there was a lot of shiftwork, that was an issue.

'It was interesting from our perspective,' the policewoman said, 'in that even though the crime was a one-on-one domestic relationship, it still conjured up that fear in the community. There was a lot of horror and, I guess, there was like a town pride issue that the town would be associated forever with this macabre thing that had happened.'

Martha Jabour has short dark hair and sparkling eyes, and the thing people remember about her enough to comment on is her big, open smiling face. It is a face that has comforted grief-stricken and traumatised men, women and children who have lived through the reality of murder. Jabour had been the executive director of the Homicide Victims' Support Group since August 1993. She was invited to run the then volunteer group two months after it was formed by the parents of two murdered girls, Anita Cobby and Ebony Simpson. Martha understood their grief. Her second son, a six and a half week old baby named Michael, had died of sudden infant death syndrome (SIDS) in 1986. She had been training police and health care professionals on how to deal with SIDS when Garry and Grace Cobby and Peter and Christine Simpson needed a coordinator. Martha took the job.

Even with her personal and professional experience, Martha Jabour was struck by what she found at the Aberdeen RSL that cold, wet Thursday night: 'When we walked in you could feel the fear in the air – What can I do to make my home safe? What can I do so that this doesn't happen to us?' Martha said. '[They were] not really thinking about how isolated this sort of incident is; where a woman would murder her partner, de facto partner, and in such gruesome circumstances. And a lot of them felt quite fearful for their lives.

'[There was also] the fact that all the people that were there knew both the victim and the offender, so there was this mixed loyalty. A lot of people couldn't believe that Katherine could do such a thing. And then the other side was, you guys are saying she did it, she must have done it, how do we cope with surviving knowing that someone that we really cared about and perhaps socialised with, and we liked, has done something so gruesome? It was a very unreal thing for them to believe had happened.

'Their fears were that it was going to happen again and she would get bail and come back and maybe murder some of them. The fear was that they had never had a murder like this in their town.

'And the other thing was, there was some guilt that came out from some people . . . who had known there was quite a lot of domestic arguments between them and saying things like, I wished I had done something about it . . . or checked when I saw the car in the driveway a bit earlier. All that hindsight type of stuff. It was a very caring community . . . there was a lot of concern for the victim's family and how people could cope with them and what to say.

'What we had to put across to people was that it wasn't happening to them. This was something that had happened to poor John and his family and in order for their family to survive, all those people basically had to be strong and help them. At the same time, [we were] validating their feelings, saying to them how normal they were.

'A lot of people were having nightmares about it. A lot of people were having flashbacks about it. It's a bit like if you read something, it's left up to your imagination to imagine what it would look like, and that's exactly what it was. In each person's mind the horrificness of the murder was very different,' Martha said.

The flashbacks, the tears, the grief: it was all normal. The locals were on a roller-coaster ride with their emotions, particularly those who had been friends with Katherine Knight or Pricey, or Kathy and Pricey as a couple.

'There were people there who supported Katherine, but that was because there was history there before. They said very little. It was support out of loyalty, the fact that they had known her for many years rather than support for what she'd done. There was more anger than hate. It was anger and anger that she could do such a thing.'

Pricey's son Johnathon and his partner, who was in the latter stages of her pregnancy with their second daughter, also attended. That surprised and impressed Martha Jabour. Johnathon was given the last word of the night. At twenty-six, he handled himself with dignity and grace. He remembered what a top bloke his dad was and thanked everyone who came for their support. The thing that struck Martha was how the people who attended the debrief managed to hold it together on such an emotional night. They would be talking about the legal issues or the grief, and then in true town meeting style, someone would pipe up with a yarn about Pricey. It broke the tension.

'And so they would talk about the nice things about him, which was really nice, which meant it became a very personal gathering where you weren't just talking about the horrificness,' said Martha. 'And that was what was so fantastic about Johnathon getting up right at the very end and he had the last word. And he got up and just thanked everybody and talked about what a great guy his dad was and didn't deserve what happened to him.'

~

There was only ever one suspect but Detective Bob Wells had to make sure the case against her stuck and that it wouldn't be lost in court on a defence of substantial impairment or automatism. Every move he made was freighted with the knowledge that one wrong step could blow the case out of the water. It was another reason why he danced carefully in the police interview with the suspect on Saturday 4 March. He never came straight out and said, 'Why did you stab John Price thirty-seven times? Why did you skin his body, and why did you decapitate him and cook him?'

Police prosecutor Phil Lloyd and Bob Wells had a strategy. Bob had to let Katherine tell them what she knew, and let her reveal how she was going to play her hand. As it turned out, her strategy was to say she could remember barely a thing. Wells played along. Had he said anything during the interview that influenced her answers, or put thoughts in her mind, the defence could have used that to their advantage.

'Phil Lloyd and I came to the opinion that [we'd] be on dangerous grounds in case she continues to say, "I can't remember, I can't remember",' Bob Wells said. 'If she later . . . confesses to it and tells people what she's done, it might come back to bite us on the arse at trial . . . [that] she only said it because we put it in her mind.' If that happened, any confession would have been lost.

Katherine was next due in court on 4 April and by then Bob Wells had eighteen witnesses in the bag and a list of dozens more to interview. The date was significant. John Price should have been celebrating his 45th birthday but instead, his ex-wife Colleen and their daughters Rosemary and Jackie attended Muswellbrook Local Court to show he had not been forgotten as a victim. Knight didn't show up. She was back at Mulawa in Sydney.

It had only been three weeks since John Price's funeral and the three Price women were raw with grief and shock, but they wanted to know exactly what had happened. They had spoken to Kylie Henry, the solicitor who was handling the committal hearing for the Director of Public Prosecutions, and told her they wanted to find out as much as they could about what happened that night. They already knew quite a bit, but Colleen and her two girls didn't want to hear about Pricey's last hours in dribs and drabs cobbled together from the gossipy country grapevine or from selective reporting in the media. It would be shocking, they knew, but they *had* to know.

A witness assistance officer from the Director of Public Prosecutions (DPP) Newcastle office was with Ms Henry just in case the family broke down. As the five women sat in a private office at the courthouse, Ms Henry told them the details of the crime. Jackie, who was three weeks from her fifteenth birthday, cried, as did Colleen. Kylie asked them if she should go on. Rosemary, the strongest of the three, asked questions but she broke down as Kylie revealed the extent of Kathy's viciousness. Only a few weeks earlier, Katherine Knight had held Rosemary's little boy in her arms at his fifth birthday party. It didn't make sense.

After the meeting, Colleen, Rosemary and Jackie walked into the courtroom and took a seat for the short procedural hearing. Kylie Henry, who had taken over the case from Phil Lloyd and would be working in the Supreme Court alongside Mark Macadam, QC, simply asked for another court date. Knight's lawyers did not apply for bail. Over and out in a few minutes. Each side was building its case.

From the get-go, Macadam and Henry believed the case should go to a murder trial for a jury to decide whether to accept a lesser plea of manslaughter once they had heard all the evidence. Macadam, who was eighteen months away from retiring, and Henry, in only her third year with the DPP, were reluctant to accept a straight-up plea of manslaughter on the evidence that was before them, thanks to Bob Wells' exhaustive investigation. A jury, quite feasibly, could decide it was a cold-blooded, premeditated murder. But, under section 23A of the Crimes Act, 1900, the murder charge could be knocked down to manslaughter if the jury believed that at the time of the killing Kathy Knight had suffered a substantial impairment caused by an abnormality of the mind from an underlying cause. It's a convoluted legal term, but a simple concept.

To cop a plea to a lesser charge of manslaughter, Knight's abnormality of mind had to have impaired at least one of the following: her capacity to understand events; her ability to judge whether they were right or wrong; and, whether she could control herself. If, on the balance of the evidence before them, a jury decided Katherine Knight warranted being found guilty only of manslaughter on the basis of substantial impairment, that would be that. As much as the case relied on the evidence excavated by Bob Wells and his investigation, it would hang on Katherine Knight's mental state at the time of the murder. Enter the psychiatrists.

20

In her nature

Forensic psychiatrists are body doctors first, mind doctors second. Before going behind bars to get inside the minds of the criminally insane, the mad or the bad, they have gone to medical school and qualified as doctors, then specialised in psychiatry, before branching off again into forensic psychiatry. It is a science and an art. Dealing with criminals and violent people requires a certain amount of professional scepticism to be able to find the truth in a lantana of lies. Sometimes there are no lies, only insanity or mental illness. At other times, there is no truth. Criminals are not known for their candour.

Psychiatrists rarely use the word 'evil', preferring to leave it to theologians and philosophers and the man in the street. They prefer to look at the causes and effects in human behaviour and 'generally see the human being as a creature who is affected by powerful internal forces and not always free to make rational decisions', writes psychiatrist Robert Simon in *Bad Men Do What Good Men Dream*. However, Simon concedes that:

> . . . the great majority of violence and mayhem in this world is done not by the mentally ill but by individuals and entire societies not considered to be sick, at least not by any known measure of mental illness. The answer to why

such violence occurs lies beyond the psychopathology of evil. No competent psychiatrist is so arrogant as to think that human motivation and behaviour can be fully explained by current medical and psychological theories. Only God knows the human mind and heart.

Robert Delaforce graduated from the University of New South Wales with undergraduate degrees in medicine and surgery in 1971. In 1976, he became a member of the Royal Australian and New Zealand College of Psychiatrists and in 1986 he got more acquainted with the criminal class when he became the visiting medical officer at Grafton Correctional Centre. Ten years later, backed by his solid experience with prisoners, he was appointed to the Director of Public Prosecutions' panel of psychiatrists. It was in that guise that the DPP asked Dr Delaforce to interview Katherine Knight in the murder case of John Price. Delaforce has also frequently acted for the defence in trials and in some cases, even when he was called as a prosecution witness, his evidence has favoured the defendant.

Dr Delaforce stands about five feet ten and has a gentle forward lean when he walks. His greying beard is trimmed short, and his fingers constantly come to rest in a steeple when he talks. On 21 and 22 June 2000 Dr Delaforce visited Katherine Knight in prison. She'd been there three and a half months, housed in the Mum Shirl Psychiatric Wing, away from the general prison population. On 11 August 2000 he furnished a 68-page report to the DPP – the results of his nearly nine hours with Katherine Knight.

His job was to examine Katherine Knight from the psychiatric– legal point of view to see if there was any evidence that her culpability would be reduced by substantial impairment. Prosecutors don't like taking a case to a jury trial if there is a good chance they will lose. It doesn't look good on their résumé and it wastes the community's money. It's as much about saving court resources as it is about ensuring the law works as fairly as possible for all involved. It is not uncommon for defendants to mount a defence of automatism (an automatic act without intent) or mental illness under the M'Naughten rule. Mental illness is a legal term – psychiatrists do not use it in a clinical sense – and applies if, under the M'Naughten rule, the person did not know the nature and quality of the act they were committing, or if they did know, they didn't know that it was wrong.

Psychiatrists search the human mind like an archeologist digs for fossils – dusting away debris to find a piece of the jigsaw. Dr Delaforce, like all psychiatrists, would have started with general questions about where Katherine Knight was born, what her childhood and schooling were like, her family background, her work, her children, and her relationships. Standard questions. Building rapport.

At one stage during his two days with Katherine Knight, Dr Delaforce conducted the structured interview for diagnosing mental disorders from the American Psychiatric Association's manual. Knight, he concluded, suffered post traumatic stress disorder and had borderline personality disorder which was related to what she had said was her traumatic childhood.

In his original report he wrote that there was a significant chance that Knight's personality disorder could give rise to a defence of substantial impairment, and he likened what she did, in parts, on the morning of 1 March 2000 when she killed John Price, to how she behaved in 1976 when she was admitted to Morisset psychiatric hospital. Back then, he said, it was a clear case of borderline personality disorder: 'Her behaviour then and related to Mr Price is characteristic of the violent and inappropriate behaviour that can occur in persons with borderline personality disorder when abandonment in a relationship occurs or is feared,' he wrote in his first report.

Fourteen months later, at Katherine Knight's sentencing hearing, Dr Delaforce pointed out that even though he noted a possible defence of substantial impairment, he had also emphasised in that original report that it was worth considering the possibility of the significance of Katherine Knight having very violent fantasies and related interests and activities. He pointed to her work at the meatworks, and her repeated contact with a man who would 'stick' pigs. He also noted the level of peace she felt when sitting among dead animal parts hanging from the walls of her home, and how she told him during their interviews that she repeatedly 'escaped' by watching violent television programs and videotapes.

On top of that, the psychiatrist told the court, as Katherine

Knight listened intently from the dock, of her 'repeated consider-
ations with her nephew of violence to Mr Price, her talk of killing
Mr Price and getting away with it by claiming she was mad, her
vindictive nature such that she was prone to move into payback
mode when her relationship was in difficulty, such as when she
video-tape recorded items stolen by Mr Price from his employer
and gave the video tape recordings to his employer, and the
possibility of her having extremely violent fantasies of mutilating
Mr Price.'

He also testified that he had 'considerable doubt about the
reliability of the information she gives'.

As he told the New South Wales Supreme Court, when he
asked Katherine Knight what happened to John Price, Katherine
Knight said she didn't know. She was still wearing his engagement
ring. He dismissed a diagnosis of dissociative amnesia. Forgetting
could just be a defence mechanism to protect herself from the
unspeakable things she had done.

'To the extent that her amnesia is genuine, it may only be the
result of a final realisation that what she did, as pleasurable as it
was, is quite shocking. If I could use an analogy of marital infidelity; the pleasures are there, the shock and guilt afterwards can
bring people down and distress them a lot,' Dr Delaforce told the
court by way of explaining amnesia after the event.

'If there is genuine amnesia there it may have come as a result
of the eventual realisation of what she had done, and confronting
the gruesome nature as to what she had done. But what causes me
some concern as to that being a likely outcome is that, with her
interest in violence – and it does seem to be very considerable, as
indicated for example, by violent movies – she would have a great
capacity to tolerate violence.'

Justice O'Keefe addressed the psychiatrist: 'Now, can you
assist me . . . whether or not what was done to the body and the
posing of the body and cooking the parts might be regarded or
would be regarded by you as a manifestation of power in relation
to this particular male, that is the deceased?'

'Very probably so. The control and power is usually present in
crimes of this nature. It is a fundamental feature of it – and, yes,'
he replied.

Dr Delaforce is a thorough man. As he testified later, his first report dated 11 August 2000 was guarded and he noted in it that if, and when, further material was presented, he might need to provide a second opinion based on the new evidence. It was still early days when Dr Delaforce wrote his report. Bob Wells' police investigation was ongoing and about to pick up pace. Within months, more evidence would be found that would significantly change Dr Delaforce's opinion.

He would soon come to the conclusion that Katherine Knight's borderline personality disorder had nothing to do with the murder of John Price, nor was she insane. 'What she did on the night was part of her personality, her nature, herself, but it is not a feature of borderline personality disorder, it is not even significantly connected,' he told the Crown Prosecutor Mark Macadam in October 2001.

21

Mad versus bad

It was the beginning of winter and the winds had turned on Aberdeen. Pricey had been dead for nearly three months. His best mate Laurie Lewis was sitting at home sorting through the paperwork of Pricey's life. The 'little fella' had made Laurie the executor of his will when he and Colleen broke up in 1988 and since then, Laurie had helped him with his financial affairs. Everything was kept in a brown cardboard shoebox – Dunlop Volley, UK Size 9. 'Pricey's life in a box,' Laurie called it.

On 15 May 2000, Laurie had the balance of Pricey's bank account at the Upper Hunter Credit Union paid to the Estate of John Price, which would eventually be worth a healthy six figure sum. The account statements from the credit union arrived a few weeks later. Laurie was having a cuppa with his wife Fran and reconciling the balance, ticking off the cheques he'd made out to finalise his mate's outstanding debts against the debits column on the statement. He checked off the familiar payments he had made to Telstra, the Scone Shire Council, Energy Australia and one for $1200 to BVM Clean Scene, which spent sixteen hours cleaning Pricey's house after the murder. All legit.

But he paused as he noticed two withdrawals for $500 each. He checked the dates. 1 March 2000. He looked at Fran. Pricey was dead on 1 March. Laurie drove down to Muswellbrook to the credit union and spoke with the manager.

'I said there must be some discrepancy in the account . . . there was money drawn out on the first of March and that man was dead, and I want to know what time it was drawn out,' Laurie said. The money was withdrawn at exactly 2.34.29 and 2.35.28 am. It said so on the printout. Laurie put two and two together. Kathy!

'This just shows you that she has really planned it and how calculated she was,' said Laurie. 'She's killed him, I don't know whether she's cut him up then or not, but . . . she took the card out of his wallet and drove to town, cleaned up, went to town. Well I suppose she cleaned herself up – you wouldn't walk around the streets with blood and guts on her, surely to God. Then again, she's Kathy Knight.'

Laurie called the local policeman Troy Conway at Aberdeen to report the discrepancy, and Troy got a message to Detective Sergeant Bob Wells, who was on sick leave suffering post traumatic stress syndrome. On 27 November, Bob Wells was back on deck and went through the times and dates of the withdrawal with Laurie. He came to the same conclusion as Pricey's mate – Katherine Knight had robbed Pricey's account of $1000. She had a motive and she had the opportunity, and it fitted into Bob Wells' timeline of Katherine Knight's movements on the night of the murder. The last withdrawal was at 2.35.28 am. Kathy was seen walking up the hill under a street-light to Pricey's at 3.30 am by his neighbour Lisa Logan, who had got out of bed to let her dog out of the house for a wee. That gave Kathy an hour to get home from the bank, park the car in the back yard at MacQueen Street where it was found the next morning, and walk back to Pricey's. The drive from Muswellbrook takes no more than fifteen minutes at that time of night. The walk from MacQueen to St Andrews Street takes another ten.

Pricey's wallet was found by police on the breakfast bar in the kitchen with all his cards in it the morning his body was discovered. During his interrogation of Katherine Knight eight months earlier in Maitland hospital, Wells ruled out the possibility that anyone else had come into the house that night.

'Are you aware, did anybody come to the house while you were watching "Star Trek" that evening?' the detective asked.

'Not that I recollect,' Kath answered.

'Okay. Do, do you recall if there was anyone, other person there besides yourself and Pricey?'

'No.'

Up until then, Bob Wells had always wondered about a small, square bit of paper lying on the floor of Kathy's red van when the New South Wales police video crime scene unit filmed it the day Pricey's body was found. Now he thought he knew; it could have been one of the receipts from the credit union but it was too late. The car had been cleaned out months ago.

Katherine Knight's committal hearing was held at Newcastle Local Court before Magistrate Steve Jackson at the end of October 2000. Sydney was still self-indulgently triumphant over the 'most successful Olympic Games ever' and the weather promised another perfect summer ahead. Solicitor Kylie Henry, who was running the committal hearing for the Director of Public Prosecutions, planned to call only two witnesses, one of whom was Dr Bob Delaforce. The other was Dr Timothy Lyons, the forensic pathologist who conducted the postmortem on Pricey and returned his reconstructed body to his family for burial. Colleen Price and her two daughters travelled from Tamworth for the hearing.

Dr Delaforce was sworn in on Tuesday 31 October 2000. *The Newcastle Herald* reported the hearing the next morning on page 5 under the headline: 'Expert rejects memory loss over death'.

A former abattoir worker alleged to have stabbed her husband to death before cooking his head in a pot had been inconsistent about her memory of the 'bizarre and gruesome' events, a psychiatrist told Newcastle Local Court yesterday . . .

Robert Delaforce . . . said he was sceptical of [Katherine Knight's] claims that she had no memory of what happened on the day of the alleged offence . . .

Dr Delaforce rejected assertions from the defence counsel that she had profound memory loss known as dissociative amnesia disorder over Mr

Price's death, saying he believed she was not being truthful.

He believed that when Ms Knight was in hospital recovering from the overdose, she moved from a 'telling mode' to an 'I'm not going to tell any more mode'.

'Ms Knight is one of the most inconsistent people I have ever interviewed,' Dr Delaforce said. 'Of all the thousands of people I have been involved with as a psychiatrist, Ms Knight is outstanding in the extent of her inconsistent answers. You cannot rely on what she is saying.'

. . . There was genuine distress when the accused was asked about details of what happened to Mr Price after his death.

'Perhaps that's a realisation of the gruesome nature of what was done to Mr Price rather than dissociative amnesia,' Dr Delaforce said.

On 1 December 2000, Magistrate Jackson committed Katherine Knight to stand trial on the charge of murder and improperly interfering with the body of John Price and a trial date was ultimately set for Tuesday 16 October 2001.

~

September 2001 was a busy time for Katherine Knight inside Mulawa Women's Correctional Centre. It was a month before her trial and she was in preparation mode. On the morning of the 12th, she had agreed to a meeting with another forensic psychiatrist for the Director of Public Prosecutions, Rod Milton. And on the 28th, she would receive a visit from a third psychiatrist, Leonard Lambeth, who had been engaged by her legal team.

She didn't look to the interviews as a break in the monotony of prison life. She enjoyed being there and was making the most of the opportunities afforded by the Department of Corrective Services, taking courses in woodwork and literacy. She was also working as a cleaner at the Governor's office. 'Here I am happy for the first time. I love it here. It's exciting to me, helping, I like helping people,' Knight told Dr Lambeth, which he later told the New South Wales Supreme Court.

Kathy liked to please. It was part of her complex personality which could be so giving and generous and yet so volatile and violent. So she sat down in a private interview room with Dr Milton for three hours to talk about her life.

Dr Delaforce, the first forensic psychiatrist employed by the Crown, was about to furnish his second report based on the new evidence that had been uncovered by Laurie Lewis and Bob Wells – the stolen $1000 – what Delaforce would later call in court the 'grubby money'. As well, he had watched three of the horror movies collected from Knight's home – *Resurrection, Idle Hands* and *Oxygen* – which involved gruesome murders, decapitation and bodies hung up on hooks. Taken together, the weight of the material changed his opinion about Kathy's motive and actions on the night of the murder. He noted copycat elements in the crime from the videos.

'Probably, her killing of Mr Price and the mutilation of his body were premeditated acts of revenge and perverted pleasure derived from her grossly violent fantasies,' Dr Delaforce wrote in his second report dated 12 October, which he read to the New South Wales Supreme Court during Knight's sentencing hearing two weeks later.

'She has an obvious interest in extremely violent movies, consistent with her work and interest at the meatworks and the pleasure of her surrounding herself in her home with animal parts. There is little now to indicate that at the time of the offences she acted without planning, or acted impulsively, involuntarily, without control, or with considerable difficulty rationally deciding between the right and wrong of her actions, and as a result of the effects of her mental disorders. The sugges- tion that she was the person who withdrew the money from his account during the night Mr Price died introduces a grubby and enormously selfish motive that is inconsistent with the loss of control of her mind because of her mental disorders. There is now much that can be presented to the Court for consideration of her . . . acting during the offences with purpose to personally profit in a grossly perverted way.'

In most matters, the court relies on two psychiatric reports: one from the Crown and one from the defence. With the evidence in front of them, Macadam and Henry believed they had a strong murder case to take to a jury, and Katherine Knight had given no indication she would plead guilty. They sought special approval from the DPP bean-counters to organise a second opinion. They brought in Dr Rod Milton, who has more than thirty years experience as a forensic psychiatrist. He spent three hours with Katherine Knight on 12 September and his report, dated 14 October 2001, ran to 55 pages.

'The problem is not that she did not know that it was wrong to do such a thing, but that she did not care about doing them. Callousness is not an absence of what is right or wrong,' Dr Milton wrote in his report, which was quoted by Justice O'Keefe when he sentenced Knight on 8 November 2001. 'Mrs Knight did not lack the ability to control herself . . . I am of the view that Mrs Knight had the ability to control herself at the time she killed Mr Price. She could have decided not to kill him. I do not believe her ability to control herself was impaired.'

Six weeks later during Knight's sentencing hearing, Dr Milton was sworn as a witness after the court resumed from a lunch break at 2 pm on 26 October. Katherine Knight claimed to remember nothing about the murder, and Dr Milton testified that he did not put a lot of stock in the DSM-IV classification of borderline personality disorder. Sometimes, he said, people do things because it is in their nature to do so. He also said he dismissed dissociative amnesia.

'What now, doctor, is your view in relation to her claim now that she does not remember what happened during that night?' the Crown prosecutor Mark Macadam asked.

'I remain of the view that I think that it is simulated . . . there are a number of other issues that I think go to the amnesia, and that is the notion of planning. There seem to be some indications that the event was planned, or at least thought about and if that is the case it is more likely to be remembered.'

'So it is premeditated, in other words.'

'Premeditated . . . I have noted too that I think she obtained some satisfaction from the act. I realise that is not a very charitable thing to say, but I think it is the fact. If one looks at Ms Knight's history there is good reason to think that there was some satisfaction or enjoyment in carrying out the kind of acts that characterise those taking place on the night of the 29th or the morning of the 1st, and I have noted things like using the word "pigs", saying their throats were cut, cutting the puppy's throat, just referring to it as a clean cut without remorse or anything like that,' said Dr Milton. 'I think threatening to kill the puppy that Sarah had from her father, or was going to have. Perhaps some satisfaction from revenge, because revenge had been important to Ms Knight in the past. And then satisfaction, I think, too, to do with dead things, that in her home there was a lot to do with death.'

The courtroom was silent as the psychiatrist continued: 'So if the act provided satisfaction, then that suggests it is likely to be remembered. And going back I think to planning and premeditation, there was some motivation, motivation for revenge, and also extreme anger at Mr Price. There didn't seem to be much doubt that there was a lot of anger at the deceased, and that all suggests that things ought to be remembered.

'. . . And I have just noted here that there was, I think, the killing, skinning, the decapitation, preparing notes, preparing what I suppose one could only refer to in a dreadful way as meals, place names for the meals, cooking the head, cleaning herself up afterwards, going to the bank, parking her car, I think walking to Mr Price's home, and then taking a certain quantity of medication which altered the way she behaved. There is very complex behaviour, and again, it illustrates satisfactory cognition, therefore memory, being part of cognition, should be present,' he said.

'. . . It is not uncommon to find that someone commits a homicide and they say, I think as I have said in my report, "I saw this person, I picked up a knife, I don't remember anything until seeing the body". That sort of thing is relatively common, but for someone to say the amnesia began, I think, at the time of or shortly after the act of sexual intercourse and then the amnesia ceased many hours later is not in accord with what one usually sees. Taking it overall, I really felt I couldn't support the notion that this is genuine amnesia.'

Dr Milton also introduced the potential of Katherine Knight's future risk to the mix and ended his report with a chilling warning that, again, Justice O'Keefe noted in his sentence: 'Ms Knight's personality characteristics are well established and are unlikely to change by the intervention of doctors or psychologists, a view expressed at least 25 years ago.' He was referring to the psychiatrist who treated Katherine Knight at Morisset hospital in 1976 after she was admitted for attacking Margaret Perry.

'Ms Knight will retain a capacity for violence and for being affronted by any challenge to a relationship, and she will continue to feel entitled to express herself in any way she deems appropriate (violent or otherwise) to gratify her feelings. There is particular concern about John Price's children and other members of his family.'

Later that afternoon, Mr Macadam addressed the issue of the prisoner's potential for further violence arising out of Dr Milton's report.

'Doctor . . . would it be reasonable to say that the very nature of the offence itself speaks or suggests strongly of future danger-ousness, just from the very nature of the offence itself?' Macadam asked.

'It does,' Dr Milton replied.

'Is it eloquent of future dangerousness?'

'It is.'

'And finally, doctor, in terms of the bizarre nature of this offence . . . the ordinary man might see the circumstances of this case such that "the person that carried out these acts must be mad". That would be the reaction immediately, I think you would probably agree with that?'

'That is a common reaction, yes it is.'

'But in this case do you have any view as to whether Ms Knight had the ability to create a situation such as to make it appear that she was mad?'

'I think there were elements of that, I do.'

'You do know . . . that at one point in time she said to her brother . . . words to the effect, "I'm going to kill Pricey and I'm going to get away with it because I'll make it out that I'm mad"?'

'Yes, I'm aware of that.'

'Do you think that any of the actions, bizarre as they may seem, after the killing may have been in pursuit of that object?'

'I think that is very likely . . .'

Macadam was done. Katherine Knight's lawyer, Peter Thraves, QC, rose from his seat and began his cross-examination of Dr Milton.

'On your estimation of the personality traits of Mrs Knight, you are concerned for the future?' said Mr Thraves.

'Yes,' Dr Milton replied.

'And I understand that concern. My interest is in whether, from your observation, there is the capacity to not necessarily cure it but to improve Mrs Knight's relationship skills, if you like, in the future?'

'I am sorry, I would have to say no, I don't think there is.'

'Now, it is logical to assume that psychiatry will continue to advance, to expand, to develop more effective diagnostic tools and, with understanding, to develop means of even improving people's lot who are psychiatrically abnormal?'

'One certainly hopes so.'

'There is a real possibility that in two decades from now, for instance, someone can come along and examine someone who is exactly the same as the prisoner, Mrs Knight, and say, "Yes, we have got the means to ameliorate this condition now and make this person sane" – that is a possibility, isn't it?'

'It is possible.'

'Would you agree that again it is quite possible that Mrs Knight's condition could ameliorate over the passage of time, she being now forty-four years of age?' Mr Thraves asked.

'I don't feel hopeful. Given the intensity of what we have seen, no I don't.'

Prosecutor Mark Macadam had been sitting at the Bar table, making notes. Every now and then he looked up and conferred with his associate, Kylie Henry. At the end of Mr Thraves' questioning, Mr Macadam re-examined the witness.

'Doctor, my learned friend asked you some questions directed towards . . . the future dangerousness of the prisoner . . . but at page 17 (of your report) . . . you said "the personality problems demonstrated in the history of Ms Knight's life are not in my view psychiatric disease, they are her nature"?'

'Yes.'

'Is it likely, doctor, even as a remote possibility, that science would be able to change the nature of the human species?' the prosecutor asked.

'I am not hopeful that that will apply. I think it is most . . .'

'So may I take it, it is not a reasonable possibility at all?'

'I think it is very unlikely.'

'So, doctor, as the situation now is then, is it such that your opinion as demonstrated in the final paragraph of your report is still your view, where it reads: "Ms Knight's personality characteristics are well established and they are not likely to change by the intervention of doctors or psychologists"?'

'Yes.'

'Now and ongoing?'

'Yes.'

The same day, Justice O'Keefe would ask Dr Delaforce to make a prediction on Katherine Knight's potential for future danger. The psychiatrist said that when things don't go her own way, there would be a risk of extreme violence.

'Doctor, one of her daughters visited her in prison – Natasha . . . and according to the daughter the prisoner said . . . that she could kill her daughter and no one would be able to stop her . . . Does it bear at all on your view . . . in relation to future risk concerning this prisoner?'

'Yes, it has to, it must . . . One interpretation is that she is expressing her power, her control: "I could kill you. It doesn't matter who you are, I could do that",' Dr Delaforce replied. 'And that (is a) characteristic of the prisoner, that she will get her way, beware of crossing her, she will pay you back.'

It is not known why Katherine Knight threatened her daughter in prison, but that she did, the psychiatrists said, was 'very worrying'.

Psychiatry is an evolving discipline and open to argument even by those who practise it. Often, it's a case of semantics. What one psychiatrist calls a person's 'nature', another calls their personality disorder. The American Psychiatric Association's DSM-IV lists ten personality disorders plus a group of disorders 'not otherwise specified'. Patients can have more than one disorder at a time, or have elements of several. The disorders include paranoid personality, schizoid personality, schizotypal personality (which are clustered together as a group), antisocial personality (previously known as a psychopath), borderline personality, histrionic personality, narcissistic personality, avoidant personality, dependent personality, and obsessive personality.

The borderline personality is clustered with antisocial, histrionic and narcissistic disorders and people who have them are often dramatic, emotional or erratic. To be classified with any disorder, the traits must be evident by early adulthood. Some psychiatrists report that childhood sexual abuse is often present in people who later present with various personality disorders. The DSM-IV states that borderlines are prone to angry disruptions in close relationships, self-destructiveness, chronic feelings of deep emptiness, loneliness and marked impulsivity. They also make frantic efforts to avoid real or imagined abandonment.

Carl Malmquist in his book *Homicide: A Psychiatric Perspective* described the changes in behaviour thus: 'Another contributing variable to violent behaviour – the smoldering resentments and enduring hatred – may seem incongruent with the theory that BPD individuals frequently vacillate between opposites. In line with this characteristic, these individuals often do not seek just a vindication or victory, but sometimes a total annihilation of a selected target who becomes a hated object and once again is seen as responsible for their unhappy plight.'

For three hours and fifty minutes Katherine Knight was interviewed by Dr Leonard Lambeth at Mulawa Women's Correctional Centre on 28 September 2001, less than three weeks before her scheduled trial date. He had been hired by Knight's lawyer Peter Thraves, QC, and his report, dated 15 October, came in at sixteen pages long. It shared some of the same diagnoses as Dr Delaforce, notably, borderline personality disorder and post traumatic stress disorder.

Four weeks later, at Katherine Knight's sentencing hearing in the Supreme Court, Dr Lambeth said that she was suffering from a mild depression when he interviewed her, possibly because of her incarceration, but he was surprised her depression wasn't greater as a result of being jailed. On the mental status examination, he said she was essentially a normal person of average or low intelligence. He concluded she had experienced dissociative amnesia on the night of the murder, however he couldn't say when it began.

He said he could find no evidence of her violent fantasies, and indeed, she told him her favourite video was *Lady and the Tramp*.

She did tell him about killing David Saunders' pet dingo pup – 'All I know, he's telling me to kill him. I had the knife in my hand,' she told him – but not about stabbing him in the stomach with the scissors or about threatening to cut the throat of a new puppy he had wanted to give to his and Katherine's daughter as a pet. She also told Dr Lambeth about offering to pay her nephew Jason Roughan $500 to throw acid in Pricey's face, something Jason never did.

Justice O'Keefe then ran through a catalogue of things that Knight and Dr Lambeth discussed during their interview.

'[Had she told you about a] previous attack on Price with a knife leading to the wounds . . . which is on the left breast, to the left of the sternum?' the judge asked.

'No,' Dr Lambeth answered.

'Did she tell you about the Mondeo?'

'No, not at all.'

'Did she tell you about engaging somebody for $500 to throw acid in Price's face?'

'This was her nephew, I believe.'

'Yes. She indicated that?'

'Yes.'

'Well, on one view that suggests a selectivity on her part in relation to events?' said Justice O'Keefe.

'Yes.'

'Now what, if anything, is the significance of that, other than perhaps in relation to her credibility?'

'The only other view is that she may well have dissociated these things out; in other words, she may have genuinely forgotten them as part of the personality disorder. That is a view that is possible. I am not saying it is probable.'

The prosecutor Mark Macadam took over: 'In terms of her credibility, doctor, did you think she was being genuine with you? Was your impression a favourable one?'

'Well, I must admit, at the time I interviewed her, yes, because it was consistent. It was consistent and there was no attempt that was visible to avoid, there was no hesitation in answering, there were none of the things that you usually see when people are attempting to lie to you.'

'Well, sometimes somebody may be a very good liar?'

'It means either they are a very, very good liar or they are telling the truth.'

Justice O'Keefe spoke: 'Or that they may have been through it a number of times before with various people?'

'Yes, that is possible,' Dr Lambeth answered.

'So that they have got the story off pat, as it were?'

'Yes.'

Detective Bob Wells was preparing to go to court. He had faith in the two Crown prosecutors, Mark Macadam and Kylie Henry. They'd never wavered in their decision to let the jury decide whether Katherine Knight was guilty of cold-blooded murder. For a cop, that's a good thing. Too often, police work themselves into the ground to build a strong case only to have the lawyers who take the matter to court accept a lesser plea. It's known as 'charge bargaining', and it infuriates them. Police believe crooks generally get the charge they deserve.

But there were two things bothering Bob Wells. Despite the hours he had put into the case, he hadn't found Pricey's stolen $1000, nor could he pin down the final sequence of steps in Kathy Knight's last tango in Aberdeen. Even with the forensic analysis and testing on Pricey's body and the pot on the stove-top, which was still between 40° and 50° Celsius when police arrived, Wells didn't know if the accused defiled and cooked John Price's body before she robbed him, or afterwards, when she came back from robbing him. Wells is a cop, he doesn't like loose ends.

'We don't know, we don't really know if she killed him, cut him up, while naked, then dressed in those clothes – because she was found in the clothes she was wearing the day before – and showered, drove, got the money, went back and dropped the car and went back and took the overdose,' Wells said. 'Or, killed him, left him there, went away with his wallet, dressed, then went to the bank, came back and sliced him up and did the business.

'I believe that she's killed him and cut him up because she's had that rage, and really done her 'nana. I couldn't see her getting changed twice. I reckon she started when she had that black nightie on, because if she's done the whole job with the black nightie, it would have been absolutely caked. It just had a few flecks of flesh on it. But she's realised and taken it off, done the job while she's been naked. And then she's showered, left the nightie in the bathroom, showered, then put those clothes back on – the light denim, shirt and the shorts – and then gone away and come back.

'She's not going to change them twice. She's not going to put them on, go there, come back, take 'em off, cut him up again and put them on. So that's why I think she's done it with a bit of rage. She's come back in to the house and thought ah, what have I done, and then she's gone and taken the tablets which were never going to kill her anyway. That's my opinion as to the circumstance of the events.'

It wasn't just Detective Wells who was confounded by the missing money. The judge raised it with the lawyers at Katherine Knight's sentencing hearing as the court was about to play the videotape of the search at her home in MacQueen Street.

Justice O'Keefe: 'Does it show anything in relation to the $1000?'

Prosecutor Macadam: 'No, your Honour. The $1000 I can indicate has never been located.'

Knight's lawyer Peter Thraves, QC, added: 'Not for want of trying, your Honour. We have all tried to find it.'

22

No remorse, no mercy

Murder trials never start with the theatre of a television court-room or the drama of the big screen. Instead, they putter to life like a 1971 Holden HQ with the choke at half throttle on a frosty morning. And so it was with Regina v. Katherine Mary Knight, case number 70094/00 in the New South Wales Supreme Court, Criminal Division, sitting high on a hill at East Maitland in the spring of 2001.

Day one, 16 October, had hardly got going when it was over. Learned counsel for the Crown and the defendant respectively, Mark Macadam and Peter Thraves, announced their appearances to Justice Barry O'Keefe. The sitting was largely to discuss the content of the necessary warning the judge would issue to poten-tial jurors the next day due to the horrific nature of the murder of John Charles Thomas Price.

Day two: Justice O'Keefe issued the warning to the assembled jury pool but then at least an hour into proceedings, called them to a halt. He asked the potential jurors to return the next morning. 'I do apologise,' Justice O'Keefe said. 'It is unusual but the circumstances that have arisen are unusual as well.'

The legal equivalent of a cliffhanger.

At 10 am on day three, Thursday 18 October, Pricey's three

children walked into court together with their mother, Colleen. They were anxious. They took their seats in the public gallery at the back of the courtroom on the right side looking towards the judge. They were about 10 metres away from the woman accused of murdering their father but couldn't see her face. Katherine Knight sat on a hard wooden bench with her back to them, alone in the middle of the courtroom in a wooden dock – a rectangular chest-high enclosure with a door that swung open to let the accused in and out. Two Corrective Services officers sat in chairs behind her, for security purposes. From where the Price family sat, they could never see her face unless she turned around, and she didn't. The journalists covering the hearing sat in old-fashioned pews to the judge's left, and when witnesses were sworn in they sat one rung lower in front of them. Katherine Knight could look at them directly.

Spot on ten o'clock, Justice O'Keefe walked to the raised bench at the front of the court from a side door that led to his temporary chambers. The court fell silent and rose as one. The judge nodded to the Bar table, and the assembled lawyers nodded back, as did the court officers and journalists who knew the drum. The public, unfamiliar with the required formality, stood still before sitting when the judge sat down.

The indictment was read by the judge's associate and Katherine Knight was asked for her plea.

'Guilty,' she replied.

Pricey's family members were overwhelmed with emotions; joy collided with relief and mixed with sorrow. They held hands in triumph. Tears welled in their eyes and spilled down their cheeks. Colleen, wearing a crisp white top and a string of black beads, her hair neatly pulled back in her signature braid, rifled through her handbag for tissues. They had been bracing themselves for a three-week murder trial but at the very last minute – just after the jury selection process had started the day before – Katherine Knight indicated she would plead guilty. They'd prayed for it but wouldn't allow themselves to think it possible. Knight's youngest brother Shane sat quietly on the other side of the courtroom.

Justice O'Keefe spoke: 'You understand, Mrs Knight, do you, the effect of that plea?'

'Beg your pardon?'

'You understand the effect of that plea – that is, that you are admitting to the charge of murder?'

'Yes, your Honour.'

'You have taken counsel's advice, have you?'

'Yes, your Honour.'

'And I understand that you have had the opportunity to consider that matter overnight?'

'Yes, your Honour.'

'And you are content to lodge that plea, is that correct?'

'Yes, your Honour.'

She sat down and said nothing while the lawyers talked about procedural matters at the end of which Justice O'Keefe again turned to her and asked her to stand up.

'Mrs Knight, you have pleaded guilty to a charge of murder and I have accepted that plea. As a consequence, I judge you to be guilty of murder and a conviction for murder will be recorded accordingly. Do you understand?'

Katherine Knight stood alone in her legal corral. 'Yes, your Honour.'

Justice O'Keefe told her that she would be brought to court each day during the sentencing hearing which would start the next morning, and court was adjourned. She was led back to the cells.

Minutes later outside the courthouse, Colleen, Rosemary, Jackie and Johnathon Price embraced. Tears streamed down the girls' faces. Rosemary spoke for her family and never once mentioned the murderer's name. 'Simply to lose Dad at such a young age was terrible. But for her to do what she did to him makes it really hard to bear,' Rosemary said as the cameras whirred and clicked and newspaper reporters took notes. 'I don't want people to just think about what she did to him when they think about this crime. Dad was a person, a great bloke, a grandfather who loved a laugh and a good time.

'Not a day goes by when I don't think of Dad and miss him. He didn't deserve this. Dad wouldn't hurt anyone.'

Rosemary's words were printed in a story written by Frances O'Shea beside a picture of a grim-looking John Price in the next morning's edition of Sydney's *Daily Telegraph* under the headline 'A horror murder that was too awful too imagine'. Pricey, with a beer in his hand, stood next to a double-chinned Katherine Knight, his body angled away from her. She leaned against a railing, smiling. She had a cigarette in one hand and was wearing black stretch bike shorts and a T-shirt with Tweety Pie on it.

Katherine Knight faced a certain future in prison, but she did not know whether she would get a life sentence or a fixed sentence with the chance of parole. Since the truth-in-sentencing legislation was enacted on 12 January 1991, if a person is sentenced to life in prison, the intention is, pending appeals, they will die there.

With her guilty plea to murder, Katherine Knight had abandoned the defence of substantial impairment caused by an abnormality of the mind, but her QC, Mr Thraves, still hoped to use it in mitigation at sentencing: 'We accepted with our plea of guilty that it was not sufficient to diminish a plea of guilty to manslaughter. We abandoned that,' said Mr Thraves in court. 'But in my submission, I am entitled to explore that position, in view of putting all the available material before your Honour to weigh in the balance of sentencing.'

When an accused person pleads guilty, the judge, after considering all the facts, has the power to give them a discount on the sentence they would have received had a jury found them guilty. But, it's not a guarantee. Mr Thraves didn't say it, he didn't need to, but it was clear that Katherine Knight did not want to spend the rest of her life in prison.

Day four, Friday 19 October. Death threats had been made against the convicted murderer, Katherine Knight, and security at the East Maitland courthouse was increased to ensure her safety. An airport-security metal detector gate was installed outside the entry to court and checked everyone who entered. Barricades had also been set up in the form of a makeshift race from the court benches to prevent access from the public area to the dock where the prisoner sat.

It was 10 am. The sentencing hearing began. A 52-minute videotape of the crime scene at St Andrews Street was played on a television suspended from the wall over the reporters. Justice

O'Keefe sat in his red high-backed chair looking down at a portable television monitor on his bench. The prisoner, as she was now known, had permission from the judge to be spared from watching the horror she created unfold on the television screens and was led out of court to the bright yellow cells at the side of the courtroom.

She waited in Cell 1. It had a stainless steel toilet and hand basin on the back wall and a concrete bench on which she could sit or lie down. It had no mattress or pillows or cushions. Comfort was not a priority. The front of the cell was covered with perspex glass which offered no privacy, and the door was locked by a heavy brass padlock, recalling crime and punishment of an era long past. A camera was mounted high in one corner and took in the entire cell. Katherine Knight was completely alone but every move she made was monitored.

The court was in total silence. The crime scene footage was graphic, no commentary was needed to describe the unspeakable acts captured on it. A white noise hummed in the background as the video opened with an external shot of the front of John Price's house. It cut to the bedroom, where the assault had begun after 'pleasurable sex' between the couple. It panned over the blood-stained sheets, light green in colour. The camera operator traced Pricey's last steps down the hallway, training the camera on his escape route and focusing on the blood sprays on the white walls. No one was in the frame, but those who saw the film could imagine the terror that John Price felt as he fled down the hallway to meet his death in the entrance foyer of his home.

A pool of blood filled the hallway. Sticking out from the archway into the lounge-room were the legs of John Price, his left ankle crossed over the right. The camera moved over Pricey's skinned and decapitated corpse, and then walked through to the kitchen and dining area, where it focused on the 'suit' of skin hanging from the architrave that separated the kitchen from the lounge-room. Gash wounds testified to the assault. The camera operator panned over to the kitchen sink; an ant trail crawled around cooking utensils and vegetable peelings. It tracked around to the bench-top by the stove where two baked dinners had been laid out for Johnathon and Jackie. A baking tray was left on the stove-top next to a big pot. The lid was lifted to reveal the cooked head of John Price.

It was the most rudimentary and honest of any horror film ever made, and a shockingly powerful way to start the sentencing hearing.

Katherine Knight returned to the dock. Mr Macadam tendered Post Mortem No. 00086, which was written by Dr Timothy Lyons. It read: 'Cause of death: Multiple internal injuries secondary to multiple stab wounds. There has also been almost complete post mortem skinning and decapitation.'

The next day the story had travelled across an ocean and continent. In London, the racy tabloid newspaper *The Mirror* ran a 283-word story on page 29 under the headline 'Mrs Hannibal: Jilted Kath cooks lover's body and serves it up for his family'. The story, written by Isobelle Gidley in Sydney, stated:

> Jilted Katherine Knight stabbed her lover, cut off his skin, then cooked his chopped up body and served it up on dinner plates.
>
> . . . The scenes in the house, reminiscent of Hannibal the Cannibal in *Silence Of The Lambs*, were so gruesome that police officers are still having counselling a year later, a court in East Maitland, near Sydney, was told yesterday.
>
> Knight admitted murder, sparing Mr Price's children . . . from hearing further horrific details.
>
> Rosemary said later: It would have haunted the jury for the rest of their lives like it haunts us.

~

Detective Sergeant Bob Wells was the last witness on Tuesday 23 October, sworn in at 4.06 pm. His extensive investigation would put Knight behind bars for a long time, but walking into the witness box to testify was almost an anticlimax. It had been the biggest case of his career and this marked the beginning of the end.

Wells gave a brief summary of the case to the court, recapping how the police investigation began with the 7.45 am phone call from Pricey's boss Geoffrey Bowditch to Senior Constable Matthews at Muswellbrook police station.

Pricey's children listened. They had gotten to know the detective well and knew that he had suffered as a result of the carnage he'd had to investigate. In many ways they were irrevocably bound together by Katherine Knight's atrocity. They listened intently. Shane Knight, loyal, was there too, in a show of support for his sister. Bob Wells continued, offering a stark and frightening catalogue of the prisoner's plan.

'Geraldine Edwards and Amanda Pemberton both described the prisoner as jealous of Price,' said Bob Wells, his policeman's voice echoing through the courtroom. When he looked up, he looked straight at Katherine Knight, who sat prim and proper in the dock.

'Tracey Knight, niece of the prisoner, described the prisoner as vindictive. The prisoner's ex-partner David Saunders described the prisoner as violent. Another ex-partner, John Chillingworth described the prisoner as cold and calculating and vengeful . . .

'The prisoner made the following comments regarding her intentions towards Price; to her daughter Natasha, "I told him that if he took me back this time, it was to the death". "If I kill Pricey, I'll kill myself after it".'

'To her neighbour Geraldine Edwards, "If I ever catch Pricey playing up on me I told him I'd kill him and cut his dick and balls off".

'To Price and heard by her friend Amanda Pemberton, "If you leave me I'll cut your balls out".

'To her brother Kenneth (Charlie) Knight, "I'm going to kill Pricey and the two kids too". "I'm going to kill Pricey and I'm going to get away with it. I'll get away with it 'cause I'll make out I'm mad".

'Said to Price and heard by Trevor Lewis, "You'll never get me out of this house, I'll do you in first".'

Bob Wells was finished and left the witness box.

The court did not sit the next day. It was Wednesday 24 October – Katherine Knight's 46th birthday.

Each night at 6 pm the horror of the day's hearing was broadcast on the evening news, and in the morning, the newspapers repeated the story with their headlines spelling out the evil that could not be undone. Aberdeen was reeling again. Old wounds had been reopened and this time, the details from the court hearing branded forever on their memory the truth of what had happened to Pricey. Martha Jabour at the Homicide Victims' Support Group received calls from Aberdeen residents wanting to know what Katherine Knight's guilty plea meant for them. Would she come home?, they wanted to know. It was as if a blanket of misery had descended on the town, smothering it and shaming it once more. Kathy's house had been sold to help pay her legal fees and the boards on the windows were an allegory for her life: what was hidden behind those walls?

Katherine Knight had been the perfect model of suburban mediocrity as she walked into the dock at the beginning of each new day in East Maitland Court. Some days she wore her hair up in a ponytail that spilled like a fountain from the top of her head. She had a range of outfits that were alternated during the thirteen-day hearing, including a white two-piece suit that she had made on her sewing machine at home. She teamed it with black stockings and white shoes. She had a black pantsuit, and occasionally wore a Laura Ashley-style floral sundress with a white cardigan. There was nothing sinister about the way she dressed or carried herself.

Her impressive height and proud carriage commanded attention, but as she sat quietly day after day alone in the dock with her hands clasped on her lap, she looked like a woman you might run into at the shops or in the doctor's office. Not a killer capable of the gruesome acts that were being discussed by lawyers, doctors, police and pathologists at the front of the court.

The prisoner paid attention to the evidence as it unfolded. The lawyers, who sat at the Bar table directly in front of her, rarely paid her any attention nor did she request it. The Sheriffs and Corrective Services officers, whose job it is to guard the accused and ensure the safety of the court, had come to know her and let her spend part of one lunch break talking with her brother Shane, who was in the courtroom almost every day. The prisoner was no trouble.

That changed on day six. The morning opened with the court being shown the videotape Katherine Knight had made at her daughter Natasha's house about six hours before she killed Pricey. It included scenes shot at a school concert for Sarah, and

Kathy shook her head in time with the music, obviously enjoying the memory. She watched intently the images of her grand-daughter bouncing on her knee accompanied by the little girl's delighted giggles. It showed happy scenes with her two youngest children Sarah and Eric playing on the floor, then a group shot in the hallway. At one point, Katherine's face filled the screen and she said: 'I hope to see all my children again.' Jarring. Was it a farewell video?

At 2.05 pm, the prosecutor called his third witness to the stand: Detective Senior Constable Peter Muscio, the scientific officer then attached to the Maitland Crime Scene Section. Muscio led the court through the forensic evidence he had collected and the method with which he conducted the investigation. Muscio said later that he arrived at St Andrews Street at 10 am and was still at Muswellbrook Police Station at 4 am the next morning booking his exhibits. He had brought into court the three knives that had been used to murder John Price and dissect his body, and the meat-hook on which Knight hung his skin. 'She showed a great deal of interest in the knives . . .' Muscio remembered later, 'she showed a lot of interest in that hook, too, the stainless steel hook.'

Katherine Knight sat in the dock and watched as Muscio pro-duced the first knife, the 31.5 centimetre yellow-handled knife. The handle had been stained black by the fingerprinting process, Muscio explained as he passed the knife to Justice O'Keefe, who had donned plastic surgical gloves before taking it.

'There is a broken piece and I can see what appears to be a finely honed edge. There is blood, perhaps skin and some hair adherent to the knife,' the judge said, examining the weapon.

'Your Honour will see in some of the postmortem photo-graphs there is one there of the skull which has a little chunk of it cut out, so that may explain . . . the gap in the blade,' the pros-ecutor Mark Macadam offered.

Muscio then produced the smaller yellow-handled knife that was found on the kitchen sink, its handle similarly stained by the fingerprinting process, and the small black paring knife with the blunt edge that was found on the kitchen breakfast bar. Muscio said the DNA profile taken from the three knives was consistent with that of the victim, indicating all had been used.

'As to the actual purposes I can't be sure, but the smaller knife, there was no major staining of the blade, and it may have been used in the preparation of the vegetables,' said Muscio. 'The other two were quite capable of doing the major damage to the deceased.'

'The large knife was fairly close by the body?' asked Mr Macadam.

'Yes.'

Muscio was asked for his opinion of the events on the night Pricey was killed and he said Knight dragged Pricey onto the carpet where she skinned and decapitated him. As he talked, the prisoner started making low keening noises in the dock. She had her eyes closed and her teeth clenched, like they were chattering. Justice O'Keefe studied her silently. Peter Muscio thought to himself, 'When you're finished . . .', and continued with his evidence. It was graphic and detailed.

'He has then been decapitated and his head carried into the kitchen and placed into an aluminium boiler. Vegetables have then been added to the mixture which was cooked and left on the stove-top,' said Muscio. 'At some stage later the pelt has been hung from the top of the dining/lounge-room doorway with a stainless steel hook.'

Katherine Knight had started a short, sharp rocking motion in her chair, moaning, her eyes still closed, her top teeth crunching against her bottom. The lawyers looked around at her.

Muscio continued. He said he believed John Price's head had been put in the pot on the stove before his 'suit' of skin was hung from the architrave over the doorway. He reasoned the drops of blood leading from the body to the stove went through the middle of the door so it made sense it was clear at the time. The human pelt, when it was found the next morning, hung from the centre of the door and took up most of the passageway. Muscio later took it down. 'It was quite heavy . . . I wasn't looking forward to it,' Muscio remembered.

Mr Thraves had been watching Katherine Knight and interrupted from the Bar table.

'Excuse my interrupting, your Honour, but I have some concerns for the prisoner.'

'I'm sorry, Mr Thraves, but the prisoner will have to stay here while the evidence relating to these matters is given,' said Justice O'Keefe.

'I was going to ask your Honour, if your Honour could adjourn for five minutes so that I can assess, in a layman's way, the state she is in.'

'All right.'

After the short adjournment, Justice O'Keefe told the court that Mr Thraves was concerned about the effect of the police-man's evidence on Knight, who Mr Thraves thought could be experiencing a dissociation or, at least, a non-receptiveness to the material being presented. Mr Thraves would argue his client had suffered amnesia regarding the murder. The judge declined to adjourn the hearing for the day and said it was central to the case to determine if the prisoner did indeed have amnesia or could recollect the night of the murder.

'If she doesn't, the recounting itself may assist her recollection even if there be a genuine amnesia,' said the judge. 'The events being recounted are those in which she was intimately involved and [is the] only living witness . . . Finally, there may well be a real suggestion that there is an element of play-acting on the part of the prisoner. That has been foreshadowed by the Crown. I have not formed any view in relation to such a matter but I need to do so.

'For these reasons I am of the opinion that it would not be in the interests of justice to further defer this evidence and I do not think it would be appropriate to allow the prisoner not to be present while it's given.'

Mr Thraves sat down at the Bar table and Muscio went back to his evidence, producing the meat-hook on which Pricey's pelt had been hung. He said DNA testing on slivers from the two 'steaks' that had been laid out as meals proved they were consistent with the victim and had come from his right buttock. Katherine Knight continued to groan and increased the speed of her rocking. She rolled her eyes back in her head and threw her arms over her head. Johnathon Price was a few rows behind her, watching. The prisoner's brother Shane Knight was also watching, growing concerned.

The prosecutor continued: 'Detective Muscio . . . is there anything about the scene that could tell you one way or another whether or not the act of the stabbing and killing of Mr Price and his decapitation and mutilation was a consistent series of acts or whether or not –' Mr Macadam broke off as Knight increased the volume and velocity of her mumbling, rocking, huffing and puffing.

'Continue, Mr Crown,' Justice O'Keefe ordered.

'– or whether it was,' Mr Macadam started. He stopped. 'Your Honour, perhaps the prisoner is showing some signs of –'

Knight had started yelling and threw herself on the floor of the dock, bucking her body. She kicked at the dock, and flailed her arms. Her brother Shane shouted 'do something for her', and three court officers helped her from the courtroom. One observer thought she was screaming 'blood' but couldn't be sure. Paramedics were at the courthouse within minutes and rushed to her aid. She was treated for a panic attack. It was 2.50 pm. Justice O'Keefe adjourned court for the day and Peter Muscio was told he would have to return to finish his evidence.

After ten minutes, the paramedics left and Katherine Knight was given a cup of tea with lots of milk and sugar. She spent the night in a less than salubrious cell at Newcastle court, and was back in court the next morning having been given a mild sedative by a doctor – as neat, prim and quiet as before. Said one observer of the prisoner the next day: 'She was as bright as a button.'

Robert Delaforce was the fourth witness for the prosecution. He was a familiar face to Katherine Knight, having spent nearly nine hours interviewing her at Mulawa Women's Correctional Centre the year before. She sat quietly in the dock as Dr Delaforce raised his right hand and swore on the Bible to tell the truth. Soon the courtroom turned into an ersatz movie theatre with a private screening of the 1999 film *Resurrection*. Dr Delaforce effectively took the role of film critic, commenting on the horror movie that was collected as evidence from Katherine Knight's home.

The video starred French actor Christopher Lambert in the role of a detective on the hunt for a serial killer and was directed by Australian Russell Mulcahy. The tagline for the movie on the cover of the video came from Ecclesiastes 6:1: 'There is an evil which I have seen under the sun, and it is common among men'.

Mr Thraves objected to the videotape being played because it could not be proved that the prisoner had seen it and she may only have picked it up from her sister on the day before the murder. Justice O'Keefe, who admitted he found the video 'disturbing', overruled the objection and said the videotape had come from her house, along with several other horror videotapes.

The judge asked Dr Delaforce what an affection for such movies might mean about a person and the psychiatrist reassured him that most fans of the horror genre were gratified by the harmless escapism and that that was perfectly healthy. 'But for some people it is an absolute morbid interest which excites them . . . they are preoccupied with it in an absolutely pathological way, they want to do what is going on in that movie,' he said.

Delaforce had the run of the courtroom while certain sections of *Resurrection* were played. He stopped the film at points that he believed related to Katherine Knight's case, and elaborated. He pointed out that one line of dialogue was significant: 'he bled him like a stuck pig'. He stopped the video again when the killer used a stun-gun to zap his victim into unconsciousness before mutilating him. 'The significance of that relates to what happens at abattoirs,' he said.

During the course of Delaforce's evidence, the prosecutor Mr Macadam said: 'I think you were at pains to say . . . during the showing of the videos, in her case what might be seen perhaps as an unusual but a harmless interest, in her case it is more of a morbid fascination type?'

'It certainly was, yes.'

'And you considered that to be relevant in your assessment of her behaviour in this case?'

'Yes I did. Definitely, definitely . . . If she had just killed Mr Price, even, say, one stab wound, even the more than 30 stab wounds that were apparently sustained, one could say, well, she had had a lot of anger because of all that has happened to her throughout her life. Maybe she just totally lost control and could not stop stabbing,' said Dr Delaforce. 'But you would think then after the stabbing it would all stop; she would walk away, perhaps with a lot of remorse . . . but it becomes more than that.

It is more than just stabbing, cutting, the knife going in and out, many, many times. The skill, the time, the focus that must have been required to cut off the head . . . to be able to take virtually all of the skin off . . . must have shown her purpose, her intent and her desire . . . ' he went on. 'And to continue doing that, one would want to do that. I couldn't find any other explanation – that was pleasurable, and I think that is a critical thing.'

Katherine Knight sat motionless, listening intently. The Price family was in the back of the courtroom, listening in horror as the psychiatrist described the woman they had let into their lives, the woman who had made delicate baby clothes for Pricey's grandchildren.

'Are you saying, Dr Delaforce, that she enjoyed what she did?' asked Mr Macadam.

'There is much to indicate that . . .'

'What, got some form of excitement of whatever type, some type of excitement, some type of thrill, would that be . . .?'

'Yes. It is probably that she thought about doing things like that for a long time, perhaps many years. Remember, up until the mid eighties she worked at the abattoirs, and you of course introduce the idea there of dealing with the animal parts, and she told me how she would enjoy getting out the blood from the bone marrow, cleaning that out; she enjoyed slicing, she enjoyed that work,' said Dr Delaforce. 'Not many people do, or would, but she enjoyed it. She particularly enjoyed going to the old man who was involved in killing the pigs.'

Macadam: 'The behaviour we have been dealing with in terms of what she did, . . . is there a term to describe the behaviour exhibited by her?'

'Yes there is.'

'What is it?'

'It is called picquerism,' and Dr Delaforce spelled it out for the court recorder.

'What is that?'

'It is the satisfaction – it is referred to in the context of the sexual satisfaction, but it doesn't have to be sexual – the satisfaction from stabbing, cutting, slicing another person or animal, and the related consequences, blood spurting, blood flowing . . . the consequences of blood spurting and death. It is describing a behaviour of course, an absolutely perverted behaviour.'

Justice O'Keefe broke in: 'Where does picquerism come from, as a word? Is it somebody's name?' he asked.

'I am not aware of that.'

'Do you spell it with a capital P?'

'No.'

'Then it suggests it might have been derived from the French.'

Macadam helped out: 'It is described, is it not, by a person called Robert D. Keppel, who is a person involved in forensic investigations in America?'

'Yes.'

Robert Keppel was the primary investigator on the case of serial killer Ted Bundy and is the author of *Signature Killers: Interpreting the Calling Cards of the Serial Murderer*. He has studied the minds of some of the most terrifying murderers and serial killers in the United States. In the book's foreword, written by leading American crime writer Ann Rule, Keppel says the thing he learned from Bundy and other killers was that the process of murder for these types of criminals goes on longer than our perception of it. 'One of them told me, "the murder ain't over until I say it's over".'

In an interview from his office in between investigations, Keppel, who is now the president of the Institute for Forensics in Seattle, Washington, said picquerism, fortunately, was rare. Perhaps more frighteningly, he said that people choose it – it doesn't choose them. Picquerism is not an illness.

'It's the sexual excitation that some people get from stabbing or penetrating holes in people . . . Anytime anyone does this kind of stuff, they choose to do it, so you don't get picquerism like you get a cold. You have chosen this, you have thought about it, you have made a conscious decision. Doing it makes you feel good and so obviously if a person goes through all that effort and it makes them feel good, they continue on with it. So I think it's more a case of choice, of making someone feel good.'

Asked about Katherine Knight, he was blunt. 'I think she would have been feeling pleasure. What a woman gets out of a sexual experience is different to a man, but certainly the same kind of pleasure.'

Peter Thraves opened his case for the defence on Tuesday 30 October and called Katherine's brother-in-law John Hinder, and then his estranged wife Joy, Kathy's twin. The couple had broken up the previous July, a few months after the murder, but they were united in their testimony that they had received the videotape of *Resurrection* the day before the murder, and that Katherine had only picked it up from them several hours before she killed John Price.

Mr Thraves then called his third witness to the stand. Dr Len Lambeth was sworn in by the court Sheriff at eight minutes to three in the afternoon.

Knight's guilty plea effectively meant that she could not rely on the defence of abnormality of mind to get a lesser conviction of manslaughter, but Mr Thraves argued his client's borderline personality disorder should be used by the judge towards mitigation. Mr Thraves asked Dr Lambeth what role her personality disorder played in determining her behaviour that night.

'You don't have a little bit of personality disorder. You have personality disorder. The main criterion for personality disorder is that it is pervasive, so it affects all parts of the patient's life,' Dr Lambeth told the court. 'And with personality disorder we see that the patient's decisions, the patient's actions and the patient's feelings are dependent upon the personality, which in this case is disordered, and we believe has been formed by factors early in the patient's experience. So that to look at the acts perpetrated by Mrs Knight and try and say that personality disorder has no relevance is, in my opinion, ridiculous.'

Justice O'Keefe interrupted from the bench: 'But, doctor . . . You see, there are plenty of people – you have given the percentages in your report – in the community who have borderline personality disorders?'

'There are.'

'In nigh on fifty years in the law I have not struck one that resulted in a stabbing followed by a skinning followed by a decapitation followed by a cooking of a supposedly loved one,' Justice O'Keefe continued. 'In other words, if what you say is right, then one would have expected to have found perhaps more of such behaviour . . . ?'

'I think, your Honour, that the personality disorder very possibly determines, if you like, the decision – "I will do this". The way that decision is carried out, if you like, the plastic part of the decision, is determined by other factors, not including the personality but also including experience, social mores and generally the way the person lives.'

'But if we take this case . . . she had a joyous day apparently filled with loving grandchildren and children, followed by enjoyable sex, with no hint of any aggression, then a claim not to remember anything, but the most frightful events then occurring?' asked Justice O'Keefe.

'Yes.'

'Now, does that suggest that there is a planning that is part of the personality disorder but that the circumstances of when that plan will be implemented et cetera at adventitious, or does it indicate something else?'

'It may indicate what you suggest, your Honour, and then I believe there would need to be a trigger to start the actions off.'

'We don't have a trigger,' said Justice O'Keefe.

'We don't have a trigger?' asked Dr Lambeth.

'We don't have a trigger at all. The only trigger that we have in this case that is apparent on the evidence as I presently see it . . . is that there was an event on the preceding Sunday involving violence and a threat to get her out of the house. That is forty-eight hours before. Now, is that sufficient or appropriate in a timeframe for that to be a trigger?'

'In my opinion it is sufficient for that to be the trigger for the killing. It certainly does not explain, nor I think can one explain, the full circumstances of the killing.'

The following day in court, the judge returned to the issue for clarity's sake.

'Doctor, if I understand correctly what you said yesterday, it is this. The events of the Sunday preceding the death appear to have been the defining moment or event; that her response to the threat of break-up . . . and exclusion from the house was that she would kill Price?'

'Yes,' answered Dr Lambeth.

'And that determination was a function of the whole person, including the personality disorder that she had?'

'Yes.'

Throughout his evidence Dr Lambeth went to lengths to explain borderline personality disorder and the frantic efforts that people with it went to to avoid loss. But surely, the judge said, there couldn't be anything more permanent than 'doing an act that would drive the loss; there can't be a loss any more permanent than killing a person?'

'No, there can't,' Dr Lambeth answered. 'And there may be many other interpretations that may be placed on this. This is an extraordinarily bizarre act.'

'If the apprehension of loss increased and that proved to be the trigger, then it is a bizarre way of preventing loss of a particular person . . . to kill that person?'

'It is, but it also means that no one else can have that person.'

'So that is part of the narcissism as well?'

'Yes.'

'And possessiveness?'

'Yes.'

'And retribution?'

'Yes . . . certainly that concept of payback, but your Honour must be aware that payback also applies to good deeds. So that in the borderline –'

He was interrupted by the judge: 'Well, I hope people don't kill others because they said something nice.'

'No, I mean in the borderline when someone does something that they perceive as nice, and that is usually something which strokes the ego – remembering a birthday, or something nice like that –'

'Or, as in this case, being very gentle and having sex that was mutually enjoyable. One could have thought that might well have fitted in that very category that you are talking about.'

'Yes, that is one of the things we can't understand.'

'And then, like the black widow spider almost, the mate is killed,' said Justice O'Keefe.

For the final minutes that he was in the witness stand, Dr Lambeth was cross-examined by the prosecution about whether

Katherine Knight would be a danger to society. Mr Macadam's questions were devastatingly direct, and the psychiatrist answered them with his trademark honesty. He had already said that the prisoner had been less than frank with him and said she told him her favourite video was *Lady and the Tramp*, a film that couldn't be more removed from the one that was shown in court as evidence, *Resurrection*.

'May I take it, doctor, that from the way in which you have expressed yourself here today, the chance of that dangerousness being ameliorated in any particular way does not stand a very good chance?' said Mr Macadam.

'No, that is true.'

'So whichever way we look at it, the court is confronted with a prisoner who is and will continue to be of great danger to the community if she were permitted to return to it?'

'Yes.'

'So it comes down to this, doctor, that regardless of whether her behaviour is governed by borderline personality or, as the other doctors suggest, just by her love of violence and the like, really, at the end of the day it doesn't matter all that much?'

'Without treatment, no,' said the psychiatrist.

'And you speak in that regard . . . as a person who has had considerable experience in places where forensic patients have been kept?'

'Yes.'

'I don't propose to ask any further questions.'

~

It was the first Monday of November and Australians were just six days away from returning Prime Minister John Howard to office for the third time. The front pages of the nation's newspapers were awash with stories about the children overboard incident, the political ramifications of the refugee crisis, and Kim Beazley's future as leader of the Australian Labor Party, which would either start again on Saturday with an unexpected victory in the Federal election or come to a crushing end. It was also Melbourne Cup week, when the entire nation stands still at 3.20 pm to watch a field of twenty-four thoroughbreds in the most prestigious and richest horserace in the southern hemisphere.

Katherine Knight was back at Mulawa Women's Correctional Centre and probably oblivious to most of it. As a convicted killer, she could neither vote nor bet and she had no access to newspapers which were carrying details about her murder sentencing.

First thing Monday morning, Knight had been transported to Newcastle Supreme Court for the final days of the hearing in which the prosecution and defence would make their closing submissions. The old courthouse on John Street in East Maitland had already been booked for another matter, so Justice O'Keefe took his court to the more modern surrounds at Newcastle.

It had been a long and emotional journey for John Price's children but they were intent on being in court for the final days of the sentencing. On Monday morning, they took their seats in the public gallery in Courtroom 1. Shane Knight was also there, still a few metres away from his sister sitting in the dock.

As is customary in closing arguments, the defence lawyer would make the first submission to the court. At 11 am on Monday 5 November, Peter Thraves stood before Justice O'Keefe and asked that Katherine Knight be shown some mercy. Yes, he said, her acts were horrific and they had hurt many innocent victims, but he said a life sentence should be avoided. He cited her plea of guilty, which prevented a long trial and also spared jurors hearing the frightening details of what she had done. He also pointed out that the prisoner had no prior criminal history and asked the judge to consider her personality disorder. 'It will be the defence submission to give a very long sentence but one which is finite, allowing the possibility that in the future this offender could be assessed as being able to be released,' said Mr Thraves.

Prosecutor Mark Macadam had twenty-four hours to polish his closing submission in which he argued that Katherine Knight had shown no remorse, so the judge, in his wisdom, should show her no mercy. Her crimes had fallen into the worst case category and deserved a sentence commensurate with that. Mr Macadam had been prosecuting criminals for twenty-five years, he told Justice O'Keefe, and never, ever, had he seen anything like this before. It was wicked, atrocious and evil, he said, his voice reverberating through the courtroom. She showed no contrition, Mr Macadam said, and the prospect of rehabilitation was remote: 'The punishment must fit the crime,' he said. Katherine Knight should spend the rest of her living days behind bars, Mr Macadam said.

The judge thanked Mr Thraves and Mr Macadam and adjourned court until Thursday at 11 am when he would hand down his sentence. Katherine Knight was led into the bowels of the courthouse to wait for the prison truck to return her to Mulawa, and the courtroom emptied. There was nothing more anyone could do but wait. The Price family returned to Aberdeen, and the lawyers went back to their chambers.

Around Australia, the nation stopped to watch a mare named Ethereal romp down the home straight at Flemington to win the 2001 Melbourne Cup.

23

For the term of her natural life

It was judgment day, Thursday 8 November. A full 618 days had passed since John Price was murdered by Katherine Knight, and his children felt the agony of his death every single day. A piece of them was missing, a gnawing emptiness that time could not fill. Johnathon, Rosemary and Jackie had each written to the judge explaining their sense of loss but words on paper seemed somehow hollow and inadequate to describe the black hole of grief they had been thrown into. They arrived in court with their mother Colleen, hoping and praying that Justice O'Keefe's sentence would fill the void, or at least a tiny bit of it.

Shane Knight arrived with his father Ken Knight, and they walked through the metal detector and into court united in their own torment and sorrow, taking a seat in the public gallery on the other side of the centre aisle from the Price family. They were still struggling to understand what Kathy had done and feared they never would – how could they, and how *could* she? And as much as they were horrified at her actions, she was still family, and family is family. It was one of the hardest moments of Ken Knight's life, especially when he and Shane were jeered at as they entered the courthouse.

The courtroom fell silent at precisely 11 am. Justice O'Keefe strode through the side door to the deep purple chair in the middle of the bench, his red robe flowing behind him. He nodded, showing the top of his powdered wig, and sat down. He had had a lot to consider. There was little doubt that the murder fell into the worst case category and under the Crimes Act 1900, the judge could either send Katherine Mary Knight to prison for the term of her natural life or he could show her mercy and impose a fixed sentence that might see her a free woman in many years to come. If he chose the former, Katherine Knight would be the first woman in Australian history imprisoned for the term of her natural life.

Justice O'Keefe began to read from his lengthy judgment. With the turning of each page came yet another reminder of what happened in the early hours of 1 March 2000. Katherine Knight sat silently in the dock staring straight ahead, impassive. She wore a black-patterned dress and a black jacket. The judge recounted the facts that had been presented and summarised the evidence of the witnesses who gave sworn testimony in court. He explained that he thought the murder was so gruesome that it couldn't be anything other than of the most serious kind.

John Price's children could feel knots in their stomachs. Rosemary and Jackie sobbed as the judge described how Mr Price had been stabbed thirty-seven times and the damage the knife had done to his body as he tried to flee. Every time they heard the details, the girls cried for their father's helplessness under attack. Eventually, Rosemary broke down and had to leave the court but she composed herself and returned to hear what she had been waiting for throughout the past three weeks.

Justice O'Keefe did not believe Knight's suicide was a genuine attempt and cited the toxicology reports which revealed the drugs in her blood levels were within the therapeutic limit. He did not believe her claim of amnesia and said that what she did on the night of the murder required a steady hand, and skill and understanding in driving a car, using an ATM and getting back to Pricey's house where she showered and freshened up. Her claimed amnesia, the judge said, was emotionally and litigiously convenient for her. And he did not believe that she was an innocent victim in her relationships with men but that she was, in fact, a frequent and serious aggressor. On balance, he believed the sworn testimonies of her ex-husband and past lovers rather than hers.

The murder of John Price, Justice O'Keefe said, was premeditated and the prisoner had planned the timing and the method of murder in such a way that she thought she might escape punishment by portraying herself as mad. The judge quoted from Dr Delaforce's oral evidence in which the psychiatrist said: 'It is very important to realise that the pleasure in getting rid of him and getting away with it by making out that she is mad, that in a sense is payback, but it is the way she gets rid of him that shows the absolute depravity of what she was doing. But that does not in itself mean madness, that type of interest – not to a psychiatrist, but to a lay person it would.'

Outside the courtroom, Pricey's younger brother Bob was causing trouble. He had been seen breaking a beer glass and putting two 10 centimetre-long pieces of glass into his coat pockets. He passed through the metal detector but was stopped before entering the courtroom. Police evicted him from the building. It was an emotional and trying morning. He was charged and five months later would plead guilty to offensive behaviour and carrying an offensive implement. He was fined $800 and hit with $58 in court costs.

Bob Price's yelling could be heard inside the courtroom but it didn't stop Justice O'Keefe. He was nearing the end of his judgment. Mr Thraves had raised four matters in mitigation: Katherine Knight's guilty plea, her borderline personality disorder, her lack of a criminal record and finally, a sense of mercy in imposing a finite sentence. The judge said the prisoner's borderline personality was not inconsistent with 'either premeditation or a natural cunning which may cause a prisoner to put the best gloss or spin on the situation confronting her'.

Her lack of a criminal record was of no real significance when he considered the catalogue of violence she had perpetrated against her previous partners, and particularly against Mr Price. As to a quality of mercy, Justice O'Keefe said that was reserved for prisoners who confessed their crimes and expressed genuine remorse and contrition, and for those whom the court believed would not repeat their crimes.

'The prisoner . . . does not qualify for mercy on any of these grounds. She engaged in cruel, vicious behaviour to Mr Price. She showed him no mercy. She has not expressed any contrition or remorse. If released, she poses a serious threat to the security of society,' said Justice O'Keefe. 'I am satisfied beyond any doubt that such a murder was premeditated. I am further satisfied in the same way that not only did she plan the murder but she also enjoyed the horrific acts which followed in its wake as part of a ritual of death and defilement.

'The things which she did after the death of Mr Price indicate cognition, volition, calm and skill. I am satisfied beyond reasonable doubt that her evil actions were the playing out of her resentments arising out of her rejection by Mr Price, her impending expulsion from Mr Price's home and his refusal to share with her his assets, particularly his home, which he wanted to retain for his children. I have no doubt that her claim of amnesia forms part of her plan to affect madness in order to escape the consequences of her acts and to provide a convenient basis on which to rely to avoid detailed questioning by the police and escape punishment.

'As I have said, the prisoner showed no mercy whatsoever to Mr Price. The last minutes of his life must have been a time of abject terror for him, as they were a time of utter enjoyment for her. At no time . . . did the prisoner express any regret for what she had done or any remorse for having done it; not even through the surrogacy of counsel. Her attitude in that regard is consistent with her general approach to the many acts of violence which she has engaged in against her various partners, namely "they deserved it".'

The judge had been speaking for more than an hour and was drawing to a close. The sobbing of the two Price girls had subsided.

'. . . The only appropriate penalty for the prisoner is life imprisonment and that parole should never be considered for her. The prisoner should never be released.'

Justice O'Keefe looked up from his judgment and asked the prisoner to stand. She did. She stared straight ahead. The courtroom was silent.

'Katherine Mary Knight, you have pleaded guilty to and been convicted of the murder of John Charles Thomas Price at Aberdeen in the State of New South Wales on or about 29 February 2000.

'In respect of that crime, I sentence you to imprisonment for life.'

John Price's children burst into applause. Katherine Knight blinked. She said nothing until she leaned over to Mr Thraves and whispered in his ear. As Corrective Services officers led her away into the cells below the courtroom, she looked over quickly at her father who was crying, and nodded. And then she was gone.

The aftermath

Katherine Knight's life will forever be measured by one of the most shocking murders in Australian criminal history. No other person – man or woman – has done what she did. She chose not to give evidence in her sentencing hearing as is her right, and by law she could not be compelled to do so. To this date, she has not spoken about what she did to her lover of six and a half years that night. All we know is that she said they had good sex and that they both climaxed. She said she remembers that Pricey got out of bed to 'go for a pee', and she watched him come back from the bathroom. Then, she said, she presumes she fell asleep.

Detective Bob Wells never found the $1000 that Katherine Knight stole from Pricey's credit union account after she killed him. What did she do with it? And why did she skin her victim and hang his human pelt from the architrave? Why did she boil his head in a pot on the oven? Were they the ultimate acts of degradation and humiliation of the former lover who had scorned her, or was it another twist in her evil and cold-blooded act of revenge against his children? Or did she go to the lengths she did because she wanted to add them to the artifacts in her home, parts of which were a ghoulish showcase of necrophilis?

John Price's three children, Johnathon, Rosemary and Jackie, regularly visit his grave and lay fresh flowers. Pricey's best mate Laurie Lewis pops up every couple of weeks to have a chat. Colleen drops in whenever she passes through Aberdeen. For her, the town will never be the same and she can't bear the thought that Katherine Knight is alive and Pricey is dead.

His 6 pm drinking mate at the top pub, Frank Heap, waters the tree that was planted in Pricey's memory in the Lions park on MacQueen Street and his mates at Bowditch Earthmoving still refer to the work truck he drove as 'Pricey's ute'. The little fella had unit 009. It's still going, and every now and then back at the double-storey tin shed office on Sir Thomas Mitchell Drive in Muswellbrook, they raise a Lite beer in his memory and laugh over their memories of the good times with Pricey.

Detective Bob Wells received a citation for his work, and still sees a psychiatrist to cope with the stress of the investigation. One of his fellow officers has never returned to work after taking fingerprints at the bloody crime scene at St Andrews Street.

In the aftermath of the life sentence, several Aberdeen locals rang the Homicide Victims' Support Group wanting to know if it was true that life meant life and that Katherine Knight would never return to Aberdeen.

Every few months Katherine Knight receives visits at Mulawa Women's Correctional Centre from her second eldest daughter Natasha. Her father Ken, Katherine's twin sister Joy, and her brother Shane also make the several hundred kilometre round trip when they can, as do Knight's three other children, two of whom live interstate. The prisoner rings the homes of her four children just about every other Sunday to talk with them.

Knight's evil acts have also had an impact on her own family and caused deep rifts that will never be healed. 'It ripped the family apart, the murder,' said Shane Knight. 'Just seemed to fall to bits.'

Shane and Ken Knight are no longer in contact with most of the family apart from Katherine's twin sister Joy, whose marriage disintegrated in the months after the murder. Katherine's half-brother Barry Roughan's marriage also ended not long after. Barry is no longer in touch with his half-brother Shane Knight, who also does not speak to his older brother Charlie Knight. Charlie was the brother who told police that Katherine threatened to kill Pricey and make out she was mad not long before the murder.

Barry Roughan has not visited his sister in prison since Christmas 2000 when she had a bit of a 'sook' on his shoulder. She has not admitted the murder to her family.

'What she done would be pure evil . . . It devastated everyone,' Barry said. 'No one believes the damage . . . I can't forgive Kath after finding out exactly what she did, you know. At first we thought it was one of these domestics [but] she thought it out . . . and then taking money out of the bank . . . this was not a murder,' said Barry. 'I don't hate her but I can't forgive her.'

~

As proscribed by her sentence, Katherine Knight will live the rest of her days in a single cell. All her possessions must fit into a 68-litre box with the lid on. Her daily routine starts between 6 and 7 am. She presents for three roll-call musters each day – early morning, late morning and once each evening just before lock-in at 7.30 pm. She has the opportunity of at least two hours of daily recreational time and the benefit of TAFE courses and training. Since being at Mulawa she has worked in the Governor's office as a cleaner. Prisoners can also work in the nursery or make headsets for airlines. It is unlikely Katherine Knight will ever get a job in the prison kitchen. Katherine Knight told her family and the psychiatrists who interviewed her that she has found peace in jail and she likes it there.

But she does not want to die there. Less than two months after she was sentenced to life in prison following her plea of guilty to the murder of John Price, Knight appealed against the severity of her never-to-be-released sentence. Her case is currently before the Court of Criminal Appeal.

Bibliography

Books

Davis, Carol Anne, *Women Who Kill: Profiles of Female Serial Killers*, Allison & Busby Ltd, 2001.

Diagnostic and Statistical Manual of Mental Disorder, Fourth Edition, Text Revision: DSM-IV-TR, American Psychiatric Association, 2000.

Douglas, John E. & Olshaker, Mark, *Journey into Darkness*, Pocket Books, 1997.

Douglas, John E. & Olshaker, Mark, *Mindhunter*, Pocket Books, 1995.

Douglas, John E. & Olshaker, Mark, *The Anatomy of Motive*, Pocket Books, 1999.

Gaute, J.H.H. & Odell, Robin, *Murder: What Dunit*, Harrap Ltd, 1982.

Gunn, John & Taylor, Pamela J., *Forensic Psychiatry: Clinical, Legal and Ethical Issues*, Butterworth Heinemann, 1993.

Hickey, Eric W., *Serial Murderers and Their Victims*, Wadsworth, 2002.

Kelleher, Michael D. & C.L., *Murder Most Rare*, Dell, 1999.

Keppel, Robert & Birnes, William J., *Signature Killers*, Arrow, 1998.

Kirwan, Barbara R., *The Mad, the Bad, and the Innocent*, Harper Paperbacks, 1997.

Lane, Brian, *The Encyclopaedia of Forensic Science*, Headline, 1992.

Lewis, Dorothy Otnow, *Guilty by Reason of Insanity*, Ivy Books, 1998.

Malmquist, Carl P., *Homicide: A Psychiatrist's Perspective*, American Psychiatric Press Inc. (www.appi.org), 1996.

Mannheim, Hermann, *Pioneers in Criminology*, Stevens & Sons Ltd, 1960.

Michaud, Stephen G. & Hazelwood, Roy, *The Evil that Men Do*, St Martins Paperbacks, 1998.

Moir, Anne & Jessel, David, *A Mind to Crime*, Signet, 1995.

Pearson, Patricia, *When She was Bad: How and Why Women Get Away with Murder*, Penguin, 1998.

Simon, Robert I., *Bad Men Do What Good Men Dream*, American Psychiatric Press Inc. (www.appi.org), 1996.

Newspaper sources

Dan Proudman, 'Slaying of a battler: Father's headless body found in house', *The Newcastle Herald*, 2 March 2000.

AAP, 'Man's head put in pot', *The Newcastle Herald*, 3 March 2000.

'Police to question woman', *The Newcastle Herald*, 6 March 2000.

'Woman, 44, charged with man's death', *The Newcastle Herald*, 7 March 2000.

'Woman on slay count', *The Newcastle Herald*, 5 April 2000.

'Kept in custody', *The Newcastle Herald*, 17 May 2000.

'Murder hearing', *The Newcastle Herald*, 13 September 2000.

'Expert rejects memory loss over death', *The Newcastle Herald*, 1 November 2000.

'Murder charge for trial', *The Newcastle Herald*, 1 December 2000.

'Jurors warned to expect "grisly, graphic evidence"', *The Newcastle Herald*, 18 October 2001.

Frances O'Shea, 'A horror murder that was too awful to imagine', *The Daily Telegraph*, 19 October 2001.

'Former abattoir worker pleads guilty to murder', *The Newcastle Herald*, 19 October 2001.

'Woman serves up her lover for dinner', *The Courier Mail*, 19 October 2001.

Isobelle Gidley, 'Mrs Hannibal: Jilted Kath cooks lover's body and serves it up for his family', *The Mirror* (London), 20 October 2001.

'Skinned partner had 37 wounds', *The Newcastle Herald*, 20 October 2001.

Greg Wendt, 'Gruesome taste in video rack', *The Newcastle Herald*, 24 October 2001.

Natalie Williams, 'Snuff films found in killer's home', *The Daily Telegraph*, 24 October 2001.

'Killer carried from court', *The Newcastle Herald*, 26 October 2001.

Natalie Williams, 'Murderer dragged from Court', *The Daily Telegraph*, 26 October 2001.

Natalie Williams, 'Mother's perverted pleasure – Court hears of "paybacks" in previous relationships', *The Daily Telegraph*, 27 October 2001.

Greg Wendt, 'Thrill killer would kill again', *The Newcastle Herald*, 27 October 2001.

'Sex sadist in a black nightgown', *The Newcastle Herald*, 30 October 2001.

'Killer partial to Disney and horror', *The Newcastle Herald*, 31 October 2001.

'Killer's necrophilia', *The Daily Telegraph*, 31 October 2001.

'Killer a "black widow spider"', *The Newcastle Herald*, 1 November 2001.

'Killer for sentence next week', *The Newcastle Herald*, 2 November 2001.

Frances O'Shea, 'Jealous, foul-mouthed with a very short fuse – inside the grisly world of Katherine Knight', *The Daily Telegraph*, 3 November 2001.

'Cold killer in plea for mercy', *The Newcastle Herald*, 6 November 2001.

Frances O'Shea, 'Life term urged for "wicked" killer', *The Daily Telegraph*, 7 November 2001.

'Sentence must fit evil crime', *The Newcastle Herald*, 7 November 2001.

Frances O'Shea, 'Jail for the term of her natural life, judge rules', *The Daily Telegraph*, 9 November 2001.

Greg Wendt, 'Macabre killer first woman to get life', *The Sydney Morning Herald*, 9 November 2001.

Greg Wendt, 'Cruel, evil killer sentenced to life,' *The Newcastle Herald*, 9 November 2001.

Peter Lalor, 'Meet the black Knight', *The Daily Telegraph*, 9 November 2001.

Donna Page, 'Life for a killer', *The Newcastle Herald*, 9 November 2001.

Donna Page, 'No sign of emotion from black widow', *The Newcastle Herald*, 9 November 2001.

Donna Page, 'A good mother but no excuse for murder', *The Newcastle Herald*, 9 November 2001.

Associated Press, 'Woman gets life term for butchering spouse', *The Toronto Star*, 9 November 2001.

Peter Lalor, 'Black Knight who murdered for fun', *The Daily Telegraph*, 10 November 2001.

Michelle Coffey, 'Unspeakable', *Who Weekly* magazine, 26 November 2001.

Greg Wendt, 'Macabre killer appeals against life', *The Newcastle Herald*, 21 December 2001.

'Man fined over hidden glass shards', *The Newcastle Herald*, 4 April 2002.

Acknowledgments

In writing Beyond Bad, I wanted to interview Katherine Knight to ask her, simply, why she did the horrific and savage things she did; why she charted a course of vengeance that ended with the symbolic defilement of the body of a man she is said to have loved dearly. No person is two dimensional – even the truly bad – and I wanted to understand her as much as possible. I have always believed that the best way to know someone and what motivates them is to talk to them, to hear first hand what they have to say.

I wrote to Knight in prison saying I was writing about her crimes and wanted to get to know her character – good and bad – and that I wanted to understand the forces at work in her life that led her to where she is now – inarguably, among the most notorious murderers in Australian history. But she declined my repeated invitations to tell her side of the story.

C.D.B. Bryan, the author of *Friendly Fire*, one of the most profoundly personal books on the Vietnam War, recently told me two things. Firstly, that writing a book is never as easy as reading one – he's right – and secondly, that the author is never as alone as he or she might think – and again, he's right.

While writing *Beyond Bad*, I interviewed more than seventy

people and was blessed by friendships, old and new. As well, I was fortunate to receive assistance from people in places I never knew existed.

Unlimited gratitude firstly goes to the families and close friends of John Price who, through their pain and sorrow, spoke to me in order to help me write a book about a crime so shocking that it has changed them forever. Particular thanks go to Pricey's youngest daughter who cannot be named by court order but whom I have called Jackie, Pricey's ex-wife Colleen Price, his best mate Laurie Lewis, his bosses who spent twelve hours every day with him, Geoffrey Bowditch and Peter Cairnes, and his drinking mates Frank Heap and Ron Murray, all of whose closeness to Pricey gave me an insight to a man I had never met. Their honesty and willingness to tell it like it was helped paint a portrait of a man who, like all of us, had flaws but unlike most of us, was willing to acknowledge them. Having spent hours getting to know Pricey through other people's memories of him, I discovered that he's the type of straight-up, decent bloke I'd love to have had the chance to have a drink with at the top pub.

Gratitude also to Katherine Knight's father, Ken Knight, and her brothers, Shane Knight and Barry Roughan, who bravely answered my questions about a woman who committed a murder they will never be able to understand. Thanks also to the numerous others who spoke to me on the record or on the condition of anonymity.

It would have been impossible to write about the life of Katherine Knight without the support and assistance of her ex-husband, David Kellett, and her former partners David Saunders and John Chillingworth. The courage and unstinting honesty of these good men in baring their lives – even when it must have hurt them and did not portray them through rose-coloured glasses – has earned my utmost respect and deserves my most profound thanks.

No true crime book is ever complete without a cop whose service went beyond the call of duty, and Bob Wells is that man. My thanks to him, and thanks also to the many other men and women in blue who did a great job and who assisted me, including Beverley Blanch, Troy Conway, Vic Ford, Phil Lloyd, Lloyd

Lyne, Scott Matthews and Peter Muscio. I am also indebted to the people of Aberdeen and beyond who trusted their memories to me, and to those who helped me understand how an abattoir works. Special thanks to Robert Delaforce, Len Lambeth, and Rod Milton for opening the doors to the world of psychiatry.

Thank you Kimberley Ashbee, Henry Krum, Valerie Malka, Joe Diflue, Kylie Henry, Martha Jabour, Geraldine Edwards, Tim Lyons, and Bob Keppel for your assistance; and a special thanks to journalists Isobelle Gidley, Frances O'Shea, Donna Page, Dan Proudman and Natalie Williams, who allowed me to use elements of their original work in this book, and editors Bruce Guthrie and Alan Oakley.

Writing a book is a solo pursuit, but producing one is not. A bouquet to my incredibly supportive agent, the indefatigable, the indomitable and the never-call-me-before-9 am Selwa Anthony whose encouragement, guidance, and pep-talks were as fearless and frank as they were needed. Thanks to the team at Random House led by Jane Southward, and to my editors, the enormously creative Jo Jarrah, and the always calm Zoe Walton.

Importantly, a big thanks to my dear friends across two continents who kept me sane and laughing, and in good company and lots of bubbles: in the United States, authors Sharon Krum and Courtlandt Bryan (whose mentoring and advice from the front line of writing a book about someone else's life was indispensable), and Anna Raine. And in Sydney, Tim Blair, David Burgess, Lynne Cossar, Miranda Devine, Helen Jackson, Chris Murphy and Nadia Santomaggio. And for adding a little sunshine when it was most needed, 'my' boys, Max and Darcy Burgess and Tom and Frankie Cutler.

Lastly, it is impossible to thank enough my two first readers, über editor Linda Smith and true crime fanatic Debbie Hammon, both of whose early suggestions and spelling corrections were always right.